THE ARDEN SHAKESPEARE

TITUS ANDRONICUS

Edited by
JONATHAN BATE

The Arden website is at
http://www.ardenshakespeare.com

The general editors of the Arden Shakespeare have been
W. J. Craig and R. H. Case (first series 1899-1944)
Una Ellis-Fermor, Harold F. Brooks, Harold Jenkins and
Brian Morris (second series 1946-82)

Present general editors (third series)
Richard Proudfoot, Ann Thompson and David Scott Kastan

This edition of *Titus Andronicus*, by Jonathan Bate
first published in 1995 by Routledge

Published by The Arden Shakespeare
Reprinted 2003

Arden Shakespeare is an imprint of Thomson Learning

Thomson Learning
High Holborn House
50-51 Bedford Row
London WC1R 4LR

Printed in Croatia

British Library Cataloguing in Publication Data
A catalogue record for this book is available from the British Library
Library of Congress Cataloguing in Publication Data
A catalogue record has been requested

ISBN 1-904-27114-6 (hbk)
ISBN 1-903436-05-2 (pbk)
NPN 9 8 7 6

THE ARDEN SHAKESPEARE

THIRD SERIES

General Editors: Richard Proudfoot, Ann Thompson
and David Scott Kastan

TITUS
ANDRONICUS

THE ARDEN SHAKESPEARE

ALL'S WELL THAT ENDS WELL	edited by G. K. Hunter*
ANTONY AND CLEOPATRA	edited by John Wilders
AS YOU LIKE IT	edited by Agnes Latham*
THE COMEDY OF ERRORS	edited by R. A. Foakes*
CORIOLANUS	edited by Philip Brockbank*
CYMBELINE	edited by J. M. Nosworthy*
HAMLET	edited by Harold Jenkins*
JULIUS CAESAR	edited by David Daniell
KING HENRY IV, Parts 1 and 2	edited by A. R. Humphreys*
KING HENRY V	edited by T. W. Craik
KING HENRY VI Part 1	edited by Edward Burns
KING HENRY VI Part 2	edited by Ronald Knowles
KING HENRY VI Part 3	edited by John D. Cox and Eric Rasmussen
KING HENRY VIII	edited by Gordon McMullan
KING JOHN	edited by E. A. J. Honigmann*
KING LEAR	edited by R. A. Foakes
KING RICHARD II	edited by Charles R. Forker
KING RICHARD III	edited by Antony Hammond*
LOVE'S LABOUR'S LOST	edited by H. R. Woudhuysen
MACBETH	edited by Kenneth Muir*
MEASURE FOR MEASURE	edited by J. W. Lever*
THE MERCHANT OF VENICE	edited by John Russell Brown*
THE MERRY WIVES OF WINDSOR	edited by Giorgio Melchiori
A MIDSUMMER NIGHT'S DREAM	edited by Harold F. Brooks*
MUCH ADO ABOUT NOTHING	edited by A. R. Humphreys*
OTHELLO	edited by E. A. J. Honigmann
PERICLES	edited by F. D. Hoeniger*
THE POEMS	edited by F. T. Prince*
ROMEO AND JULIET	edited by Brian Gibbons*
SHAKESPEARE'S SONNETS	edited by Katherine Duncan-Jones
THE TAMING OF THE SHREW	edited by Brian Morris*
THE TEMPEST	edited by Virginia Mason Vaughan and Alden T. Vaughan
TIMON OF ATHENS	edited by H. J. Oliver*
TITUS ANDRONICUS	edited by Jonathan Bate
TROILUS AND CRESSIDA	edited by David Bevington
TWELFTH NIGHT	edited by J. M. Lothian and T. W. Craik*
THE TWO GENTLEMEN OF VERONA	edited by Clifford Leech*
THE TWO NOBLE KINSMEN	edited by Lois Potter
THE WINTER'S TALE	edited by John Pitcher

*Second Series

CONTENTS

The Editor

Jonathan Bate is King Alfred Professor of English Literature at the University of Liverpool and a former Fellow of Trinity Hall, Cambridge. He has written several books on Shakespeare, including *Shakespeare and Ovid* (1993) and *The Genius of Shakespeare* (1997). Well known as a reviewer and broadcaster, he is also the author of *Romantic Ecology* (1991) and a novel, *The Cure for Love* (1998).

LIST OF
ILLUSTRATIONS

GENERAL EDITORS' PREFACE

The Arden Shakespeare is now nearly one hundred years old. The earliest volume in the first series, Edward Dowden's edition of *Hamlet*, was published in 1899. Since then the Arden Shakespeare has become internationally recognized and respected. It is now widely acknowledged as the pre-eminent Shakespeare series, valued by scholars, students, actors, and 'the great variety of readers' alike for its readable and reliable texts, its full annotation and its richly informative introductions.

We have aimed in the third Arden series to maintain the quality and general character of its predecessors, preserving the commitment to presenting the play as it has been shaped in history. While each individual edition will necessarily have its own emphasis in the light of the unique possibilities and problems posed by the play, the series as a whole, like the earlier Ardens, insists upon the highest standards of scholarship and upon attractive and accessible presentation.

Newly edited from the original quarto and folio editions, the texts are presented in fully modernized form, with a textual apparatus that records all substantial divergences from those early printings. The notes and introductions focus on the conditions and possibilities of meaning that editors, critics and performers (on stage and screen) have discovered in the play. While building upon the rich history of scholarly and theatrical activity that has long shaped our understanding of the texts of Shakespeare's plays, this third series of the Arden Shakespeare is made necessary and possible by a new generation's encounter with Shakespeare, engaging with the plays and their complex relation to the culture in which they were – and continue to be – produced.

THE TEXT

On each page of the play itself, readers will find a passage of text followed by commentary and, finally, textual notes. Act and scene divisions (seldom present in the early editions and often the product of eighteenth-century or later scholarship) have been retained for ease of reference, but have been given less prominence than in the previous series. Editorial indications of scene have been removed to the textual notes or commentary.

In the text itself, unfamiliar typographic conventions have been avoided in order to minimize obstacles to the reader. Elided forms in the early texts are spelt out in full in verse lines wherever they indicate a usual late twentieth-century pronunciation that requires no special indication and wherever they occur in prose (except when they indicate non-standard pronunciation). In verse speeches, marks of elision are retained where they are necessary guides to the scansion and pronunciation of the line. Final -ed in past tense and participial forms of verbs is always printed as -ed, without accent, never as -'d, but wherever the required pronunciation diverges from modern usage a note in the commentary draws attention to the fact. Where the final -ed should be given syllabic value contrary to modern usage, e.g.

> Doth Silvia know that I am banished?
> (*TGV* 3.1.221)

the note will take the form

221 **banished** banishèd

Conventional lineation of divided verse lines shared by two or more speakers has been reconsidered and sometimes rearranged. Except for the familiar *Exit* and *Exeunt*, Latin forms in stage directions and speech prefixes have been translated into English, and the original Latin forms recorded in the textual notes.

COMMENTARY AND TEXTUAL NOTES

Notes in the commentary, for which a major source will be the *Oxford English Dictionary*, offer glossarial and other explication of verbal difficulties; they may also include discussion of points of theatrical interpretation and, in relevant cases, substantial extracts from Shakespeare's source material. Editors will not usually offer glossarial notes for words adequately defined in the *Concise Oxford Dictionary* or *Webster's Ninth New Collegiate Dictionary*, but in cases of doubt they will include notes. Attention, however, will be drawn to places where more than one likely interpretation can be proposed and to significant verbal and syntactic complexity. Notes preceded by * involve readings altered from the early edition(s) on which the text is based.

Headnotes to acts or scenes discuss, where appropriate, questions of scene location, Shakespeare's handling of his source materials, and major difficulties of staging. The list of roles (so headed to emphasize the play's status as a text for performance) is also considered in commentary notes. These may include comment on plausible patterns of casting with the resources of an Elizabethan or Jacobean acting company and also on any variation in the description of roles in their speech prefixes in the early editions.

The textual notes are designed to let readers know when the edited text diverges from the early edition(s) on which it is based. Wherever this happens the note will record the rejected reading of the early edition(s), in original spelling, and the source of the reading adopted in this edition. Other forms from the early edition(s) recorded in these notes will include some spellings of particular interest or significance and original forms of translated stage directions. Where two early editions are involved, for instance with *Othello*, the notes will also record all important differences between them. The textual notes take a form that has been in use since the nineteenth century. This comprises, first: line reference, reading adopted in the text and closing square bracket; then: abbreviated reference, in italic, to the earliest edition to adopt the accepted reading, italic semi-colon and noteworthy alternative reading(s), each with abbreviated italic reference to its source.

Conventions used in these textual notes include the following. The solidus / is used, in notes quoting verse or discussing verse lining, to indicate line endings. Distinctive spellings of the basic text (Q or F) follow the square bracket without indication of source and are enclosed in italic brackets. An editor's name in brackets indicates the originator of a textual emendation. Stage directions (SDs) are referred to by the number of the line within or immediately after which they are placed. Line numbers with a decimal point relate to SDs more than one line long, with the number after the point indicating the line within the SD: e.g. 78.4 refers to the fourth line of the SD following line 78. Lines of SDs at the start of a scene are numbered 0.1, 0.2, etc. Where only a line number precedes the square bracket, e.g. 128], the note relates to the whole line; where SD is added to the number, it relates to the whole of a SD within or immediately following the line. Speech prefixes (SPs) follow similar conventions, 203 SP], referring to the speaker's name for line 203. Where a SP reference takes the form e.g. 38+ SP, it relates to all subsequent speeches assigned to that speaker in the scene in question.

Where, as with *King Henry V*, one of the early editions is a so-called 'bad quarto' (that is, a text either heavily adapted, or reconstructed from memory, or both), the divergences from the present edition are too great to be recorded in full in the notes. In these cases the editions will include a reduced photographic facsimile of the 'bad quarto' in an appendix.

INTRODUCTION

Both the introduction and the commentary are designed to present the plays as texts for performance, and make appropriate reference to stage, film and television versions, as well as introducing the reader to the range of critical approaches to the play. They discuss the history of the reception of the texts within the theatre and scholarship and beyond, investigating the interdependency of the literary text and the surrounding 'cultural text' both at the time of the original production of Shakespeare's works and during their long and rich afterlife.

ACKNOWLEDGEMENTS

For their kind permission to reproduce copyright material, I am very grateful to those indicated in the list of illustrations. I would also like to thank Mary White of the Shakespeare Centre Library in Stratford-upon-Avon for her assistance in obtaining photographs of the Peter Brook and Deborah Warner productions. Thanks also to: Stephen Siddall for inviting me to act as dramaturg for his 1991 production of the play at the Arts Theatre, Cambridge; Heather James (one of the play's best living critics) for the stimulation of valuable conversations and for enabling me, through the good offices of Brian Payne, to see a video of Mark Rucker's 1988 Santa Cruz production; students in my Renaissance Drama Workshop at the University of Liverpool for helping me to work out the staging of the first act; Edward Burns for reading the introduction; Anne Barton, Al Braunmuller, Tom Craik, Andy Gurr, Peter Holland, George Hunter, John Kerrigan, Laurie Maguire, Jeremy Maule, Benjamin Thompson and Stanley Wells for local advice; my research assistant, Sonia Massai; my general editors, Richard Proudfoot and Ann Thompson; Jane Armstrong at Routledge; Kate Harris, librarian to the Marquess of Bath at Longleat House; staff at the Beinecke, Cambridge University, Folger and Huntington Libraries (especially Laetitia Yeandle at the Folger, for examining the unique copy of the first quarto with me). My time at the Beinecke was made possible by my being awarded the James M. Osborn Fellowship, for which I am most grateful.

Some of the material in the introduction was first presented in more detailed form in papers delivered at conferences in Montpellier, Ferrara and Liverpool, and published as follows: 'The performance of revenge in *The Spanish Tragedy* and *Titus*

Andronicus', in *The Show Within: Dramatic Insets in English Renaissance Drama*, ed. F. Laroque, 2 vols (Montpellier, 1992); 'Staging the unspeakable: four versions of *Titus Andronicus*', in *Shakespeare from Text to Stage*, ed. P. Kennan and M. Tempera (Bologna, 1992); 'Adaptation as edition' in *Margins of the Text*, ed. David Greetham (Ann Arbor, forthcoming). I am particularly grateful to François Laroque and Mariangela Tempera for their invitations.

I very much regret that it was only after completing work on the edition that I saw a video of Silviu Pucarete's remarkable production for the Romanian National Theatre (Paris, Vienna, Tokyo, Melbourne, Montreal, 1993); I hope that it may be possible to refer to it in a future revision.

INTRODUCTION

> When the notices of *Titus Andronicus* came out, giving
> us full marks for saving your dreadful play, I could
> not help feeling a twinge of guilt. For to tell the truth
> it had not occurred to any of us in rehearsal that the
> play was so bad.[1]

Shakespeare's earliest and bloodiest tragedy has had a curious
history. It was hugely successful in its own time – indeed, it
perhaps did more than any other play to establish its author's
reputation as a dramatist – but it has been reviled by critics
and revived infrequently. Yet on the few occasions when it has
reappeared in the repertory it has repeated its original success:
Peter Brook's production with Laurence Olivier as Titus was
one of the great theatrical experiences of the 1950s and Deborah
Warner's with Brian Cox was the most highly acclaimed
Shakespearean production of the 1980s.

The play began getting a negative press among literary
critics in the eighteenth century because it was thought to be
in bad taste. Not only is a hand chopped off on stage: worse,
dreadful puns are made about it ('O *hand*le not the theme, to
talk of hands, / Lest we remember still that we have none').
But fashions in taste go around and come around, and in
its willingness to confront violence, often in ways that are
simultaneously shocking and playful, our culture resembles
that of the Elizabethans more than that of Dr Johnson.
Audiences may still be disturbed by the play's representations

---

1   Peter Brook, 'An open letter to William Shakespeare', *Sunday Times*, 1 Sept. 1957,
    repr. in Brook, *The Shifting Point* (1987), 72.

1

of bloody revenge, dismemberment, miscegenation, rape and cannibalism, but theatregoers who are also moviegoers will be very familiar with this kind of material.

The actress Anna Calder-Marshall played the raped Lavinia in the BBC television production in the mid-1980s, at a time when there was great concern about the ready availability of videos characterized by extreme violence, usually wrought upon the bodies of women. 'Someone said to me,' she recollected, ' "It's just like a video nasty, isn't it?" ' and it is very, very frightening.' 'But,' she went on, 'somehow, we've found – or I think we have – that the characters through their suffering get closer. Titus has committed the most appalling deeds and it isn't until he's maimed and his daughter's maimed that he learns anything about love' (BBC, 22). To understand *Titus Andronicus* thus is at once to perceive its proximity to *King Lear* and to apprehend the difference between a slasher movie and a tragedy.

In 1953 J. C. Maxwell wrote in the introduction to his Arden edition that '*Titus* is neither a play with a complicated staging nor one which will ever be widely read' (Ard^2, xvii). This completely re-edited Arden will argue to the contrary that not only the play's staging but also its aesthetics and politics are in fact complicated and sophisticated – and that it ought to be widely read and more frequently performed. The introduction begins with a critical and historical account, which explores the play's intricate structure and innovative use of theatrical resources ('Space and structure'), its historical setting and the significance of that setting for an Elizabethan audience ('Romans and Goths'), its generic context ('Revenge'), its expressive language ('Passionating grief'), and two activities which are crucial to the action ('Reading and rape'). Part two of the introduction continues the critical discussion, but in relation to the play's theatrical life; it analyses aspects of seven productions, three from within or shortly after Shakespeare's lifetime, one from the Restoration, one from the Victorian age, and the two great modern revivals mentioned at the outset.

Even those who have approached *Titus* in a spirit of scholarly enquiry rather than critical judgement have been prejudiced by their distaste for the play. In particular, they have been anxious to find grounds for devaluing its place in Shakespeare's career or even dismissing it from the canon of his works altogether. Several eighteenth-century editors denied that Shakespeare wrote any of it; there has been a persistent argument that he was merely touching up someone else's play or that it was a patched-together collaborative effort; the discovery of an eighteenth-century chapbook narrating the story allowed much of the violence to be palmed off on Shakespeare's 'source'; and nearly all scholars suppose that it is a very early work, a piece of crude and embarrassing juvenilia.

I believe that every one of these arguments is wrong. I believe that the play was wholly by Shakespeare and furthermore that it was not based on the chapbook; rather, it was one of the dramatist's most inventive plays, a complex and self-conscious improvisation upon classical sources, most notably the *Metamorphoses* of Ovid. I also suspect that it was not a piece of juvenilia but a new work performed for the first time as a showpiece in January 1594. 'Origins', the third section of the introduction, argues this position in detail. Finally, in 'Establishing the text', I describe the four early editions of the play (the Quartos of 1594, 1600 and 1611, and the 1623 First Folio), attending particularly to various revisions to the text; I also offer an analysis of my own editorial procedures, premised on the assumption that every edition is itself an act of revision.

It may seem curious to place the section called 'Origins' near the end of the introduction. I have ordered it thus because I believe that *Titus* is an important play and a living one, and that this is best demonstrated by taking the reader forward through its afterlife on the stage before turning back to its emergence out of the London theatre-scene of the early 1590s. Treatments of date, sources and text have to be concerned with minutiae and may appear technical and potentially boring, but I have tried to write about these matters in an accessible way because they reveal much about the artfulness of the play.

THE DRAMATIC ACHIEVEMENT

Space and structure

The theatres built by the Elizabethans allowed for triple-layered performance. There was a gallery or upper stage (Juliet's window is the most famous use of this 'above' or 'aloft' space), the main stage which projected into the auditorium and on which the actors – in Hamlet's image – 'hold as 'twere the mirror' up to the lives of the theatre audience, and the 'cellarage' below the stage, reached by a trap-door (through which Dr Faustus descends and the weird sisters' apparitions arise). In *Titus Andronicus* Shakespeare made bold and innovative use of all three levels.

Trumpets sound, heralding the beginning of the play. But the stage remains empty: the first entrance is that of the Roman tribunes and senators 'aloft'. The biggest theatrical hit of the early 1590s, Thomas Kyd's *The Spanish Tragedy*, had also begun with an entrance above, but there the personages on the upper stage represented a dead man and a personification of Revenge: the tragedy performed below is imagined as an acting out of revenge upon the dead man's enemies, with him as spectator throughout. The stage-manager, 'Revenge', is a figure from ancient Roman tragedy, so what Kyd offers his audience is a classicized version of the medieval image of God looking down on the theatre of the world. But where Christian iconography had God and Kyd had Revenge, Shakespeare begins with human, secular authorities in the commanding position aloft.

Below them, on the main stage, there are doors at either

4

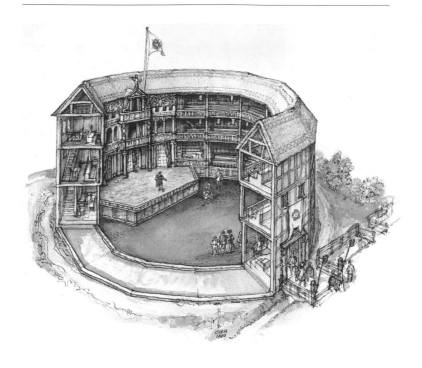

1 Reconstruction of the Rose Theatre as extended in 1592 (originally built in 1587: painting by C. Walter Hodges)

end of the tiring-house which serves as a backdrop (see impression of the Rose Theatre, Fig. 1). Through them come rival claimants for power: the use of opposite doors dramatizes the brothers' opposition in terms of the stage space. When Titus Andronicus enters in his victory procession, the third level, the darkness below the stage which figures the under-world, comes into play. His first task is to give a proper burial to his sons who have died in combat, '*They open the tomb*' and the nether world is invoked for the first time. Once buried, the dead sons would be free to cross the Styx into the underworld; once the gods were propitiated, peace could return to Rome. The city prided itself on not being barbaric: the word *civilized* comes from *civilis*, which means 'of citizens, of the city', and Rome was *the* city. The religious rituals of a civilized culture, it was believed, involved animal rather than human sacrifice. When Lucius demands that the shadows be appeased through the lopping of the limbs of 'the proudest prisoner of the Goths' and the consuming of his flesh in fire, barbarism has entered the city.[1] The first of the play's many reversals of expected linguistic and behavioural codes takes place, and the supposedly barbaric queen of Goths speaks a Roman language of valour, patriotism, piety, mercy and nobility, whereas the Roman warriors go about their ritual killing. Theirs is, as Tamora says in a telling oxymoron, a 'cruel, irreligious piety'. It will provoke the bloody requital of what Demetrius here calls 'sharp revenge'. The ground is immediately laid for the play's brutal but elegant symmetrical structure: 'Alarbus' limbs are lopped' in Act 1, so Lavinia's will be 'lopped and hewed' in Act 2; Tamora is made to kneel and plead for her son's life, so Titus will later be made to kneel and plead for his sons' lives.

To read the timing of entrances and exits is to see these patterns unfold: Titus' sons enter with their swords bloody from the sacrifice of Alarbus, their dead brothers are laid to rest and then their sister comes on. Her entrance is perfectly timed to draw her into the spiral of retribution. It also serves to link the domestic political plot with the opposition between Titus and Tamora. The opposite doors come into play again when Saturninus and the Goths take off for the upper stage just as the Andronicus boys help Bassianus bear Lavinia away through the other door. Having just been at the centre of a triumphal procession, Titus suddenly finds himself alone on

---

1 On sacrifice, hunting and the play's dissolution of the distinction between city and wild forest, see Marienstras.

stage with the body of a son whom he has slain out of a mistaken sense of honour and loyalty to the new emperor who at the very same moment has gone off to marry the queen of Goths, thus further dissolving the distinction between insiders and outsiders, civilized and barbaric. There is then a re-entry through the opposite doors in which the two sides are seen in tableau against each other. Having begun with Saturninus against Bassianus, then moved to Romans against Goths, the scene ends with Saturninus and Goths versus Bassianus and Andronici, but in uneasy truce. Since that truce has been brokered by Tamora, with her ulterior scheme revealed in an aside, we know it will not last – especially since the general departure for the double wedding has left the sinister and hitherto menacingly silent figure of Aaron alone in control of the stage.

Hunting for sport is 'civilized' society's way of getting back in touch with the wild. The second act of the play moves swiftly from a cheerful aubade, complete with hunter's peal, to a dark forest, evoked through a verbal iconography of shadowiness and banefulness – the emblem reproduced here (Fig. 2) suggests the associations of such a place. A second-act movement away from city and court anticipates the journeys not only of pastoral plays such as *A Midsummer Night's Dream*, *As You Like It* and *Cymbeline*, but also of *Lear*. Where the first act is dominated by the question of who controls the upper stage, symbolic of the Capitol, of power over Rome, the second is dominated by the pit, represented by the trap-door. Aaron is in his element here, hiding the gold, springing the trap, leading in the hapless Quintus and Martius. Attention shifts from the body politic to the human body. The forest is a place where desire can be acted out: Tamora comes to make love to Aaron, Chiron and Demetrius rape Lavinia.

The rape cannot be shown onstage, but it is evoked through the simultaneous action of the pit scene. We do not have to be card-carrying Freudians to see the connection between what

Nulli penetrabilis.

A SHADIE Wood, pourtraicted to the fight,
  With vncouth pathes, and hidden waies vnknowne:
Refembling *C H A O S*, or the hideous night,
Or thofe fad Groues, by banke of *A C H E R O N*
With banefull *Ewe*, and *Ebon* overgrowne:
  Whofe thickeft boughes, and inmoft entries are
  Not peirceable, to power of any ftarre.

2 'The woods are ruthless, dreadful ...': emblem from Henry Peacham's
Minerva Britanna (1612)

we know Chiron and Demetrius are doing to Lavinia, and
Quintus' description of a 'subtle hole', 'Whose mouth is
covered with rude-growing briers / Upon whose leaves are
drops of new-shed blood', or Martius' reference to 'the swallowing womb / Of this deep pit' where the dead Bassianus

8

lies 'bathed in maiden blood'.[1] 'This detested, dark, blood-drinking pit', 'Cocytus' misty mouth', 'this fell devouring receptacle', 'this gaping hollow' (*OED*'s earliest record of the adjective), 'the ragged entrails of this pit': the language becomes darkly obsessive, evocative not only of death and hell but also of the threatening female sexuality that is embodied in Tamora. There is a suggestion of Lear's disgust at what he calls the 'sulphurous pit' of woman's genitals.[2] The 'mouth' of the pit becomes crucial when we realize that Lavinia is not only being raped but also having her tongue cut out; throughout the play, the action turns on mouths that speak, mouths that abuse and are abused, mouths that devour.

If the onstage/offstage counterpoint of pit and rape is bold, how much bolder is the following scene in which the elaborate poetic language of Marcus is juxtaposed onstage to the physical image of Lavinia's mutilated body. The best account of the effect is by D. J. Palmer, and it is well worth a long quotation:

> Marcus' lament is the expression of an effort to realise a sight that taxes to the utmost the powers of under-standing and utterance. The vivid conceits in which he pictures his hapless niece do not transform or depersonalise her: she is already transformed and depersonalised, as she stands before him the victim of a strange and cruel metamorphosis. ... Far from be-ing a retreat from the awful reality into some aesthetic distance, then, Marcus' conceits dwell upon this figure that is to him both familiar and strange, fair and hideous, living body and object: this is, and is not, Lavinia. ... Lavinia's plight is literally unutterable ... Marcus' formal lament articulates unspeakable woes.

---

1   For a full psychoanalytic reading, see Willbern, 168: 'Here is Freud's plenty. The passage [describing the dark wood] expresses highly sadistic fantasies of sexual attack ... "The abhorred pit" will soon assume its central and over-determined symbolic significance as vagina, womb, tomb, and mouth.'

2   *KL* 4.6.128; the link is made by Serpieri, 205–6.

... Here and throughout the play, the response to the intolerable is ritualised, in language and action, because ritual is the ultimate means by which man seeks to order and control his precarious and unstable world.

(Palmer, 321–2)

I return to Marcus' speech later, in the context of Peter Brook's and Deborah Warner's very different treatments of the scene.

In terms of the structure of the play, the post-rape scene is pivotal because it shifts the balance from the language-registers associated with action to those associated with reaction. It introduces two registers which have been apparent only in passing up to this point: comedy and grief. Grief is the register of Marcus' speech, as it is of much of Titus' language in the following scene. But the first reaction to the rape is a series of jokes. Chiron and Demetrius become a sick comedy team, offering feed line and punch line:

CHIRON
Go home, call for sweet water, wash thy hands.
DEMETRIUS
She hath no tongue to call, nor hands to wash.

and again,

CHIRON
And 'twere my cause, I should go hang myself.
DEMETRIUS
If thou hadst hands to help thee knit the cord.

There is a decorum of character in this – it is not unknown for rapists to think of their actions as a bit of a laugh. There is also an anticipation of *Lear*, where Cornwall accompanies the gouging of Gloucester's eyes with some grimly witty word-play. But does comedy effect a simultaneous heightening and release of tension in the audience here, as it does in the Porter scene in *Macbeth*, which occupies a closely comparable

10

structural position? I suspect that it is intended to, but that the cultural gap between our time and Shakespeare's makes it difficult for us to share in the release. Among our few taboos are having a laugh at the expense of people who haven't got any hands or women who have been raped.

Titus' first words to his mutilated daughter are 'what accursed hand / Hath made thee handless in thy father's sight?' Features such as the relentless play on the word 'hands' from this point onwards have led some critics to suppose that the whole play is 'a huge joke', a parody in which Shakespeare watched the groundlings 'gaping ever wider to swallow more as he tossed them bigger and bigger gobbets of sob-stuff and raw beef-steak' (Dover Wilson, Cam[1], lvi). This is a wrong-headed but understandable reading. There *is* a lot of comedy in the second half of the play – it was brought out brilliantly by Brian Cox in the Deborah Warner production – but that does not make it a parody. Rather, what it does is blur the conventional distinctions between tragedy and comedy, grieving and laughing. As the decorums of Roman honour disintegrate, so do the decorums of dramatic expectation.

What do you do when twenty-one of your sons have been killed in battle, you've killed the twenty-second in a fit of pique, your daughter has been raped and had her hands cut off and her tongue cut out, two further sons have been wrongly accused of murdering your son-in-law and the remaining one sentenced to exile, you've been told that the two who are condemned will be reprieved if you chop off your hand, and you do so, only to have the hand and the heads of the two sons sent back to you in scorn? Dramatic decorum dictates that you should rant ('Now is a time to storm,' says Marcus). But human nature does not obey dramatic decorum. What Titus says is much more true: 'Ha, ha, ha!' At the end of the scene, he and Marcus carry off the heads; but, so as to be sure that Lavinia is not left out, he says 'Bear thou my hand, sweet wench, between thy teeth'. This is a visual joke, for it shows

3 'I'll play the cook': Deborah Warner production

that she has become the *hand*maid of Revenge (a role which will later involve her in dextrous work with a basin between her stumps). If we laugh at Titus' line, as the audience in all three productions I have seen certainly did, we are sharing in Titus' experience. By laughing with him, we also participate in what he calls the 'sympathy of woe'. Where Lear has his Fool and then the company of Poor Tom, Titus and Hamlet play their own fools; in each case, the moments of laughter intensify rather than diminish the passionate fellow-feeling of tragedy.

Titus certainly gets the last laugh against his enemies. He spends the fourth act sending jokey messages, first to Chiron and Demetrius, then to Saturninus via arrows and Clown. He turns the tables on Tamora in the scene in which she impersonates Revenge and he then enjoys himself playing the cook (see Fig. 3 for the stylish presentation of this in the Warner production). Comedy depends on a sense of *satisfaction*, of one thing answering neatly to another. So there is a kind of comic satisfaction in the gagging of Chiron and Demetrius and the slitting of their throats: it answers exactly to their gagging of Lavinia and cutting of her tongue. It is no coincidence that the two longest speeches in the play are Marcus' address to the raped Lavinia and Titus' address to her rapists prior to his act of retribution. Furthermore, in the preceding scene, Aaron has bragged of his villainy in what Palmer (336) aptly calls 'a parody of the need under which Titus ritualises suffering in speech and action', so that 'tragedy is transformed into jest' (the trick is learnt from Marlowe's *Jew of Malta*). Aaron's 'bitter tongue' torments his enemies until, like other tongues in the play, it is gagged and stopped. As we come to the close and reflect on the hand that Titus has played in the second half, Palmer is again our surest commentator on the game:

> Titus' passion is a continued struggle, not merely to endure the unendurable, but to express the inexpressible; he *performs* his woes out of the need to grasp what is all too real but virtually inconceivable in its enormity. The impulse to play, in other words, arises in Titus not as a retreat from the hideous world that confronts him, but as a means of registering its full significance. His more bizarre fantasies, in which his mind seems to have collapsed under the unbearable suffering, are certainly symptoms of a precarious sanity, yet far from losing his grip on reality, through these obsessive pantomimes Titus' mind becomes fixed on its object.
>
> (Palmer, 330)

Subsequently, I will suggest what the political consequences of the *performance* of revenge might be. Meanwhile, the resolution of the main political action is achieved through a structural device which Shakespeare replicated in *Coriolanus*. The successful Roman warrior is sent into exile, where he joins

4 'The poor remainder of Andronici': Peter Brook production

up with his former enemies and then marches with them against the city which has cast him out. There is a full trial run for Coriolanus in Lucius' self-description in the closing scene, with its images of banishment, closed gates, relief among

Rome's enemies, discomfort at being a vaunter, the wounded body as witness, and construction of the self as the archetype of 'the turned-forth' (5.3.103–17).

Titus Andronicus differs from *Coriolanus* in that there is no turning back outside the city gates. When Lucius is proclaimed as emperor, he has an army of Goths in support. Their role in the final scene has been insufficiently recognized, because they are silent at the climax. But they are unquestionably present, and there is every reason to suppose that when Lucius kills the emperor Saturninus, the imperial guard will rise against him and the Goths will come to his defence. It is clear from the ensuing dialogue that Lucius and Marcus move at this point to the dominating above space (see Fig. 4 for the lucid presentation of them in this position in the Brook production). I have therefore introduced the stage direction '*The Goths protect the Andronici, who go aloft*'. Where Saturninus went aloft with the 'evil' Goths in the first act, Lucius escapes aloft through the offices of the 'good' Goths in the last act. When he is proclaimed emperor and comes down on to the main stage, the symmetry which marks so much of the play's action suggests that there should be '*A long flourish till the Andronici come down*', echoing the trumpet flourish at the corresponding moment when Saturninus was proclaimed in the first act.

The wheel has come full circle. Andronicus refused the crown at the beginning of the play; an Andronicus takes it at the end. Will he usher in a new golden age? His name is propitious, as I shall show, but his final action raises questions (quite apart from the matter of how the Goths are going to be paid off for their assistance): the troubles of the Andronici began with the question of proper burial rites and the sacrifice of Alarbus; the play ends with the living burial of Aaron and the refusal of proper burial rites for Tamora. It ends on a rhyme of 'pity' with 'pity', and pity has reached its zenith in the moving farewell kisses upon the dead Titus, but what Lucius is advocating in the final couplet is an absence of pity.

15

Romans and Goths

> No subject affecteth us with more delight than history,
> imprinting a thousand forms upon our imaginations
> from the circumstances of place, person, time, matter,
> manner, and the like. And what can be more profitable,
> saith an ancient historian, than sitting on the stage of
> human life, to be made wise by their example who
> have trod the path of error and danger before us.
>
> > (Peacham, 64)

So wrote Henry Peacham, whom we will meet again, in a
handbook for gentlemen that is typical of the age. When we
speak of the Renaissance we mean above all a renewed grasp
of the ancient world. Sir Thomas North wrote in the address
to the reader at the beginning of his English version of *The
Lives of the Noble Grecians and Romans* that 'there is no
prophane studye better than Plutarke'. He dedicated his translation to Queen Elizabeth because, he wrote, there was no
other book 'that teacheth so much honor, love, obedience,
reverence, zeale, and devocion to Princes, as these lives of
Plutarke doe'.[1] Peacham approvingly cites the sentiment that,
if the world had to choose one author (in addition to the Bible)
and burn the rest, that one should be Plutarch. As England
sought to establish itself as a great nation and an imperial
power, it looked to the example of classical Rome.

Shakespeare's treatment of Roman political institutions in
Titus Andronicus has been mocked: is the state a commonwealth
or a monarchy, is succession based on election or heredity? In
T. J. B. Spencer's words,

> The play does not assume a political situation known
> to Roman history; it is, rather, a summary of Roman
> politics. It is not so much that any particular set of
> political institutions is assumed in *Titus*, but rather

---

1   Plutarch, sigs *ii^r^–iii^r^.

that it includes *all* the political institutions that Rome
ever had. The author seems anxious, not to get it all
right, but to get it all in.

(Spencer, 32)

To which the best critics of the play reply: quite so, but this
is exactly the point.[1] Far from being a matter of anxiety or
youthful incompetence, the eclecticism is deliberate. Shakespeare is interrogating Rome, asking what kind of an example
it provides for Elizabethan England; in so doing he collapses
the whole of Roman history, known to him from Plutarch and
Livy, into a single action.

The first book of Livy's Roman history narrates two key
events in the foundation of the city: first, the escape of Aeneas
from Troy and his arrival in Italy, and second the expulsion
of the Tarquins. Near the end of *Titus Andronicus*, a Roman
Lord speaks of 'Our Troy, our Rome'. According to the theory
of the translation of empire (*translatio imperii*), history consists of a gradual westward shift of the greatest imperial power;
myths are created to story that shift. Thus, when the city of
Troy fell, Aeneas escaped and founded Rome. In an effort to
sustain the pattern, British writers created the myth of Brutus,
who also escaped from Troy and founded Britain, London
serving as another new Troy ('Troynovant'): our Troy, our
Rome, this England. In order to establish Rome, Aeneas had
to reject the amorous advances of Dido in Carthage and sail
on to Italy; there, according to Virgil's *Aeneid*, Lavinia, the
daughter of Latinus, king of Latium (the region where the
Trojans made landfall), was betrothed to Turnus, but then
given by her father in marriage to Aeneas, who kills Turnus
in single combat at the climax of the poem.

According to Livy, Rome first went into decline when

---

1   See especially, Hunter, 'Sources and Meanings', and James, whose highly original
     essay on the play is further developed in her forthcoming *The Fatal Cleopatra:
     Shakespeare's Translations of Empire*.

L. Tarquinius Superbus 'usurped the kingdome, without the election, either of the Senators or the people'; but he was then expelled because of his son's rape of the chaste Lucretia. The Romans then decided that they'd had enough of tyrannical monarchs and established the republic. The man who was chiefly instrumental in expelling the Tarquins was Lucius Junius Brutus. The parallel of his names with the Brutus who was supposed to have established Britain and the Lucius who was supposed to have been the first Christian king of Britain facilitated the Elizabethan extension of the *translatio*.

The relevance of this early history to the action of the play should be readily apparent. Like Tarquin, Saturninus abuses the electoral process; like Lucretia, Lavinia is raped; as a consequence, Lucius, following in the footsteps of Lucius Junius Brutus, brings political change. Like Aeneas, Titus is 'surnamed Pius', and, as in the *Aeneid*, the main threat to him is an exotic woman from a rival empire. But in a deliberate debasement of the famous encounter between Aeneas and Dido in a cave during a hunt, Tamora's sexual involvement is with the Moor, not with a Roman, and Virgil's celebrated image of the impassioned woman as a stricken deer (*Aen.* 4.68–73) is displaced on to the rape of Lavinia: 'Chiron, we hunt not, we, with horse nor hound, / But hope to pluck a dainty doe to ground' (2.1.25–6). Virgil's Lavinia, the mother of early Rome, becomes the mutilated daughter of late Rome. The high history of the foundation of the city and the advent of its republican government, with senators balanced against tribunes, is replayed in the decadent key of the late empire. As Heather James puts it in her ground-breaking article on this theme, 'the founding acts of Empire turn out to contain the seeds of its destruction' (James, 123).

Everybody knows that the Roman empire was eventually over-run by Goths and Vandals, heralding the 'middle' age in which, according to the imaginings of Renaissance historiographers, darkness fell over Europe. But the Goths in the play are not historically specific. They are all the enemies of Rome, including the Carthaginians whose wars were a main preoccupation of Livy and the Gauls whose wars were a main preoccupation of Julius Caesar. Titus' ten-year war against the Goths is an echo of the length not only of the Trojan war but also of Caesar's Gallic wars. As the play begins, Titus has spent ten years expanding the empire, as if during its heyday; when it ends, an army of Goths is in the city, as if during its decline. But the Goths who join with Lucius are a very civilized lot in comparison with the ones who are paraded through the streets in the first act. This will seem puzzling until we know what the Elizabethans thought about the Goths.[1]

In his *Perambulation of Kent* (1570), William Lambarde wrote, 'The Saxons, Jutes, and Angles, were the Germaines that came over (as we have said) in aide of the Britons, of which the first sort inhabited Saxonie: the second were of Gotland, and therefore called Gutes, or Gottes' (Lambarde, xiii). To the Elizabethans, Jutes, Getes, Goths and Germans were not only interchangeable, they were also their own ancestors. Lambarde tells of how they established themselves in Kent, a county which, as Shakespeare reminds us, was especially associated with freedom and valour (see *2H6* 4.7.60–4; tradition had it that William the Conqueror never forced Kent under the Norman yoke). *Titus Andronicus* begins with a Roman stigmatization of Goths as barbarians, but modulates towards a very different view.

If the Second Goth is a barbarian, what is he doing gazing 'upon a ruinous monastery' (5.1.21)? For the Elizabethans, history had lessons to teach the present, so this anachronism is purposeful. It brings a Reformation context into play. The Goth's meditation upon Henry VIII's dissolution of the monasteries, the most drastic consequence of England's break with Rome, carries forward the *translatio imperii ad Teutonicos*:

---

1 What follows is much indebted to Kliger; see also Broude.

The *translatio* suggested forcefully an analogy between the breakup of the Roman empire by the
Goths and the demands of the humanist reformers
of northern Europe for religious freedom, interpreted
as liberation from Roman priestcraft. In other words,
the *translatio* crystallized the idea that humanity was
twice ransomed from Roman tyranny and depravity –
in antiquity by the Goths, in modern times by their
descendants, the German reformers. In their youth,
vigour, and moral purity, the Goths destroyed the
decadent Roman civilization and brought about a
rejuvenation or rebirth of the world. In the same
way, the Reformation was interpreted as a second
world rejuvenation.

(Kliger, 33–4)

Other passing phrases also suggest a Reformation context, most
notably 'popish tricks and ceremonies' (5.1.76), but perhaps
also the references to Lavinia as a 'martyr' (mutilation is the
keynote of one of the most-read books in Elizabethan England,
John Foxe's virulently Protestant martyrology, *Acts and
Monuments*) and even the words with which Titus slits the
throats of his victims, 'Receive the blood' (Protestants could
say that Roman Catholics were barbaric because they made the
Eucharist into a cannibalistic feast in which the wine was
literally the blood of Christ).

The most urgent question facing England in the 1590s was
the succession to the unmarried and childless Elizabeth, and
in particular the preservation of the Protestant nation against
the possibility of another counter-Reformation, like that of
Mary, which, it was thought, would inevitably lead to sub-
jugation to the Catholic power of Spain. Arguments about the
basis on which the succession should be decided – heredity,
election, desert – were widespread, as was fear of tyranny and

foreign invasion. All this suggests that the issue of succession and the mixed nature of Roman government explored in the first act of the play would have had strong contemporary overtones. The descent into imperial tyranny could well have looked like a warning as to what might happen once Astraea, the virgin Queen, had left the earth. Lucius brings back the light; in the shooting scene, his son, another Lucius, scores a direct hit on Astraea's lap. One of the writers who said that 'the christian faith' was received into Britain 'in the time of Lucius their king' was none other than John Foxe (*Acts and Monuments*, 16). The Goths who accompany Lucius, we may then say, are there to secure the Protestant succession.

They also serve as an antidote to the intrigues of high politics. Saturninus is like one of the wicked emperors described in Suetonius and Tacitus. One of Tacitus' ways of condemning imperial rule was by means of the contrasting image of wholesome, pastoral Germans who fed on berries, roots, goatsmilk, curds and whey, as Aaron plans to have his baby fed among the Goths. Tacitism was a code for political disaffection and even republicanism in certain circles in the 1590s, such as that which gathered around the Earl of Essex.[1] The emperor Saturninus, like Claudius in *Hamlet*, is very worried about the popular will slipping away from him. This, combined with the central role played in the elections in both the first and fifth acts by Marcus Andronicus, elected tribune of the people and spokesman for 'the common voice', suggests that Shakespeare's earliest tragedy may be shot through with an unexpected vein of republicanism.

Revenge

The play's interest in political institutions is not confined to its examination of Roman government. The matter of revenge

---

1 See Levy, 251, 261–2; M. James, 418–19.

raises inevitable questions about the institutions of the law.

Halfway through Kyd's *Spanish Tragedy*, Hieronimo stares an old man in the face and assumes or pretends to assume that the 'Senex' is an avenging Fury sent from hell (3.13.133–75). In *Titus Andronicus* Shakespeare picked up on this detail and decided to have a character actually impersonate a Fury sent from hell. The framing device whereby Kyd makes his whole play a performance staged by a personification of Revenge is therefore dropped and Revenge becomes a disguise assumed by Tamora (the ballad based on the play says that at this point she was indeed dressed to look like a Fury). But, as with the masque of Muscovites in *Love's Labour's Lost*, this is a disguise which is instantly seen through and then played along with to wonderful comic effect. This encounter between Titus and Tamora in 5.2 is a brilliant piece of theatre because of the way that one character takes over the other's plot, and turns it against the inventor. By a superb act of improvisation, Titus expands the cast of the masque-like show, making Tamora's companions into what they are, Rape and Murder; by the end of the scene, the device has been fully reversed – the vehicle of Tamora's revenge against Titus for the death of Alarbus has become the vehicle of Titus' revenge against Tamora for the rape of Lavinia and the deaths of Bassianus, Quintus and Martius.

By trumping one character's performance with another's, Shakespeare makes the point which he went on making throughout his career: that we are all role-players. By representing Revenge as a character's device rather than a 'reality' outside the action, as it is in Kyd's frame, he suggests that retribution is a matter of human, not divine will. This is a world in which people make their own laws; as in *Lear*, the gods are frequently invoked but never reply. When the post comes with the answer to the letters which Titus shoots into the heavens, it is in the form not of some message from the gods of the sort we get in *Cymbeline* and

The Winter's Tale, but of a Clown with a basket and two pigeons. Jupiter is replaced by a gibbet-maker and the poor fool is hanged.

In George Peele's *The Battle of Alcazar*, there is a bloody banquet complete with dish of heads, but it is performed in dumb-show and therefore has the same status as that play's other insets, such as its show of Nemesis and three Furies. In *Titus Andronicus*, however, the show is put on by a character instead of Peele's extra-dramatic 'Presenter'. Nemesis comes from within, not without. Titus is an unusual dramatist in that he knocks up a pie rather than a curtain; he plays the cook, not the author and the actor. But a dramatist he is none the less: he has written the script for the climax of his play. He doesn't hesitate to list his literary authorities for it, such as the myth of Progne and the story of Virginius (see below, pp. 90–2). Like Hieronimo's play in sundry languages at the climax of *The Spanish Tragedy*, Titus' banquet serves to render violence structured and ritualistic instead of arbitrary and chaotic. It is no coincidence that later plays in the revenge genre, notably *The Revenger's Tragedy* and Marston's *Antonio's Revenge*, perform their retributions by means of that most structured and ritualistic Renaissance dramatic form, the masque.

Would playgoers have drawn comparisons between the revenger's ritualized violence and the ritualized violence that they were familiar with in real life? Is there a paradoxical sense in which self-conscious performance serves to say not 'this is only a play' but 'this is just like life'? The ritualized violence which an Elizabethan audience would have known best was public execution, itself a highly theatrical activity. Consider a typical sentence passed on a nobleman found guilty of treason in 1589:

That he should be conveyed to the Place from whence he came, and from thence to the place of Execution, and there to be hanged until he were half dead, his

> Members to be cut off, his Bowels to be cast into the
> Fire, his Head to be cut off, his Quarters to be divided
> into four several parts, and to be bestowed in four
> several Places.[1]

Such dismemberment takes us very close to the world of *Titus
Andronicus*. Furthermore, it could elicit the same kind of black
wit as that of Shakespeare's play – on being told at the end of
his trial that his head and quarters would be disposed at her
Majesty's pleasure, Essex replied: 'I think it fit my poor
Quarters that have done her Majesty true Service in divers
parts of the World, should be sacrificed and disposed of at her
Majesty's Pleasure' (*State-Trials*, 1.173). Essex plays on quarters and parts very much in the manner of Titus' puns on hands.

The resemblances between tragedy of blood and live
execution did not escape notice in the period: in *Basilicon
Doron*, James I famously wrote that 'a King is as one set on a
skaffold, whose smallest actions and gestures all the people
gazingly doe behold', but in later editions 'skaffold', with its
simultaneous summoning of theatre and place of execution,
was changed to 'stage'; Stephen Orgel suggests that the emendation was the result of 'the danger James must have felt to
be inherent in the royal drama' – 'To mime the monarch was
a potentially revolutionary act' (Orgel, 45, 47). The players
who represent the enactment of revenge undertake the same
kind of usurpation of the law as the revenger himself does. By
casting revenge in the form of an elaborate public performance,
the drama reveals that the public performance known as the
law is also a form of revenge action; the submission of one
kind of action to critical scrutiny opens the way for the
submission of the other to similar scrutiny. The audience that
shares in Hieronimo's and Hamlet's troubled inquiries as to
whether they should take vengeance into their own hands or

1 'The Tryal of Philip Howard, Earl of Arundel, the 18th day of April, 1589[,] and
   in the 31st Year of the Reign of Queen Elizabeth', in *State-Trials*, 1.140–4.

leave it to God is in a position to reflect upon the insufficiencies and inequalities of the law.

In this regard, it is highly significant that Hamlet is a prince, that Hieronimo is not some marginal or subversive figure but the Knight Marshall, one of the senior law officers of the land. So, too, is Titus a patron of virtue, Rome's best champion, a potential emperor and an actual arbiter of emperors. According to the late sixteenth-century perception of Calvinist political theory, which was widespread in the early 1590s, revolt against the civil order was justified when led by magistrates. God may use those in positions of lesser authority as 'avengers' who will 'punish the tyranny of vicious men and deliver the oppressed from their wretched calamities; at other times he turns the frenzy of men who intended something quite different to the same end' (Calvin, 4.20.30). An Hieronimo or an Andronicus acting beyond the law was a very different proposition from a Jack Cade or a Roman mob doing so.

This is where Fredson Bowers's influential position in his book on *Elizabethan Revenge Tragedy* fails to catch the complexity of the drama. As far as Bowers is concerned, both the law and the drama are unequivocal in their condemnation of blood-revenge. It is the product of malice prepense and as such it is murder in the first degree. Private action undermines the authority of the state:

> Elizabethan law felt itself capable of meting out justice to murderers, and therefore punished an avenger who took justice into his own hands just as heavily as the original murderer. The authorities, conscious of the Elizabethan inheritance of private justice from earlier ages, recognized that their own times still held the possibilities of serious turmoil; and they were determined that private revenge should not unleash a general disrespect for law.
>
> (Bowers, 10–11)

Bowers is confident in his application of this principle to the drama, suggesting that whenever the revenger acts above the law the Elizabethan audience would condemn him. Quite apart from its questionable assumption that the Elizabethan audience all felt the same about such matters, this argument is flawed by its reliance on a rigid distinction between private revenge and legal retribution.

This distinction must be made more subtly, as in fact it was by Bacon in his brief essay 'Of Revenge'. That essay begins with an apparent endorsement of the views summarized by Bowers: revenge is a kind of wild (uncultivated) justice; it puts the law out of office, so the law should weed it out; revenge is perhaps 'tolerable' if it is for a wrong which there is no law to remedy, but the method of revenge had better be one which is not punishable by law. But the conclusion is surprising: 'Public revenges are for the most part fortunate: as that for the death of Caesar, for the death of Pertinax, for the Death of Henry the Third of France, and many more. But in private revenges it is not so. Nay rather, vindicative persons live the life of witches, who, as they are mischievous, so end they infortunate' (Bacon, 73). The public revengers cited – Augustus, Severus, and Henry IV of France – proved to be, according to the official Renaissance view, good and successful rulers. If we believe that Lucius will rule Rome well, then the revenges in the final act of *Titus*, which are certainly performed very publicly, come into the category of the fortunate. Like Hieronimo and Hamlet, Titus pretends to be mad, gives the appearance of having turned his vindictiveness inward in the auto-destructive fashion of Bacon's private revengers, but in fact all along he is preparing for a public act. His revenge takes place as part of a public performance which brings political change.

The necessity to revenge reveals the inadequacy of the law; the formalization of revenge in performance acts as a substitution for the law, simultaneously revealing the law to be

itself nothing other than a performance, replete with processions, costumes, symbolic geography, dialogues, epideictic
utterances, and gestures. Critics who believe that revengers
like Hieronimo and Titus are really mad read the play-within-
the-play as 'a symbol of the revenger's subjective world' and
argue that the 'entrance into this self-created illusory world is
what finally allows the revenger to act' (Hallett, 10). I would
argue on the contrary that the revenger is but mad north-
north-west and that his play or banquet serves as a mirror of
the civic world, revealing it to be not illusory but dependent
upon the performances of power.

Because of the censorship it would not have been possible
to stage a play demystifying an English courtroom or a London
execution. Strikingly, the most notable 1590s tragedy of blood
set in contemporary England, *Arden of Faversham*, ends not
with private vengeance but with the Mayor and the Watch
fully in control and the pronouncement of public death sen-
tences. Where *The Spanish Tragedy, Titus*, and *Hamlet* move
towards the wild justice of the revenger, *Arden* ends with an
affirmation of English justice – the legal system may be a little
rough, but it is eminently capable of punishing evildoers
without the assistance of aggrieved family members acting in
their own capacity. But this is not to say that revenge plays
set abroad could not comment on England. Thomas Heywood
claimed that 'If wee present a forreigne History, the subject is
so intended, that in the lives of *Romans, Grecians*, or others,
either the vertues of our Countrymen are extolled, or their
vices reproved.'[1] If their vices, why not their institutions? *Titus
Andronicus* tells a story of the failure of established legal
remedies: one notes in particular the unsuccessful appeal for
clemency in 3.1 (*'Titus' two sons bound, passing on the stage to
the place of execution, and Titus going before, pleading ... the
Judges pass by him'*) and the treatment of the Clown, whose

---

1 *An Apology for Actors* (1612), sig.F3ᵛ.

27

attempt to settle a matter of a brawl between his uncle and one of the emperor's men leads to instant hanging for himself.

Consequent upon the failure of imperial law is the revenger's establishment of an alternative procedure. Barbaric as the feast in the final scene may be, Titus still uses the language of the law: he speaks of 'precedent' and 'warrant' (5.3.43). It is as if the breakdown of established law is such that he has to create a new system of case-law, based on historical and mythological sources. The appeal to 'precedent', the bedrock of the common law, in a play set in Rome, the home of civil law, suggests something of the contemporaneity of the play's exploration of justice. It may even suggest an intervention in the late Elizabethan argument about the relative weight of civil (also known as imperial) and common law. Recent historians note that 'by the early seventeenth century the civil law was associated with arbitrary government' – 'When Coke elevated past decisions into rules which bound the present, he introduced a major new innovation, one which gave history, albeit mythical history, an importance it had not enjoyed in the sixteenth century' (Sharpe, 175–6). The play foreshadows these developments: the case of the Clown reveals the tyranny of civil or imperial law, as does Saturninus' chilling insistence that Martius and Quintus 'died by law' (4.4.53); Titus' argument from 'precedent' makes him into the voice of the English common law, a dramatic antecedent to Sir Edward Coke – whose commitment to the common law would bring him into conflict with two kings and lead to the framing of the Petition of Right in 1628.

Queen Elizabeth was mythologized as the returned Astraea of Virgil's fourth eclogue. But *Titus Andronicus* imagines a time when justice has left the earth; it locates itself in Ovid's Iron Age when *'Terras Astraea reliquit'* (4.3.4). Where Saturn was supposed to have ruled Rome in the Golden Age, the reign of Saturninus is a new Iron Age (see the wordplay at 4.3.57). The play vividly dramatizes Justice's absence when Titus shoots arrows into the air to try to bring Astraea down. As so often, the three-decker stage works as an image of the three-decker universe; to dramatize so self-consciously the search for justice above is to show that it is not to be found on the stage that is the world. The latter is an empty space which must be filled with the actor's own version of justice, his alternative juridical structure; wild at heart but supremely cultivated in action, he performs his revenge as coolly, as stylishly, and as professionally as any self-respecting judge or executioner going about his daily business.

Passionating grief

Titus resorts to laughter, ritual or self-conscious performance when his ability to express emotion in language is stretched to breaking point. The full title of the play is *The Most Lamentable Roman Tragedy of Titus Andronicus*. The original sense of 'lamentable' is 'Full of or expressing sorrow or grief' (*OED a.* 1). The classical model for 'Tragedy' which was widely available to the Elizabethans was the Roman one of Seneca.[1] Senecan tragedy was based on declamation more than on action: the expression of emotion in elaborate rhetorical form was its very life-blood. Although the explicit 'pattern' of Titus' cannibalistic banquet is Ovid's story of Tereus and Progne, not the feast of Atreus in Seneca's *Thyestes*,[2] 'Senecanism' in a broader sense is a key to the rhetoric of the drama.[3]

Two Senecan themes exercise a deep influence on the play, as they did on Renaissance high culture more generally: that death is a release into rest which is not to be feared and that

---

1 Jones (85–108) has argued for the influence on *Titus* of a Latin translation of Euripides' *Hecuba*, but there is scant, if any, evidence for Shakespeare's direct knowledge of Greek tragedy.
2 For a strong refutation of a previous generation of critics' belief that *Thyestes* was a major source, see Baker, 119–39.
3 On this, see Brower, 173–203, and Miola, 11–32; for Renaissance Senecanism more broadly, Braden.

the wise man has an inner stability which makes him immune to the blows of fortune. The Elizabethans did not doubt that the stoic philosopher Seneca who put forward these views in works such as his *Epistles* was the same man as the dramatist whose *Tenne Tragedies* were collected in English translation in 1581. When Titus discovers that his daughter has been raped, he follows Kyd's Hieronimo in speaking Latin at a moment of extreme emotional stress: *'Magni dominator poli, / Tam lentus audis scelera, tam lentus vides?'* (4.1.81–2). This means 'Ruler of the great heavens, are you so slow to hear crimes, so slow to see?' It indicates that Titus is turning himself into Senecan man, for it is from a moment of discovery of appalling sexual knowledge in the *Hippolytus* (671–2). But there the passage begins 'Magne regnator deum' – Titus' *'dominator poli'* is incorporated from a well-known passage of verse contained in one of Seneca's prose epistles on accepting death and enduring whatever nature throws at you: 'Duc, O parens celsique dominator poli, / Quocumque placuit' ('Lead me, O master of the high heavens, whithersoever thou shalt wish' – *Epistulae Morales*, 107). Philosophical Seneca's idea of submission to the will of the universe is thus skilfully combined with tragical Seneca's scene of *anagnorisis*, of terrible recognition.

Typically, the hero of Senecan tragedy undergoes an explosion of passion ('furor') which elicits on the one hand grief and lamentation, and on the other consolation in the wisdom of stoic philosophy. In a famous chorus in the *Agamemnon*, the Trojan women led by Cassandra welcome death as 'a peaceful port of everlasting rest, a refuge from woes which opens wide and with a generous hand invites the wretched' ('cum pateat malis / effugium et miseros libera mors vocet / portus aeterna placidus quiete'). It is a place where there is no fear, no storm of raging fortune, no civil war, no military wrath, no falling city (Seneca, *Agamemnon*, 589–604). When Titus lays his sons to rest, Shakespeare writes a formal imitation of this:

> In peace and honour rest you here, my sons;
> Rome's readiest champions, repose you here in rest,
> Secure from worldly chances and mishaps.
> Here lurks no treason, here no envy swells,
> Here grow no damned drugs, here are no storms,
> No noise, but silence and eternal sleep:
> In peace and honour rest you here, my sons.
>
> (1.1.153–9)

And when Duncan is in his grave Macbeth reiterates it, adapted to the new context:

> After life's fitful fever he sleeps well.
> Treason has done his worst; nor steel, nor poison,
> Malice domestic, foreign levy, nothing,
> Can touch him further.
>
> (*Mac* 3.2.23–6)

Senecan man's ability to stand still and suffer the slings and arrows of outrageous fortune is nowhere better seen than at the moment when Titus is presented with the sight of his mutilated daughter. Where Lucius faints to his knees, Titus remains firm and looks:

> MARCUS
> This was thy daughter.
> TITUS
> Why, Marcus, so she is.
>
> (3.1.63–4)

This is a man of 'metal', 'steel to the very back'. But he is 'wrung with wrongs more than our backs can bear'. And stoic restraint can be harmful, as Marcus recognizes: 'Sorrow concealed, like an oven stopped, / Doth burn the heart to cinders where it is.' Titus cannot keep his centre wholly hard; he must break into what Marcus calls 'consuming sorrow'. 'Consuming' is a key word in the play, in that it is only after sorrow has eaten away Titus' heart, his kindness, that he turns himself into a revenger and prepares himself to kill his daughter and force Tamora to devour her sons. Passion batters and pierces: the warrior's scarred body is further punctured by grief (see in particular the extraordinary image of the knife, the hole, the tears and the heart at 3.2.16–20). It erodes: Titus is an ancient building, his tears streaming down its side like rain. And it drowns: after Lavinia is brought to him, Titus stands 'as one upon a rock, / Environed with a wilderness of sea,' waiting to be swallowed by the water. After he cuts off his hand, there can be no rational restraint. Passion is bottomless and woe cannot be bound. Titus becomes the sea, the sighing Lavinia becomes the wind:

> When heaven doth weep, doth not the earth o'erflow?
> If the winds rage, doth not the sea wax mad,
> Threatening the welkin with his big-swollen face?
> And wilt thou have a reason for this coil?
> I am the sea. Hark how her sighs doth blow.
> She is the weeping welkin, I the earth.
> Then must my sea be moved with her sighs,
> Then must my earth with her continual tears
> Become a deluge overflowed and drowned . . .
>
> (3.1.222–30)

What is astonishing about these lines is the way in which, even as passion expresses itself through the overflowing imagery, reason restrains it through the controlled rhetoric, the balance of the lines, the doublings and formal repetitions. Rhetorical tragedy proposes that humankind, even in the greatest extremity, is capable of something other than the howl of the wounded animal. The grief is expressed – pressed out – yet a dignity remains.

Renaissance man is rhetorical man, whose repertoire of formal linguistic structures and accompanying physical gestures is a way of ordering the chaos of experience. In Titus' 'I am the sea' there is a kind of consolatory decorum. As the stoic Edgar says in *Lear*, 'The worst is not / So long as we can *say*, "This is the worst"' (*KL* 4.1.27–8). When Titus says 'I am the sea', the worst is still to come: the moment his speech ends, a Messenger enters with his severed hand and the heads of the sons he thought he had saved. Marcus, the voice of decorum, recognizes that now is the time 'to storm', that he should no longer 'control' his brother's griefs, that a full tragic performance is called for: 'Rend off thy silver hair, thy other hand / Gnawing with thy teeth'. But, as we have seen, Titus breaks this decorum and laughs instead. One reason why he does so is suggested in the fly-killing scene:

> Thy niece and I, poor creatures, want our hands
> And cannot passionate our tenfold grief
> With folded arms.

> (3.2.5–7)

Rhetorical tragedy demands hand gestures to help perform the passion. Dismemberment denies these and forces Titus into his alternative course of black comic theatricality. When language no longer works for him, he takes to literalizing metaphor: instead of crying to the elements and the gods, as Lear will do, he writes his message about universal injustice down on arrows and shoots them in the air; instead of talking about 'consuming sorrow', he makes Tamora consume her own children.

Reading and rape

Titus Andronicus has been despised by great Shakespearean critics from Samuel Johnson, who thought that 'The barbarity of the spectacles, and the general massacre which are here exhibited, can scarcely be conceived tolerable to any audience'

(Johnson, 6.364), to T. S. Eliot, who called it 'one of the stupidest and most uninspired plays ever written' (Eliot, 82). There have, it is true, always been glimmers of praise: A. W. Schlegel, for example, found 'no want of beautiful lines, bold images, nay, even features which betray the peculiar conception of Shakespeare' (*Romantics*, 543). But only in the second half of the twentieth century did criticism begin to do justice to the play's sustained artfulness. Hereward Price (1943) was the first critic fully to appreciate its highly-wrought structure, Eugene Waith (1957) the first to hear its Ovidian language, David Palmer (1972) the first to catch its tone scene-by-scene, Albert Tricomi (1974) the first to draw attention to its distinctive way of literalizing its metaphors, G. K. Hunter (1983) the first to perceive the purposeful eclecticism of its Romanness, Heather James (1991) the first to discern the translation of empire. Theirs have, however, been isolated voices; most general books on Shakespearean tragedy still pass the play quickly by.

The linguistic turn taken by post-1960s literary theory put criticism in a position from where it could begin to catch up with the play's characteristically Renaissance obsession with the problem of meaning. The silencing of Lavinia raises exactly that problem: 'I can interpret all her martyred signs,' claims Titus in the manner of a confident semiotician, but he finds that gesture is more ambiguous than spoken language. Only when a text is inscribed upon the ground can interpretation be confirmed. At times the play seems to dramatize the movement from speech to writing: 'See how with signs and tokens she can scrawl', says Demetrius after the rape, 'scrawl' seeming to suggest not only the gesture of spreading the limbs abroad in a sprawling manner, but also scrawling handwriting and perhaps a scroll, a written text.[1]

When the characters are not revenging or raping, they spend their time reading – reading events, reading texts and citations,

---

1   But see note to 2.3.5 regarding dates of *OED*'s first citations.

reading the book of Ovid in which the narrative of the drama is pre-written. Writing demands to be read but it is always open to misconstruction: when Titus sends a message on a scroll to Chiron and Demetrius to the effect that he has deciphered their action, they misinterpret its meaning (though that cunning reader, Aaron, does not). This interest in the signifying potential and the limitations of language plays straight into the hands of the playful deconstructive interpreter:

> *Arms* means offensive and defensive gear, the stuff of war and wounding; it also designates the part of the body which deploys such stuff and which connects the hands with the body. Hence, the word designates both instruments and instrumentality. In the case of *tears*, we need a context to pronounce the word correctly. It can mean the act of rending and separating, or the bodily sign of mourning a loss. In *Titus Andronicus* such dual meanings and plays on words are frequent (as for example, 'hue' and 'hew' or 'hands' and 'handle'); the play goes further still to *dis*play words – to literalize them by writing out on stage, as when the ravished Lavinia writes her Latin lesson on the dusty ground of Rome. Words are embodied and disembodied through this work. One person becomes the text for another's explication, a challenge for interpretation.
>
> (Fawcett, 263)

There is no doubt that the text is full of word games, puns and verbal sleights, and in this respect *Titus* takes us towards the extraordinary linguistic self-consciousness of *Hamlet*. But it is important to register that it does not end in some hermeneutic blockage or deconstructionist's 'aporia'. There is a truth behind the words, a meaning which through painful interpretative work can be unfolded: 'But I of these will wrest an alphabet / And by still practice learn to know thy meaning.' That truth is rape.

Where Lucrece sometimes seems to disappear in the 'helpless smoke of words' of her poetic complaints (*Luc* 1027), Lavinia is a 'Speechless complainer' but a bodily presence. Her body is at the centre of the action, as images of the pierced and wounded body are central to the play's language. It is in reflection upon the display of the woman's body (complicated by the fact that in the original staging it would have been a boy actor's body) that another late twentieth-century critical practice, feminist reading, has much to offer to our apprehension of *Titus*. In two provocative articles, Nancy Vickers has suggested links between voyeurism, rape and dismemberment and the poet's part-by-part enumeration of his mistress' beauties in the Petrarchan convention of the blazon. For all that it is an attempt at empathy, might Marcus' perversely Petrarchan display of the raped Lavinia be a kind of second rape upon her? Again, Stephanie Jed has read the Lucrece story as an example of how the price of 'progress' towards the male republic of Rome is the rape and death of a woman. So, too, the rape and death of Lavinia may be read as the price of Lucius' knitting together of Rome. Frequently in the play the female body is figured – in proto-Freudian fashion, one has to say – in terms of absence, severance and open wounds. The pit containing the corpse of the husband, over which Chiron had previously planned to perform the rape, is one figuration of Lavinia's body. But what are we to make of Lavinia being forced to put her father's hand in her mouth, which is as wounded as her genitals? And of her uncle then making her put a stick in that mouth, with which she writes the word 'rape'? These moments seem 'to reenact her rape in a way that oppressively reinscribes her absence from the sphere of articulation and action'.[1]

---

1 Katherine Rowe, in an essay in *SQ* (Fall, 1994) which usefully criticizes the tendency of some feminists to read Lavinia as an emblem of the absolute oppression of the female, seeing her instead as an emblem for the general loss of agency in the play and thus Titus' counterpart, not his opposite.

And, it might be said, if woman is not silenced and mutilated, then she must be demonized, as she is in the figure of Tamora. Heinrich Heine noticed the way in which 'Shakespeare places two women of entirely different mould next to one another, in order that we may read their characters by the force of contrast' (*Romantics*, 544). Are not such contrasts typical of a male need to cast all women as virgins or whores? But, then, Tamora is a victim, too, a mother whose child is heartlessly wrenched from her. Heine thought that she had the charisma of Milton's Satan: 'a bewitching, imperial figure with the marks of a fallen divinity on her brow' (*Romantics*, 544). I would say that she also has touches of the complexity which makes Lady Macbeth and Cleopatra no mere demons but rather two of the most rewarding female roles in the repertory of world drama.

THE THEATRICAL LIFE

Early stagings

The available evidence strongly suggests that *Titus Andronicus* was written for Henslowe's Rose Theatre. The excavation of the foundations of that theatre in 1989 revealed that the shape of its stage was rather different from those of the Fortune and the Globe, which we know about from documents relating to their construction. The Rose had a wide but shallow stage, tapering towards the front (see Fig. 1). This is a more difficult space to unify than a deep but narrow or a square stage, where the centre can easily dominate the audience's attention.

The opening scene of *Titus* has four focal points: the doors at either side upstage, the tomb of the Andronici in the centre and the gallery aloft, also centre. The action consists of movements within and between these spaces: there are conversations above, conversations below and conversations between above and below. There are actions to the right and actions to the left and still points in the middle. When Saturninus is freeing the Goth prisoners on one side of the stage, Bassianus and the Andronicus boys are going off with Lavinia on the other side. In cinematic terms, this is like a split-screen effect; in contrast to it, on the two occasions when sons of Titus are laid in the tomb there is something like a freeze-frame. Such techniques suggest that Shakespeare had given very careful thought to the problems and potentialities of the Rose stage. Throughout the play, the action shifts between fluidity and stillness. The rising and falling fortunes of the first and last acts are dramatized in vertical movement between main stage and aloft space. Horizontal movement across the width of the main stage takes a variety of forms, notably processions (Titus' triumphal entry, the Judges passing by, Lucius marching with the Goth army) and chases (Lavinia running away from Marcus, the Boy running away from Lavinia). But on other occasions the eye is fixed on the centre: on the tomb in Act 1, the pit in Act 2 and the banqueting table in the final scene. It is not only things which hold the central focus; it is also people, though people frozen into tableaux that make them like pictures, like emblems. We cannot recapture the fluidity of the original performance at the Rose, the figure of Lavinia running across that shallow stage, but by turning to another piece of evidence we can gain some idea of an Elizabethan view of the play's pictorial aspect.

Titus Andronicus is the only Shakespearean play for which we have a contemporaneous illustration. It consists of a single folio sheet, at the top of which is the carefully executed ink drawing reproduced here (Fig. 5). Below the drawing is the heading 'Enter Tamora pleadinge for her sonnes going to execution', then a transcription of forty lines of verse, with speech prefixes. The text consists of Tamora's plea for Alarbus' life (1.1.107–23), a three-line speech for Titus which collapses his reply to this (1.1.124–9) into the single line, 'Patient your

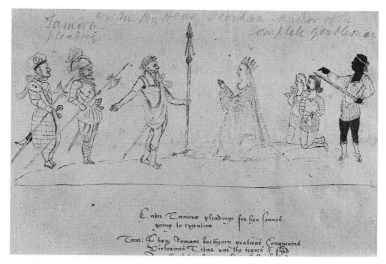

5 The earliest illustration of Shakespeare: Henry Peacham's drawing

self madame for dy hee must', and adds to it an invented two-line transition ('Aaron do you likewise prepare your selfe / And now at last repent your wicked life'), and Aaron's twenty-line boast of his wickedness (5.1.125–44). The page ends with the speech prefix 'Alarbus'.

It is known as the 'Peacham drawing' because in the left-hand margin near the bottom of the sheet is written 'Henricus Peacham'.[1] Among some pencil annotations, apparently made by a nineteenth-century librarian to the Marquess of Bath,[2] is the ascription 'Written by Henry Peacham – author of The Complete Gentleman' (a book published in 1622). This Peacham, who was born in about 1576, was also author of the first English book of practical instruction in drawing and of a published emblem book (from which my Fig. 2 is taken) as well as many other holograph emblems. Ability as a draughts-

---

1 The hand seems to be the same as that which copied the extracts from the play, though the signature is in italic script whereas the transcription uses mainly secretary forms.
2 See Metz, 'Watermark', 451–2.

man and an interest in visual signification thus support the identification.

Below the signature, in the same hand, is a date: 'Anno m°q°gq^{to}'. This has usually been interpreted with the benefit of a later annotation on the page opposite the drawing, 'Henrye Peachams Hande 1595'. But this annotation seems to have been made by the highly unreliable John Payne Collier, who in the nineteenth century tampered with many documents associated with Shakespeare. The authenticity of the drawing and transcription themselves are not in doubt, but Collier's dating most certainly is. The first two letters of Peacham's Latin abbreviation indicate *millesimo* (1000) and *quingentesimo* (500); the last could be *quinto* (5), but if 1595 were the date the third letter ought to be 'n' for *nonogesimo* (90), not 'g'. I suspect that 'g' is intended to stand for *gentesimo*: if *quingentesimo* is 500, *gentesimo* is 100 (i.e. a variant spelling of *centesimo*). If the final letter indicates 5, then, on the analogy of MDCV, the date would be 1605. But the last letter and its superscripts could also indicate *quarto* (4), *quarto-decimo* (14) or *quinto-decimo* (15); 1604, 1614 and 1615 are therefore alternative possibilities.

From what text did Peacham make his transcription? At the beginning of Aaron's line 'I have done a thousand dreadfull thinges', he has 'Tut', the reading of the second and third quartos (1600, 1611), not 'But', the reading of the first quarto (1594). This strongly suggests that the transcription was not made in 1595, when only the first quarto would have been available. Furthermore, in another line of the transcription, the spelling 'haystackes' reproduces Q3 and is close to Q2's 'haystakes', whereas Q1 has 'haystalks'. Consultation of Q3 supports 1614–15, dates which fit well with Peacham's other writings.

But, then, the fifth line of Tamora's speech is 'Oh thinke my sonnes to bee as deare to mee', which corresponds to the first folio of 1623, whereas all the quartos have a singular 'sonne'. To J. Q. Adams, these details suggested consultation of F and therefore a date after 1623.[1] That two sons are mentioned in the heading and shown bound and kneeling in the drawing raises the possibility that an error in F determined the content of the illustration. On the other hand, the many references to sons, together with the absence of Alarbus from the entry direction in the quartos (see p. 103), may have caused Peacham's confusion. I do not see any way in which the Latin date could be, say, 1625, so my best guess is a date between 1604 and 1615 and Q2 or Q3 as copy-text.

The interest in classical history and in the code of honour evinced in *The Complete Gentleman* make it highly likely that Peacham would have read the play and sketched a quasi-emblematic representation of it. There is no evidence that he ever saw *Titus* on stage (beyond the possibility that seeing it was what led him to read it), but the drawing may still be described as an early 'production'. Even if it is a production in Peacham's mental theatre, it demonstrates how a contemporary of Shakespeare's visualized the play – and such a visualization must have depended on some experience of the real theatre. When he was a schoolboy, Peacham saw Tarlton act in London; later, he wrote an epigram to Ben Jonson and received one from Thomas Heywood.

The text's conflation of passages from the first and last acts suggests that the drawing is a composite representation, analogous to the woodcut on the title-page of the 1615 edition of *The Spanish Tragedy* which juxtaposes two key moments in the play. Indeed, I think that the illustration may offer an emblematic reading of the whole play. To read it from left to right is like reading the play from first act to fifth. One begins with two Roman soldiers, who represent Titus' victory in war and service to the state; they may be thought of as members of his ceremonial entrance procession. One then sees the figure

---

1   Adams, 37–40. Wilson ('Stage') supposed that the drawing was made in 1595 and the transcription after 1623, but the unified composition of the page and the similarity of ink make this unlikely.

of Titus himself. He is wearing the laurel bough mentioned at
1.1.77 and the sword which he later hands over to Saturninus.
He has a toga, sign of his civic dignity, over a breastplate or
tunic, sign of his military prowess. He carries a decorated
ceremonial spear or staff, symbol of his 'triumph'. At the base
of it, lying on the ground, is the 'sceptre to control the world',
the token of the empery, which he has rejected at 1.1.202. The
centre of the illustration is a foursquare confrontation between
him and the enemy against whom he is pitted throughout the
play. They are represented as opposites: male against female,
laurel against crown, plain Roman garb against the flowing
dress of the exotic Goth. The long spear or staff divides the
picture down the middle, Romans one side, Goths the other,
just as the play as a whole begins from these two opposed
nations. The opposed gestures of Titus and Tamora are also
the central gestures of the play: authoritative command against
supplication on knees with hands in a gesture of pleading.

Behind Tamora are two kneeling sons, bound for execution.
Peacham seems to have intended to continue his transcription
with a speech from Alarbus; perhaps he broke it off because he
couldn't find one, Alarbus being a mute. That he remembered
Alarbus' name makes it curious that he seems to have forgotten
that only one of Tamora's sons is sacrificed in Act 1. I suspect that he was influenced here by his memory of the play's
repeated stage-images of pairs of sons and large numbers of
characters on their knees. The two youths behind Tamora
become emblems of all the play's sons: they are simultaneously
a kind of doubled Alarbus on the way to execution, Chiron
and Demetrius pleading together with their mother for their
brother's life, and Titus' two middle sons, Quintus and Martius,
whose death is the *quid pro quo* for that of Alarbus (and for
whom Titus later kneels in supplication, echoing Tamora here).
Aaron is instrumental in their execution, and so it is that the
eye then moves to him. He points to his sword, which is raised
(whereas that of Titus is sheathed) to indicate the deaths he

has instigated; there may also be a recollection of the moment when he draws his sword to defend his baby. As the soldiers, symbol of Roman authority, stand at one side of the picture, so Aaron, double outsider, both Goth and coal-black Moor, stands on the opposite margin, just as he stands silently on the margin watching the vicissitudes of the opening 500 lines of the play. He stands defiantly, but at the end of the play he will pass into the hands of the Roman guards.

The Peacham drawing provides us with valuable evidence about costumes: as the play addresses issues in contemporary history via a Roman setting, so the costumes mingle ages. Titus wears a toga but his soldiers are Elizabethan men-at-arms with halberds, while Tamora's dress is vaguely medieval.[1] There could be no better precedent for modern productions which are determinedly eclectic in their dress, combining ancient and modern.

But, as my analysis has suggested, what is most telling about the illustration is its emblematic quality, which exactly fits the way in which the characters in the play so often seem to become emblems, to be frozen into postures that are the very picture of supplication, grief or violent revenge.[2] This sense of a strikingly visual quality is also suggested by the tiny fragment of evidence we have about another very early production. On 1 January 1596 *Titus* was performed by one of the London companies, presumably Shakespeare's Chamberlain's Men, in the household of Sir John Harington at Burley-on-the-Hill in Rutland. Harington had links with the Essex circle, so the play's exploration of the question of succession, and its possible vein of Tacitism, would have been of considerable interest to him. But what we know about the performance concerns its style, not its politics: Jacques Petit, a French tutor in the household, wrote home saying, 'on a aussi joué la tragédie de

---

1   On the costumes, see further Foakes, 50–1.
2   On this, see further Haaker, Hattaway (the latter offers a good general account of the play's use of Elizabethan theatrical resources).

Titus Andronicus mais la monstre a plus valu que le sujet'.[1]
What he valued, then, was the visual spectacle ('la monstre'),
not the narrative substance ('le sujet').

Titus Andronicus was not only the first of Shakespeare's plays
to be printed in England; it was also the first to be printed in
Germany. In 1620, possibly in Leipzig, there was published a
volume of 384 unnumbered pages called *Englische Comedien und
Tragedien*, described as 'the plays acted by the English in Germany'. The eighth play in the collection was *Eine sehr klägliche
Tragaedia von Tito Andronico und der hoffertigen Kaiserin, darinnen
denckwürdige actiones zubefinden*, 'A most lamentable tragedy of
Titus Andronicus and the haughty empress, wherein are found
memorable events'. The 'reporter' responsible for the text was
one Frederick Menius.[2] Anyone who reads it without prejudice
will conclude that it is a translation of Shakespeare's play into
plain German prose, with heavy cutting and a reduction of the
cast to twelve parts (with some doubling possible) and a couple
of all-purpose silent extras (who serve as soldiers, carriers on of
the table for the bloody banquet, and so on).

The scenic structure is in all essentials identical to that of
Shakespeare's play minus the additional fly-killing scene and
with some slight adjustments of order. The cuts are the obvious
ones which a company would make in reducing the size of the
cast. There is no Bassianus in the opening scene, no rivalry for
rule of Rome, no opposing factions requiring large numbers of
soldiers. This greatly streamlines the complex opening, with its
demanding casting requirement. The crown is offered to Titus
since he has saved Rome in war; he refuses it and gives it to the
emperor who is 'next in line'; Bassianus appears briefly and
merely as 'Husband' in Act 2,[3] where he is killed. There is no
killing of Alarbus; this might suggest that the text derives from

---

1 Ungerer, 102, spelling modernized.
2 See Braekman, 9.22–5.
3 In my description of the German play, for convenience I follow the act and scene
   divisions of the Shakespearean.

a version before Alarbus was added, but it need not, since it is an obvious self-contained cut. Quintus and Martius do not actually appear while alive: this reduces the cast size and avoids the difficult-to-stage pit scene; we are told that they have been imprisoned for unspecified crimes, and then their heads are brought on in the scene involving the business of Titus' hand.

Many scenes, however, such as the one in which the sons of the new empress vie over the charms of Titus' daughter and the Moor intervenes, and the one in which the Moor kills the nurse, are hardly altered at all. And many vestiges of the language of the English play are quite clear. For instance, when the empress and her sons come to Titus in disguise, he '*looks down from above*' and says, 'Who are you who calls out to me in this way?', which is obviously a prose version of Titus' line spoken from above in the original, 'Who doth molest my contemplation?' (G1620, 46; *Tit* 5.2.9).

The whole structure of classical allusion which underpins the play is removed. A bucket of sand and a stick – easy props for a touring company – replace the sophisticated business of turning the pages of a text of Ovid's *Metamorphoses*. A 'lower' audience than Shakespeare's is implied, one which requires a strong concentration on spectacle and action rather than ornate rhetoric. This is only to be expected in view of the language problem: in the 1590s the English actors in Germany performed in English, so much of the audience would have been entirely dependent on the visual; after 1600, they increasingly used German, but since it was not their first language they tended to use it as a vehicle for narrative, not for literary display. But, for all the simplification, the sustained structural similarity, together with the many verbal reminiscences, clearly suggests that the German text is a cut-down touring version of Shakespeare.[1] A modern-day small company wanting to perform a 'reduced' *Titus* could learn a lot from it.

---

1 For an explanation of the variations in the characters' names, see Bate, 'Adaptation', n. 15.

As a performance from within, or very shortly after, Shakespeare's own lifetime it has a kind of authority that is rare indeed. If its staging is not Shakespeare's own, it is that of a company as close to him as one is ever going to get. So its directions are of enormous interest. Probably because it was a performance for a foreign audience, there is a great deal of visual business. The bloody banquet is especially vivid: Titus wears a blood-spattered apron and carries a knife in his hand, he *'Goes to the pasties, cuts and places portions of them before the Emperor and the Empress'*, then *'walks mournfully up and down before the table'*, every bit in the manner of Brian Cox in the Deborah Warner production. But it is two bits of business in the great central scene of the third act that are most fascinating. At the end of that scene, the Andronici make an oath that they will right each other's wrongs. Eugene Waith's edition introduces the stage direction 'He pledges them', and adds a footnote to the effect that what is needed is 'A simple ritual, such as handshaking' (Oxf[1], 140). In the circumstances this suggestion seems mildly unfortunate – one can only say with Titus, 'O, handle not the theme, to talk of hands, / Lest we remember still that we have none.' Menius' description of the English actors in Germany suggests that 'ritual' is right, but that something more elaborate is needed:

> *Now* Titus Andronicus *falls upon his knees and begins to chant a dirge, all the others sitting down by the heads. Titus takes up his hand, holds it up and looks to heaven, sobs and repeats the oath softly; he beats his breast and at the conclusion of the oath sets the hand aside. Then he takes up one head and then the other, swearing by each one in turn. Finally he goes to [his daughter], who is kneeling, and swears by her also, as he did with the others, whereupon they all rise again.*

(G1620, 36)

This seems to me in keeping with the high formality of the occasion. It would be fascinating to see it staged, not least because the BBC television production showed that many other effects in the play respond extremely well to a highly ritualized style.

A little earlier in 3.1, shortly after Shakespeare's grisliest stage direction, *'Enter a Messenger with two heads and a hand'*, Marcus says 'Alas, poor heart, that kiss is comfortless / As frozen water to a starved snake' (3.1.251–2). Titus' next utterance is that key line 'Ha, ha, ha!' (3.1.265); after this catharsis of laughter he asks the way to Revenge's cave and the counter-action of the drama is initiated. This sequence is the very cusp of the play, which makes it all the more imperative to visualize the text's intentions for its staging. There is an implied stage direction at this pivotal moment. Neither quartos nor folios include one, but there must be a kiss to prompt Marcus' lines. Dr Johnson therefore introduced the direction 'Lavinia kisses him', meaning 'Lavinia kisses Lucius'; the nineteenth-century Cambridge editor changed this to 'Lavinia kisses Titus', and all modern editors include one or other of these directions.

But in the German version Titus' daughter *'is horrified, looks up to heaven and moans; then she walks to the heads and kisses them'*, after which the Marcus-character speaks (G1620, 34). Deprived of a verbal reaction like those of Marcus and Lucius, the tongue-less woman kisses the severed heads of her brothers. Perhaps she first picks them up between her stumps, in a movement paralleling her subsequent bearing off of Titus' hand between her teeth. Only the combination of mutilated sister and decapitated brothers can make sense of Marcus' image of a physical impediment that denies comfort. The word 'comfortless' should have indicated to editors that Lavinia is not kissing Titus, for earlier in the scene a kiss between father and daughter is associated with comfort: 'Gentle Lavinia, let me kiss thy lips / Or make some sign how I may do thee ease' (3.1.121–2). The German stage direction also makes more sense of Titus' next line: like Marcus, he is a spectator not a participant at this moment. What he is looking at, the scattered remains of his family, his tongueless daughter kissing his sons' severed heads, would be any father's fearful nightmare. Lavinia's motivation for the kiss may well be an attempt to communicate her brothers' innocence of Bassianus' murder, a response to Marcus' perplexity earlier in the scene, 'Perchance she weeps because they killed her husband, / Perchance because she knows them innocent' (3.1.115–16). My edition is the first to follow the stage direction of the early text for this macabre kiss.

Adaptations

It is testimony to the popularity of *Titus* on the Continent in the seventeenth century that the Dutch dramatist Jan Vos wrote an adaptation of it in 1637–8, which was staged in Amsterdam in 1641 and published that year with the title *Aran en Titus*. It was reprinted in 1642, 1644, 1648 and 1649, subsequently going through no fewer than twenty-eight editions by 1726. Its exact relationship with Shakespeare's original is not clear – a Dutch poem of 1652 claimed that a dramatist from Utrecht, Adriaen Van den Bergh, had written an *Andronicus* which was published in 1621, but this cannot be confirmed since that play does not survive.[1] Where the German version focused on Titus and Tamora, the Dutch one, as its title indicates, gave more emphasis to Aaron. It thus initiated a long stage-tradition of making the Moor the central character – it even gave the play a new climax in which he was burned alive on stage.

In common with many of Shakespeare's plays, *Titus Andronicus* was also adapted for production on the English stage after the

---

1 Braekman (10.17) conjectures that Vos based his play on Van den Bergh's, which in turn may have conflated the Shakespearean original and the German version of 1620.

theatres reopened in 1660. Edward Ravenscroft's version, subtitled *The Rape of Lavinia*, published in 1687 though performed about nine years earlier, was one of the more faithful Restoration adaptations. In comparison to the Dryden/Davenant *Tempest*, with its new characters, or the Tate *Lear*, with its happy ending, both characterization and structure are remarkably true to the original. Paradoxically, though, what marks out the theatrical excellence of this version is its chief departure from the original, namely the foregrounding of the role of Aaron which it shares with Vos.

In Shakespeare, the Moor is a brooding silent presence throughout the opening ceremonies and reversals; his first speech is the confident Marlovian soliloquy after everyone else has gone off to the feast in celebration of the marriage of Saturninus and Tamora. Ravenscroft gets him into the action earlier by giving him the speech that in Shakespeare belongs to Demetrius, encouraging Tamora to revenge herself for the death of Alarbus. The character is then brought into prominence through a new exchange in which he is accepted into the service of Saturninus:

TAMORA

> But to my Emperour this one thing I commend
> In highest care and greatest Love 'tis done,
> Receive this worthy Moor to your esteem.

EMPEROR

> Dark is the Case, but thro't a noble light
> There Shines. –

TAMORA

> First, be the place he holds in Trust and Confidence,
> His head in Counsell, and his hand in Warr
> Will never fail to do you service.

ARON

> If Blushes could be seen thro' this black Vayle,
> These undeserved praises, from your Mouth,

> Would dye my Vizage of another hue;
> Quick mounts the blood up to my swarthy Cheeks:
> Tho' not perceiv'd, the Oven glows within.
>
> EMPEROR
> Your word's a noble Warrant.
>
> (Ravenscroft, 2.1, pp. 10–11)

This is a typically strong addition to the text. It heightens the conspiratorial relationship between Tamora and Aaron, showing how it penetrates to the very seat of power; it shows up the gullibility of Saturninus and the quick-wittedness of Aaron; it has a nice dramatic irony (the praises are indeed 'undeserved'); and it introduces the motif of race. Aaron is cleverly exploiting his colour by pretending that he's blushing (a sign of modesty and honesty) but that the blushes cannot be seen because of his swarthy hue. Ravenscroft has taken the idea from a speech later in the play, when Aaron argues to Chiron and Demetrius that black is a superior colour to white because it is constant and because it doesn't betray itself by blushing: 'Coal-black is better than another hue...' (4.2.101–2, 117–20). Ravenscroft retains these arguments in his fifth act, but makes additional use of the idea by showing early how Aaron cunningly turns to advantage his inability to blush.

Shakespeare's Aaron only gets around to celebrating blackness in the fourth act, when he wants to save his child. There is a certain dramatic force in this sudden revelation of the schemer's humanity – it makes us reassess our judgements on the action – but in terms of consistency of characterization it would perhaps have been better to set up much earlier in the play the idea of Aaron as a member of an oppressed minority wreaking his revenge on the established powers. That is of course what Shakespeare did with Edmund in his 'gods, stand up for bastards' soliloquy early in *King Lear*, and it is what Ravenscroft achieves by inserting the following lines into Aaron's 'Now climbeth Tamora' soliloquy:

> Hence abject thoughts that I am black and foul,
> And all the Taunts of Whites that call me Fiend,
> I still am Lovely in an Empress Eyes.
>
> (2.1, p. 15)

The vulnerability revealed in this has an exact counterpart in the Bastard's touching recognition that 'Edmund was beloved' (*KL* 5.3.240). It introduces the possibility that the villainy is a cry for attention, that it stems from a desire to be loved.

Ravenscroft's subtle modulations of the character of Aaron are apparent throughout the play. Where in Shakespeare the Moor lures Quintus and Martius to the pit with the promise of one kind of sport ('I espied the panther fast asleep', 2.2.194), in Ravenscroft it is with another. Aaron slips the brothers a letter, promising them that if they 'attend a while at the Mouth of the Vault which is called the *Serpents-Den*', they will be 'rewarded with the Company of two Ladies, Young, and in our own opinions not unhandsome, whose sight shall not displease you; Love gives the Invitation, and we believe you both Gallant Enough to know how to use it, and to conceal our favours' (3.1, p. 23). Anne Barton has shown how this feigned assignation is part of a translation of the woodland scenes of the play into the world of Restoration comedy or Rochester's 'Ramble in St James's Park'. But it also serves to blur the moral distinction between Romans and Goths. Shakespeare initiated that blurring with the lopping of Alarbus' limbs; Ravenscroft extends it to the other brothers: his Quintus and Martius are not rapists like Chiron and Demetrius, but their predilection for casual sex has a certain decadence about it. What is more, it is Aaron who points the moral once the Andronicus boys have been lured into the pit and thus framed for the murder of Bassianus:

Ha, ha, ha, Poor easy loving fools,
How is their Amorous Expectation cross'd,
Death wayted for their coming here, not Love,
Woman's a sure bait to draw to ruine.
How Easily men are to confusion hurl'd,
'Tis gold and women that undo the world.

(3.1, p. 26)

To give such a moralization to the villain is at once to make him
more complex and to parody the sort of play that makes moral
distinctions appear easy. Ravenscroft's technique is comparable
to that of William Wycherley, who liked to put moral platitudes
into the mouths of characters of doubtful moral pedigree. His
innovation obeys the first rule of strong theatrical reinvention: it
at one and the same time grows from the original text and speaks
to the concerns of the age in which the new production takes
place. What is offered is a distinctively Restoration twist to a
dimension that is already there in Shakespeare, namely a ques-
tioning of the assumption that Rome represents all that is civilized while the Gothic and Moorish outsiders are pure
barbarians.

Shakespeare's principal method of breaking down that
assumption in the case of the Moor occurs with the blackamoor
child; Ravenscroft accentuates this by moving the substance of
5.1 (Lucius getting Aaron to reveal the truth by threatening the
child) to the final scene – there, thanks to the technology of the
Restoration stage, Aaron is discovered on a rack; he is stretched
and stretched again, and still will not speak, but he finally does
so when 'Marcus *holds the child as if he wou'd Kill it*' (p. 54).
Aaron's spilling of the beans enables Ravenscroft to squeeze yet
one more revenge action out of a play that already in Shakespeare
is packed with revenges and counter-revenges: the dying Tamora's final act is to call for the blackamoor child supposedly in
order to give it a parting kiss, but in fact to stab it with the words,

'Dye thou off-spring of that Blab-tongu'd Moor' (p. 55). Aaron's response to his son's death is bizarre. He says:

> She has out-done me in my own Art –
> Out-done me in Murder – Kill'd her own Child.
> Give it me – I'le eat it.
>
> (5.1, p. 55)

This is a variation on the motif of the bloody banquet. Ravenscroft's Tamora has unwittingly eaten the hearts and tongues of two of her sons (Titus, with commendable culinary economy, having kept back the rest of them so that at a strategic moment a curtain can be drawn discovering their heads and hands hanging up against the wall and *'Their bodys in Chairs in bloody Linnen'*). Now Aaron seems to be implying: 'You're not having our son too, I'll eat him in order to prevent you doing so' or, less literally, 'You bore him and killed him, but I begat him and now I'm going to consume him so that at least something of him remains mine, not yours'. Extraordinarily, cannibalism appears for a moment to be something other than mere barbarism. In contrast to both Titus and Tamora, who stab their own children, Aaron has a truly consuming love for his baby. The play cannot of course be allowed to end with such unorthodox thoughts, and Aaron soon returns to cursing all the Romans and repenting of any good deeds he's ever done; in a final spectacle that parallels the Vos adaptation, he is himself consumed by flames, still on his rack. But it is hard to condemn outright an Aaron whose vulnerability has been revealed from early in the play and who has finally seen his baby first threatened by one character and then stabbed to death by a second, its own mother. Ravenscroft has executed a neat reversal of Shakespeare: in the original play the blackamoor child remains alive and is pointed to by Marcus ('Behold the child' – 5.3.118) as a token of Aaron's villainy; in the adaptation, its death serves as a token of others' villainy and Aaron's unexpected humanity.

In view of all this, it comes as no surprise that the revivals of Ravenscroft's version in the period around 1720 owed their success largely to James Quin's performance as Aaron (it was such a favourite in his repertoire that he chose it for his benefit in March 1724). Ravenscroft saw that the sophisticated audience of his age would respond favourably to a compelling villain who was on the one hand scheming and worldly-wise, but on the other oddly vulnerable and tender. He knew at the same time that the convention of poetic justice required that the positive features should be but an under-current, an opportunity for the good actor to win over his audience, and that ultimately the villain would have to be destroyed in spectacular style. The rack and flames symbolically consign him to hell, yet he remains proud and defiant: Aaron effectively becomes Milton's Satan. But to say that is of course instantly to raise the possibility that he also becomes the hero of the play.

Ravenscroft achieved his ends by a degree of reordering and rewriting, but each element of the character – the scheming, the asides, the defiance and bravado, the unexpected vulnerability and tenderness – is there in embryo in Shakespeare. The adaptation is an activation of potential that is latent in the text, and in this respect it may be described as 'faithful' despite all its innovations.[1]

The same may be said of Ira Aldridge in the nineteenth century, though his liberties were greater still. His agenda was slightly different from Ravenscroft's, equally theatrical but more overtly ideological. Where Ravenscroft expanded on what might be described as Aaron's 'Black Power' speeches merely in order to render his villain more interesting and sympathetic, Aldridge did so in order to make the Moor's blackness more prominent. The actor himself was black, and wanted to generate a stronger black tradition in the English theatre. Thus, where

---

1 Ravenscroft is more directly faithful in many of his stage directions: see, for examples, my notes on 1.1.171, 4.2.136 and 5.3.145.

Ravenscroft back-projected on to Aaron some of the characteristics of Edmund, Aldridge attempted to bring him into line
with Othello, his own greatest role (one indeed with which he
became so closely associated that it was widely believed that
the actor himself fetched his life and being from men of royal
siege in Senegal). He had also distinguished himself in the
second major black role in the classic repertory, that of Zanga
in Edward Young's *The Revenge*. This play, which had held its
place on stage for a hundred years (it was first performed in
1721, and Zanga was a celebrated vehicle for Quin in the 1740s
and Edmund Kean during the Regency), was essentially a
compound of *Othello* and Aphra Behn's *Abdelazar, or the
Moor's Revenge*, the latter itself adapted from a *Titus*-influenced
play with a lascivious queen and a scheming Moor, Dekker's
Lust's Dominion. It provided an established precedent for
the theatrical fusion of earlier texts. Aldridge accordingly
commissioned C. A. Somerset, a popular dramatist, to produce
for him an Aaron-centred *Titus* which would not offend
Victorian sensibilities.

According to the most extended surviving review (the text
itself is lost),

> The deflowerment of Lavinia, cutting out her tongue,
> chopping off her hands, and the numerous decapi-
> tations and gross language which occur in the original
> are totally omitted and a play not only presentable but
> actually attractive is the result.
>
> Aaron is elevated into a noble and lofty character.
> Tamora, the Queen of Scythia, is a chaste though
> decidedly strong-minded female, and her connection
> with the Moor appears to be of a legitimate descrip-
> tion. . . . Mr Aldridge's conception of the part of Aaron
> is excellent – gentle and impassioned by turns; now,
> burning with jealousy as he doubts the honour of the
> Queen; anon, fierce with rage as he reflects upon the

6 A nineteenth-century Aaron: Ira Aldridge

wrongs which have been done him – the murder of Alarbus and the abduction of his son; and then all tenderness and emotion in the gentle passages with his infant.[1]

1 *The Era*, 26 April 1857, quoted in Marshall & Stock, 172.

7 A twentieth-century Aaron: Anthony Quayle

Another commentator, J. J. Sheahan, recorded that Aldridge's aggrandizing of Aaron was also achieved by the incorporation into the text of a powerful scene from a play that had been written for him in Dublin with the splendid title *Zaraffa, the Slave King*.

Obviously this *Titus* is not Shakespeare's, but, as with Ravenscroft, it springs from certain potentialities in the text: there is a Shakespearean rationale for Aaron's jealousy when Tamora marries Saturninus and for the 'tenderness and emotion in the gentle passages with his infant'. These are not innovations which go against the grain of the original text in the way that the relationship between Edgar and Cordelia does in Tate's *Lear*. Visually, Aldridge's Aaron, with his glistening scimitar (the ice-brook's temper?), is indistinguishable from Othello (Fig. 6). The endurance of this image of the character is suggested by the fact that one could say the same of Anthony Quayle's Aaron in the Peter Brook production (Fig. 7). But is an identification with Shakespeare's later Moor necessarily a bad thing? The fact is that Shakespeare did write *Othello* after *Titus* and that once *Othello* entered the repertory the image of the Moor of Venice could not be erased from the English theatrical imagination. Zanga and Alonzo in *The Revenge* only have meaning in relation to Othello and Iago, and by the same account every post-*Othello* production of *Titus* comes with the knowledge of the later play in which Shakespeare redistributed the characteristics of Aaron, giving his racial identity to the noble but gullible Moor and his villainy to the demi-devil with a black heart in a white skin. Most productions emphasize the embryonic Iago in Aaron, while Aldridge's serves to remind us that there is also an embryonic Othello in him.

Where Aldridge's version did go against the Shakespearean grain was in its Bowdlerization. The price of getting an Aaron on to the Victorian stage was the removal of the rape and mutilation of Lavinia. For simple reasons of taste – of moral decorum – the nineteenth century could not bring on a rape victim as Shakespeare could in the late sixteenth century and Ravenscroft could in the late seventeenth (the latter's stage direction was as uncompromising as Shakespeare's: '*Enter* Chiron, Demetrius, Lavinia *her hands Cut off, and her tongue cut out, Loose hair, and Garments disorder'd, as ravisht*' – 3.1,

p. 26). In the Victorian age, then, the rape of Lavinia was quite literally unstageable.

Stylization or intimacy?

In the twentieth century, with its looser decorums, the rape has been restored to the stage, but until recently the rape victim's entry and her uncle's verbal response to it have remained deeply problematic for directors. Whilst no longer unstageable, the scene was still thought to be un*speak*able. That is to say, Marcus' long lyric monologue was regarded as indecorous: what place has such poetry in the face of such a sight of horror? An influential critical statement of this position came in 1957 with Eugene Waith's article, 'The metamorphosis of violence in *Titus Andronicus*'. Waith skilfully showed that the play was much more Ovidian than Senecan, but as part of his argument he claimed that the post-rape scene was an aesthetic failure since it was written in an opulent Ovidian language which was all very well on the page of the *Metamorphoses* but grotesquely inappropriate on stage.

An even more influential, because theatrical, statement of this position came two years earlier with Peter Brook's Stratford production, in which Vivien Leigh played Lavinia to Laurence Olivier's Titus. Leigh's entrance in this scene was the most striking moment in the performance. To 'the slow plucking of harp-strings, like drops of blood falling into a pool' (David, 127), she entered with scarlet ribbons trailing from her wrists and mouth (Fig. 8). The achievement of a visual stylization was brilliant – it shaped the predominant theatrical approach to the play for thirty years[1] – but in order to highlight it Brook removed the verbal stylization. The scene was made into a silent tableau in a kind of discovery space upstage centre: the

---

1 For an account of the succession of post-Brook stylized productions, see Dessen, 24–35. For a general stage history of the play, see Metz, 'Stage'; for a useful selection of reviews, see Williamson.

8 The raped Lavinia (Vivien Leigh) in Peter Brook's stylized production

promptbook has 'Enter C[entre] Lavinia stands desolate', no Marcus, and hence no verbal response, and within a very short time 'Demetrius and Chiron slowly close the column doors meeting C[entre]'.[1] Most subsequent productions have reintroduced the speech but cut it very heavily.[2] Brook's visual innovation and verbal suppression in their way represent as radical a reconstitution of the original as anything in Ravenscroft. Once again, they answer to the first rule of strong theatrical reinvention. The long red ribbons serve as a translation of the language of the text in that they stand in the same evocative but oblique relation to blood as do such similes as that of the bubbling fountain: the innovation may thus be said to grow from

1 Promptbook in the collection of the Shakespeare Centre, Stratford-upon-Avon.
2 The promptbook of the 1972 Trevor Nunn/Buzz Goodbody production reveals that twenty-nine out of forty-seven lines were cut (including all the 'poetic' ones). Friedrich Dürrenmatt's 1970 German adaptation, much of which is very close to the original, cut the speech altogether.

9 The raped Lavinia (Sonia Ritter) in Deborah Warner's realistic production, supported by Marcus (Donald Sumpter)

the original script. And at the same time they speak in the new language of the post-Artaudian theatre in which stage events are ritualized and their correspondence to reality outside the theatre is skewed and problematized.

Deborah Warner's production at the Swan in Stratford-upon-Avon in 1987, The Pit in London in 1988, and then on European tour, including a highly successful run at Brook's own Bouffes du Nord in Paris, was remarkable not least because of its textual fidelity. Not a single line was cut. What, then, was the effect of playing Marcus' monologue in its entirety? The best description of the moment is that of Stanley Wells:

> spoken in Donald Sumpter's hushed tones it became a deeply moving attempt to master the facts, and thus to overcome the emotional shock, of a previously unimagined horror. We had the sense of a suspension of time, as if the speech represented an articulation, necessarily extended in expression, of a sequence of thoughts and emotions that might have taken no more than a second or two to flash through the character's mind, like a bad dream.
>
> (Wells, *ShS*, 179)

Alan Dessen adds a helpful gloss:

> we observe Marcus, step-by-step, use his logic and Lavinia's reactions to work out what has happened, so that the spectators both see Lavinia directly *and* see her through his eyes and images. In the process the horror of the situation is filtered through a human consciousness in a way difficult to describe but powerful to experience (so as to produce what many observers felt to be the strongest single moment in the show).
>
> (Dessen, 60)

Marcus needs a long speech because in it he has to learn slowly and painfully to confront suffering. He has to make himself *look* steadily at the mutilated woman, just as we, the offstage audience, have to look at her (Fig. 9). The working through of bad dream into clear sight is formalized in Marcus' elaborate verbal patterns; only after writing out the process in this way could Shakespeare repeat and vary it in the simple, direct, unbearable language of the end of *Lear*: 'Look there, look there!' (5.3.312). And a lyrical speech is needed because it is only when an appropriately inappropriate language has been found that the sheer force of contrast between its beauty and Lavinia's degradation begins to express what she has undergone and lost.

Marcus' speech was also made to work movingly in Mark Rucker's 1988 Santa Cruz production. There, as he spoke, the actor tore his robe to make tourniquets to stem the flow of Lavinia's blood. The speech itself thus became a kind of bandage, life-preserving and wound-concealing. After this act of linguistic first aid, Marcus could then take Lavinia to join her father in the full-scale rhetorical field hospital of the third act.

The Warner version of Marcus' speech was revisionary in its effect even as it was faithful in its form because it brought the text squarely into the present. For Warner in her direction of Marcus and Sonia Ritter in her portrayal of Lavinia achieved what they did because rape matters to them as late twentieth-century women more than it could possibly have done to Shakespeare writing for Marcus and to the boy who first played Lavinia. The simple fact that Warner was (to my knowledge) the first woman ever to direct the play on stage[1] itself effects a radical revision: for a start it defuses the argument that a speech written and performed by men cannot begin to make an audience feel what rape is like. Watching Ritter and sensing

---

1 The BBC television version of 1985 was directed by Jane Howell; its particular strength was in its viewing of violent male public rituals through the eyes of a child, Young Lucius.

10 An exotic Tamora: Maxine Audley

Warner behind Sumpter, one could with Marcus begin to share
the rape victim's anguish. The scene was so powerful to so
many members of the audience because our culture is more
conscious of rape and its peculiar vileness than many previous

11 An earthy Tamora: Estelle Kohler, with Saturninus (Jim Hooper)

cultures have been: so it was that the words from the 1590s (when rape was very rarely reported to the authorities or acted upon by the courts)[1] worked a new effect in the context of the 1980s.

As Alan Dessen has argued in his valuable book on *Titus* in performance, the Brook and Warner productions represent strong alternative directorial choices. Stylization enabled Brook to bring out the play's ritualistic and emblematic qualities;

1 On this, see Gossett, 310–12.

realism enabled Warner to bring out its representation of how ordinary human beings can be driven to extraordinary extremities of violence and cruelty on the one hand, resilience and tenderness on the other. Stylistic choices have to be made at every level: does a director look for an exotic, almost operatic Tamora, like Brook's Maxine Audley (Fig. 10)? Or one who exudes an earthier sexual magnetism, like Warner's Estelle Kohler? (Fig. 11 shows a moment which nicely plays her control off against Saturninus' bemused frustration in 4.4 – in this production they've been disturbed in bed by Titus' arrows.) The text has potential for both, and it is in just this combination of exoticism and earthiness that Tamora anticipates Cleopatra.

Kohler didn't need regal paraphernalia to convey Tamora's erotic aura; the sexual revolution which occurred between the Brook production and the Warner meant that she could use her body much more freely. That freedom, in combination with the small studio spaces in which the production was staged, meant that she could activate Tamora's cunning and playfulness – the qualities which are most apparent in her asides and which look forward to Richard III as well as to Cleopatra – with a new intimacy. Indeed, intimacy was the key to the Warner production. Where Olivier was like some image of what Kent in *Lear* calls 'the promised end', Cox took the audience into his confidence with nudges and winks. The contrasting styles are well caught in a pair of reviews. Here is Kenneth Tynan on Olivier's Titus:

> Titus enters not as a beaming hero but as a battered veteran, stubborn and shambling, long past caring about the people's cheers. A hundred campaigns have tanned his heart to leather, and from the cracking of that heart there issues a terrible music, not untinged by madness. One hears great cries, which, like all of this actor's best effects, seem to have been dredged up

from an ocean-bed of fatigue. One recognized, though one had never heard it before, the noise made in its last extremity by the cornered human soul.

(Tynan, 11)

And here is Michael Billington on Cox's:

Ms Warner's wiliest tactic is to pre-empt possible laughter at the play's grosser cruelties by launching them in a spirit of dangerous jocularity . . . [Cox] combines a quirky, senescent humour with a tremendous bottled danger: he kills a fly with a savage, table-turning zest that is a terrifying prelude to his later calculated revenge.

(Billington, 24)

Brook made the boy Lucius finish off the fly in order to suggest Gloucester's 'As flies to wanton boys are we to the gods, / They kill us for their sport'; Warner's fly-killing scene, in common with her approach throughout, combined passion with comedy in the exact spirit of Titus' laugh.

The recent excavation of the Rose Theatre, where the play was first staged, suggests that Warner's intimate production may have been closer to the original than one would once have imagined, for the archaeological evidence shows that the Rose was a lot smaller than later Elizabethan theatres such as the Fortune and the Globe. But, whatever the size of the stage and the overall style of the production, there will always be intimacy and intensity at moments such as that in 3.1 when Titus looks stoically at his raped daughter: the similarity between Olivier and Cox here is striking (Figs 12 and 13). In the words of Edward Capell, one of the tiny handful of pre-twentieth-century commentators to have appreciated the play, 'The genius of its Author breaks forth in some places, and, to the editor's eye, Shakespeare stands confess'd: the third act in particular may be read with admiration even by the most

12 Father and daughter: Laurence Olivier and Vivien Leigh

13 Father and daughter: Brian Cox and Sonia Ritter

delicate; who, if they are not without feelings, may chance to find themselves touch'd by it with such passions as tragedy should excite, that is – terror, and pity' (Capell, 1.45).

ORIGINS

Date

Times were hard for the London theatre in the years 1592–4. On the evening of 12 June 1592 Sir William Webbe, the Lord Mayor of London, broke up a public disturbance within the borough of Southwark. The next morning he sent the Deputy and Constable of the borough to investigate the circumstances; it was established that 'the sayed companies assembled themselves by occasion & pretence of their meeting at a play' (Chambers, 4.310). Ten days later the theatres were closed by order of the Privy Council. Philip Henslowe's record of plays performed and receipts taken at his Rose Theatre comes to a temporary halt; Lord Strange's men did not perform for him at the Rose again until 29 December. But worse was to come. The 1592–3 winter season was cut short at the end of January when a new order went out from the Privy Council: 'Forasmuch as by the certificate of the last weeke yt appeareth the infection doth increase ... we thinke yt fytt that all manner of councourse and publique meetinges of the people at playes, beare-baitinges, bowlinges and other like assemblyes for sportes be forbidden' (Chambers, 4.313). The theatres remained closed for nearly a year as plague deaths climbed through the summer and only diminished with the cold of another winter. Once again Henslowe could open the Rose after Christmas: there was another short season from 27 December 1593 to 6 February 1594, played by 'the earle of susex his men'. One new work was introduced into the repertoire. It must have taken some preparation, for it was not until four weeks of the season had passed that Henslowe recorded: 'ne – Rd at titus & ondronicus th*e* 2[4] of Jenew*a*ry ... iij^li viij s'. New: *Titus Andronicus*, Thursday 24 January 1594, receipts three pounds eight shillings.[1]

The takings were among the best of the season (the performances immediately before and after yielded twenty-five and eighteen shillings respectively); the new play was repeated on 29 January and 6 February, forty shillings (two pounds) being taken each time. But a potential long run was forestalled: another restraining order – plague again – closed the Rose with effect from 7 February. The order was issued on 3 February; on the 6th the printer John Danter lodged in the Stationers' Register an entry for 'A Noble Roman Historye of Tytus Andronicus'; before too long the text of the play could be bought from Edward White and Thomas Millington at the little north door of St Paul's under the sign of the Gun. A likely explanation of this sequence of events is that in response to the imminent closure of the theatres so soon after the première of their successful new play, the players decided to make some money on it from another source and sold it to Danter, who rushed it into print while it was still new. If the public were to be prevented from seeing it, at least they could read it. Danter also entered a ballad on the same subject: it was common practice to produce ballads based on plays – the spin-off as teaser, a modern marketer might say (the ballad could be sold as a penny broadsheet, so that a version of the story would be available to a wider range of purchasers, some of whom might then be so hooked that they would dig deeper into their pocket and buy the play).

In early June 1594, the Admiral's and Chamberlain's men

---

1 Henslowe, 21. Recorded as 23 Jan., but as 4th play of the week, therefore corrected to Thurs. 24th on assumption that there was no performance the previous Sunday. 'New' (perhaps meaning '*n*ewly *e*ntered [the repertoire]') is the obvious interpretation of Henslowe's 'ne'. All the plays so marked between 1591 and 1594 seem to have been genuinely new; it was only from late 1595 onwards that 'ne' was occasionally written beside an older play that was either newly revised or new to the company performing it. *The Jew of Malta* was new to the repertory of Sussex's Men on 4 February 1594, just four performances after their new *Titus*, but Henslowe did not mark it 'ne'.

played together for Henslowe at Newington Butts, a theatre across St George's Fields and beyond the City jurisdiction; *Andronicus* was revived for two of these ten performances. But receipts were low out in the sticks, and in mid-June, plague having abated, the theatres on Bankside could reopen, so the two companies parted. The Admiral's returned to the Rose and the Chamberlain's, a new company, almost certainly established themselves at the Theatre north of the river. *Titus* became the property of the Chamberlain's. We do not, alas, have records of their repertory, as we do of the Admiral's in their subsequent years as Henslowe's house troupe, so it is impossible to tell how long they went on performing it. The private performance in Rutland suggests that it was still a company showpiece in 1596. That the printed text went into second and third editions in 1600 and 1611 with the title-page claiming that 'it hath sundry times beene playde' by the Lord Chamberlain's (later King's) servants, suggests that it remained popular.

Indeed, it still had a place in the affections of the theatregoing public in 1614. Ben Jonson's new play of that year, *Bartholomew Fair*, began with an Induction in which a Scrivener read out some supposed Articles of Agreement between the Spectators and the Author, one condition of which was that the audience should be 'fixed and settled' in their judgements – they shouldn't approve the play today and not approve it tomorrow; they should follow the example of those who 'will swear, *Jeronimo*, or *Andronicus* are the best plays ... whose judgement shows it is constant, and hath stood still, these five and twenty, or thirty years' (Jonson, 6.16). Such preference for old-fangled plays is ignorant, but at least it is 'a virtuous and stayed ignorance'. The best editor of *The Spanish Tragedy* (as *Jeronimo* was more frequently known) proposed the date 1590 for it (*Sp. Trag.*, xxvii); I incline to 1589. If this is correct and *Titus* was new in 1594, the two plays would have been twenty-five and twenty years old in 1614, not twenty-five or thirty. The discrepancy arises because exaggeration is the trope of these

Articles of Agreement: item one inflates length of performance, item two inflates ticket prices, item three inflates the age of *The Spanish Tragedy* and *Titus Andronicus*. Jonson's point is that these plays were all the rage a generation ago and are still what people want now, whereas he has something different to offer.

But Jonson's joke was a gift to literal-minded scholars who didn't like *Titus Andronicus* and wanted to argue that it wasn't by Shakespeare, or if it was he was just adding a few strokes to an old play, or if he was really responsible for all of it then it must have been one of his very earliest works. It seemed to give them grounds for pushing the date of composition back to about 1589. The previous Arden editor wavered over the date but, in accordance with his general contempt for the play, concluded that 'there does not seem to be anything that flatly contradicts a date of about 1589–90' (Ard[2], xxiv). Among more recent editors, Eugene Waith decides on 'a date preceding 1592 for the original composition of the play with a revision in late 1593' (Oxf[1], 10) and Gary Taylor plumps for 1592 (*TxC*, 113).

An over-literal reading of the allusion in *Bartholomew Fair* is not the only reason why few scholars have accepted the *prima facie* case that *Titus* really was new on 24 January 1594. There are two other pieces of apparent evidence for an early date.

In 1594, a text was published of a fairly successful Henslowe comedy called *A Knack to Know a Knave*. One passage reads as follows:

> My gratious Lord, as welcome shall you be,
> To me, my Daughter, and my sonne in Law,
> As *Titus* was unto the Roman Senators,
> When he had made a conquest on the Goths:
> That in requitall of his service done,
> Did offer him the imperiall Diademe:
> As they in *Titus*, we in your Grace still fynd,
> The perfect figure of a Princelie mind.
>   (*Knack*, sig.F2[v], lines 1488–95)

According to Henslowe's records, *Knack* was performed as new by Lord Strange's Men on 10 June 1592. If the text published in 1594 were reliable, Shakespeare's play (or some putative earlier version of it) would have to ante-date June 1592. But in fact the *Knack* text of 1594 has all the marks of having been memorially reconstructed by some of Strange's/Derby's Men, so the allusion cannot be relied on. If the same actors were simultaneously learning their lines for the new *Titus* and remembering the lines of the old *Knack*, contamination from one to the other is eminently plausible.

Paul Bennett suggested that there may have been a muddling of two Titus plays. In June 1592 and January 1593, *Knack* was often performed in close proximity to (on two occasions the day before) a lost play called *Titus and Vespasian*. Indeed, there seem to be allusions to this play elsewhere in *Knack*; one line refers to Vespasian having his son's hand cut off as punishment for beating a swain. *Titus and Vespasian* almost certainly concerned the two Roman emperors and the siege of Jerusalem in AD 70; the Roman historians record that when Titus returned to Rome after capturing Jerusalem he was welcomed by the senate and made joint emperor with his father, Vespasian. If this incident was dramatized in the lost play, the possibility for confusion is immediately apparent: replace 'Goths' with 'Jews' and you have an allusion to *Titus and Vespasian* as precise as that in the received text appears to be to *Titus Andronicus* – perhaps more precise, since in Shakespeare's play the offer comes not from the senate but from the people via their tribunes. In the absence of the lost play and a reliable text of *Knack*, this 'evidence' must be discounted. It tells us not that *Titus* was in existence by June 1592, but that it was in existence when *Knack* was 'Newlie set foorth' in early 1594.

The second exhibit is the title page of Danter's 1594 edition, the first quarto: *The Most Lamentable Romaine Tragedie of Titus Andronicus: As it was Plaide by the Right Honourable the Earle of Darbie, Earle of Pembrooke, and Earle of Sussex their Seruants*

(Fig. 14). It has usually been assumed that this means that the play went successively through the hands of the three companies. Thus it is said to have originated with Lord Strange's Men (Strange became Earl of Derby in September 1593), passed to the obscure Pembroke's Men, and ended up with Sussex's. We have a full record of Strange's men's performances from 19 February to 23 June 1592, and *Titus* is not included in their twenty-three-play-strong repertory, so if it had been written by then it must have passed on to Pembroke's Men.[1] Records of Pembroke's are extremely scant: the company seems to have come into existence in 1592 and to have toured in the provinces that year and the next, giving just two performances at Court in the 1592 Christmas season; they appear to have gone bankrupt by September 1593. If they played *Titus*, it was almost certainly in the provinces. On the assumption that Pembroke's was a touring offshoot of Strange's, one could postulate the sequence: pre-1592 Strange's *Titus*, 1592–3 Pembroke's touring *Titus*, 1594 Sussex's *Titus*.

But there is an alternative possibility, first put forward by David George, namely that the 1594 title-page refers to performances not by three companies in sequence, but by one company which included actors who had previously worked for the other two. Elements of Strange's and Pembroke's Men may have been absorbed into Sussex's for this season. Pembroke's broke late in 1593; Strange's went through considerable upheaval at the same time – the only records of them in 1594 are in the provinces. It seems eminently plausible that some actors from each would have returned to London and sought employment with the group who were performing for Henslowe. Sussex's Men were at Winchester on 7 December 1593, and from 27 December were at the Rose. At Winchester

---

1 The brief season of 29 December 1592 to 1 February 1593 included three performances of a *Titus*, but Henslowe did not mark it as 'Andronicus' or as 'ne', so this must almost certainly have been a revival of the *Titus and Vespasian* that was new on 11 April 1592.

they may have been a small-size touring company; by taking on elements of Strange's and Pembroke's, they would have been up to full London strength, and in a position to perform the one new play of the season – with its large cast and its emphasis on grand spectacle.

That Henslowe only mentions Sussex's Men need not be significant: Strange's and the Lord Admiral's performed in some sort of combination at various times in the early 1590s, and were sometimes known by one title, sometimes by the other. The companies went through many mutations from 1592 to 1594, and personnel only settled in the summer of 1594 when there emerged for the first time the pattern of the Admiral's (with the Marlowe repertory) at Henslowe's Rose and the Chamberlain's (with the Shakespeare repertory) at the Theatre. Sussex's disappeared, presumably absorbed into another company, after the Easter 1594 season during which Henslowe made payments to 'the Quenes men & my lord of Susexe to geather'. There is every reason to postulate the likelihood of actors from different companies coming together in the first season after the plague.[1]

The wording of the title-page is extremely unusual. The only plays printed before 1594 to mention more than one company on the title-page were Lyly's *Sapho and Phao* and *Campaspe* (both 1584), the former 'Played beefore the Queenes Majestie on twelfe day at night by her Majesties children, and the children of Paules', the latter 'Played beefore the Queenes Majestie on Shrove-tewsday, by her Majesties Children, and the Boyes of Paules'. In each case, this clearly refers to joint production. After *Titus*, the next printed plays to name more than one company were Lyly's *Love's Metamorphosis* (1601) and Dekker's *Satiromastix* (1602); in each case, the different performances are very clearly distinguished (Lyly: 'First playd by ... and now by'; Dekker: 'presented publikely, by ... and

---

1 See McMillin for a similar reconstruction of the companies at this time, though he believes that *Titus* passed from one to the next between 1592 and 1594.

privately, by'). These cases apart, there is no tradition of title-pages listing a sequence of companies through whose hands a play passed. The 1594 quarto of Greene's *Friar Bacon and Friar Bungay* (printed, as *Titus* was, for Edward White), 'As it was plaid by her Majesties [Queens'] servants', makes no mention of performance by Strange's, even though they played it many times for Henslowe in 1592–3; Peele's *Battle of Alcazar* was one of the most popular plays in Strange's repertory before the inhibition, but the 1594 quarto only mentions Admiral's. The same situation obtains with several other 1590s plays.

Furthermore, when a play was performed many times, the published text liked to emphasize its popularity by speaking of the play 'as it hath sundry times been played'. Surprisingly few publicly performed London plays went into print before 1594; typical examples of those that did were the two parts of *Tamburlaine* printed in 1590 as 'sundrie times shewed upon Stages in the Citie of London' and reprinted in 1593 as 'sundry times most stately shewed', the two parts of *The Troublesome Reign of King John* (1591) 'As it was (sundry times) publikely acted', and *Fair Em* (>1593, probably printed by Danter) 'as it was sundrietimes publiquely acted in the honourable citie of London'. Among plays first published in 1594, *A Knack to Know a Knave*, *The Taming of a Shrew*, *The Battle of Alcazar*, *Mother Bombie*, and *Edward II* all had 'sundry times' on their title-pages. The absence of the word from the title-page of *Titus* Q1 begins to look conspicuous. It becomes glaring when Q2 appears in 1600 'As it hath sundry times beene playde by the Right Honourable the Earle of Pembrooke, the Earle of Darbie, the Earle of Sussex, and the Lorde Chamberlaine theyr Seruants', and Q3 in 1611 'As it hath sundry times beene plaide by the Kings Maiesties Seruants'.[1] Why is the puff

---

1 That Q2 adds the name of the company in whose repertoire the play was in 1600 suggests an assumption of performance by the other three companies in succession, but an assumption made by a printer in 1600 cannot be taken as firm evidence of the original meaning of the 1594 title-page.

'sundry times' absent in 1594 but present in 1600 and 1611? The obvious explanation is that the play had not been performed sundry times by 1594, that Q1 refers to a brand-new play performed for the first time by a large company which included 'servants' who between them had loyalty to all three noblemen. Getting three lords for the price of one on to the title-page was a good way of making the play seem very impressive indeed and keeping all parties happy, especially since Derby and Pembroke were more prominent patrons than Sussex.

Three local details also support a composition date of late 1593 to early 1594. The image of Lavinia's husband's dead body being used as a pillow while she is raped exactly replicates a detail in Nashe's *Unfortunate Traveller* (completed 27 June 1593).[1] The rare word 'palliament' appears to have been coined by George Peele in his *The Honour of the Garter*, written for a ceremony in June 1593 and published by the end of the year; the word is used by Marcus at 1.1.185 (the play includes several other striking echoes of Peele's poem). And on 31 March 1593 two puritans were taken to the scaffold, then reprieved at the last minute, taken down again and returned to prison, only to be taken back to Tyburn and hanged seven days later. This sounds remarkably like the Clown's gossip: 'Ho, the gibbet-maker? He says that he hath taken them down again, for the man must not be hanged till the next week' (4.3.80–2).[2]

Nashe's *Christ's Tears over Jerusalem* also belongs to the summer of 1593. It alludes to Titus' and Vespasian's conquest of Jerusalem; it also speaks of a mother eating her own child and a consul called Saturninus; both the phrase '*Titus* ledde prysoncrs to Rome' (Nashe, 2.78) and a number of individual words suggest that Shakespeare may have picked up some ideas from here too (see Tobin).

---

1 Nashe, 2.292; see Burnet, who also notes that a few lines later Nashe has the phrase 'Let not your sorrow die', which is also used by Aaron (5.1.140).
2 This striking link was first noted by Politi.

The nature of the printer's copy gives further support to the hypothesis that *Titus* was new in early 1594. It is generally agreed that Danter typeset his text from Shakespeare's working draft manuscript. Consider the two following possibilities. That Shakespeare wrote this manuscript some time before the plague closure, and that a theatrical transcript of it passed through the hands of three different companies, but that the author's manuscript happened to reappear in early February 1594 and be given to a printer at the same time that the play was being revived by the third company. Or that Shakespeare wrote a new play which was ready for performance by late January 1594 and that as soon as the theatrical copy was prepared and the parts for the actors made out the working draft could be sold to a printer. The latter seems more plausible.

All this evidence suggests that *Titus*, at least in the form in which we have it, was written in late 1593 and first performed in January 1594. I believe that it was completely new at this time, though it is possible that some earlier version of the play (by Shakespeare or another) was in existence before June 1592 and that the January 1594 performance was new only in the sense that it was of a text that was newly revised.

There would have been little point in writing plays between June 1592 and the end of 1593. Shakespeare wrote his *Henry VI* plays before the closure of 23 June 1592; the theatres' future then being uncertain, he tried to make his way as a non-dramatic poet, writing and publishing *Venus and Adonis* and beginning *The Rape of Lucrece*. These works took him to Ovid and to Roman history, quite possibly for the first time since his schooldays. According to my hypothesis, in late 1593, with the prospect of the theatres reopening, he began a new play based on his classical reading – a Roman tragedy which has exceptionally strong stylistic and thematic links with *Lucrece*. With *Titus* he cut his teeth, both structurally and rhetorically, in the writing of tragedy; he was then able to go back to English history, but with a new tragic intensity. I suspect that

Richard III was his next move in historical tragedy and that it belongs to 1594, being his first tragedy for the new Chamberlain's Men.[1] Burbage played the lead and established his reputation. If my reconstruction is correct, *Titus Andronicus* emerges as *the* pivotal play in Shakespeare's early career. It is the play in which he draws on the new skills learned in his eighteen-month sabbatical as a non-dramatic poet and paves the way for his later achievements in tragedy.

Authorship

On the face of it, there ought not to be a dispute about the authorship of *Titus Andronicus*. It went with Shakespeare into the repertoire of the Chamberlain's Men; many details are paralleled in *Lucrece* or anticipate later plays such as *Lear* and *Coriolanus*; Francis Meres, a reliable witness, listed it among Shakespeare's tragedies in his *Palladis Tamia* of 1598; it was included in the First Folio.

But Ravenscroft wrote in the address 'To the Reader' at the beginning of his adaptation that 'I have been told by some anciently conversant with the Stage, that it was not Originally his, but brought by a private Author to be Acted, and he only gave some Master-touches to one or two Principal Parts or Characters'. There is no other evidence for this story and the context of the address suggests that Ravenscroft may have created a fiction about Shakespeare as improver in order to give precedent and warrant for his own practice as improver. The attribution of the play to a 'private Author' gives no support to those who have subsequently ascribed all or part of it to Peele, Kyd, Nashe, or some other professional. Furthermore, the opening scene of the play evinces a mastery of

---

1 For links between *Titus* and both *Lucrece* and *Richard III*, see Braunmuller. For a compelling argument for a late date on the basis of stylistic links to other Shakespearean works, see Mincoff, *Steps*. A date of 1594 for *R3* is not universally accepted (Ard[2] argues for late 1591).

multiple entrances and exits, including use of the 'above' stage, that surpasses anything in any previous Elizabethan play. No 'private Author' could have handled his theatrical resources with such command and such experimental bravura. But Ravenscroft's statement was pounced on by eighteenth-century critics who wanted to excise *Titus* from the canon. They had to make the excision because they thought that it was a bad play and their Shakespeare could not have written anything that was uniformly bad. For 'bad', read principally, though not exclusively, indecorous. Edward Capell was virtually alone in the eighteenth century in recognizing not only that the play is authentically Shakespearean but also that it has many excellencies and in particular that one of its principal indecorums, Titus' horrid laugh, 'has something great in it even for Shakespeare' (Capell, *Notes*, 105).

The fashion for 'disintegrating' Shakespeare in the early twentieth century gave new impetus to the authorship question. In 1905 J. M. Robertson devoted a whole book to the question *Did Shakespeare Write 'Titus Andronicus'?*, but eventually the issue resolved itself into the question 'did Shakespeare write the first scene of *Titus Andronicus*?' Dover Wilson spent much of his 1948 Cambridge edition enumerating parallel passages in that scene and the works of George Peele. In the 1953 Arden, J. C. Maxwell noted that some five or six times in the opening scene there occurs a possessive adjective or pronoun as antecedent to a relative cause. Such a syntactic structure is rare in Shakespeare but common in Peele; on the basis of this unobtrusive trick of style, together with the word 'palliament' that is shared with Peele's poem *The Honour of the Garter*, Maxwell fell into line with Dover Wilson. Then in 1979, building on earlier disintegrationist work, MacDonald P. Jackson noted the low frequency of feminine endings in 1.1, 2.1 (2.1 in the editorial tradition, that is – the scene was originally part of 1.1, to which my text restores it) and 4.1, and the high, typically Shakespearean, frequency elsewhere.

He also found a corresponding disparity in rare vocabulary links and use of compounds (Jackson, *Attribution*, 151–4). Jackson's conclusions are enshrined in the Oxford *Textual Companion*, where Gary Taylor writes that 'The parallels suggest that the first scene was written by either Peele or an imitator of Peele, but the rest of the play seems to have been written by neither' (*TxC*, 115).

Some of the parallels of phrasing are certainly striking. Compare, for instance, Titus'

> Hail, Rome, victorious in thy mourning weeds!
> Lo, as the bark that hath discharged his freight
> Returns...
> Cometh Andronicus, bound with laurel boughs,
> To resalute his country with his tears

with the lines in Peele's *Garter* poem,

> Haile Windsore, where I sometimes tooke delight...
> In my returne fro[m] France...
> Loe from the house of Fame, with Princely traynes
> Accompanied...
> I resalute thee heere, and gratulate...
>
> (Peele, 257–8)

('The house of Fame' and 'gratulate' are also in the first scene of *Titus*). But then there are equally striking parallels with anonymous plays such as *Selimus Emperor of the Turks* and *Edmund Ironside*,[1] with Marlowe's *Jew of Malta*, Kyd's *Spanish Tragedy* and Lodge's *Wounds of Civil War* – and of course with Shakespeare's works.

The problem with all the arguments based on verbal parallels is that imitation is always as likely as authorship. The Elizabethan poetic and dramatic repertory consisted of a vast stock

---

1   See the extract from *Selimus* in my appendix; Sams lists *Ironside* parallels in his edn of that play, 34–7, though his argument for Shakespearean authorship of it is unconvincing – *Ironside* seems to date from the later 1590s, so the parallels are more likely to be imitations of *Titus* than marks of the same authorial hand.

of words and phrases to which authors contributed and from which they drew at will. There is no copyright on coinages. The word 'Pallium' was used of the garment worn by knights of the Garter (see Cooper's *Thesaurus*); it therefore seems likely that Peele coined the word 'Palliament' in his poem written for that investiture on 26 June 1593.[1] What follows from this need not be that Peele wrote the first act of *Titus*, but rather that Shakespeare read the poem and snapped up the word – just as he snapped up other details from Nashe's *Unfortunate Traveller* and *Christ's Tears*, written about the same time.

All the parallels with other dramatists in *Titus* may, paradoxically, be evidence that Shakespeare was in fact the author. The one thing we know for sure about his early career was that he was notorious for making use of other writers' fine phrases. In *Greenes Groats-worth of Witte*, Robert Greene calls Marlowe, Nashe and Peele to his deathbed and complains about 'an upstart Crow, beautified with our feathers'. He means Shakespeare ('Shake-scene'), the country actor turned dramatist, and the specific accusation is linguistic filching, what Nashe in the preface to Greene's *Menaphon* called vaunting another's 'plumes' as one's own. That Shakespeare was an actor, whose trade was learning other people's lines, no doubt facilitated the process.[2]

The play's tight structural unity suggests a single authorial hand, in contrast to the form of such broken-backed collaborative plays of the time as *Sir Thomas More*.[3] Another kind of unity is at a linguistic level far less easily imitable than that

---

1   The association with the Garter ceremony is reinforced by a hitherto unnoticed third occurrence of the rare word: Peele's lines, including the simile 'like a Romaine Palliament', were reproduced in Anthony Nixon's poem, 'Prince *Frederick* created Knight of the Ga[r]ter, and install at Windsor the 7 day of February 1612', publ. in 1613 with *Great Brittaines Generall Joyes*, Nixon's celebration of the marriage of Frederick to Princess Elizabeth.

2   On *Titus* in relation to Greene's jibe, see further, Bate, *Ovid*, 102; on Greene and Shakespeare's invention of himself as an author, see the introduction to Edward Burns' forthcoming Arden edn of *1H6*.

3   Price argues convincingly for single authorship of *Titus* on the basis of structure.

of memorable words and phrases. All language-users have their characteristic but subliminal pattern of functional words – connectives, articles, prepositions and pronouns – which constitute a linguistic fingerprint as opposed to poetic plumage. Computer analysis of these suggests what literary judgement confirms: that the whole of *Titus* is by a single hand and that at this level its linguistic habits are very different from Peele's. According to Andrew Q. Morton, who undertook the analysis, the statistical probability of Peele's involvement is less than one in ten thousand million (Metz, 'Stylometric', 155).

Sources

The story of *Titus Andronicus* is not historical. It is extant in three versions, Shakespeare's play, a ballad which was entered with it in the Stationers' Register in 1594, and a prose narrative account which survives only in a mid-eighteenth-century chapbook. The orthodox view is that the order of composition was narrative–play–ballad.[1] Three scholars have, however, convincingly argued that in fact the play came first, the ballad was based on the play, and the chapbook was a re-expansion of the story based on the ballad.[2]

Five pieces of evidence are decisive in support of this view. First, there was a tradition in the 1590s of ballads based on popular plays (a ballad of Hieronimo is extant; ballads of Tamburlaine and the Jew of Malta were entered in the Register but are now lost); it is therefore highly probable that the play of *Titus* was the source of the ballad. This is the obvious inference to be drawn from the Stationers' Register entry. The ballad includes a stanza on Tamora and her sons 'clad' as

1 See Bullough, 6.7–23; Oxf[1], 28–35. Since the chapbook is readily available in Bantam, Bullough, Oxf[1] and Signet, and since I do not believe it is the source of the play, I do not reproduce it in my appendix. Bullough and Oxf[1] also print the ballad.
2 See Mincoff ('Source'), Hunter ('Sources', 'Sources and Meanings'), Jackson (*ShS*, 'Play').

furies, 'She named Revenge, and Rape and Murder they'.[1] This is unquestionably based on 5.2 of the play, since there is no equivalent for it in the narrative. Second, the prose narrative includes one verse couplet, which also appears in the ballad; since it perfectly fits the ballad's stanza form, it surely appeared there first. Point one puts the ballad after the play and point two puts the prose narrative after the ballad.

Third, the play and the prose narrative name many characters but only have three names in common (Titus, Marcus, and Lavinia) and those are the only three names in the ballad; this strongly suggests that the ballad comes between the two other versions. The fact that other characters are named in the opening chapters of the chapbook which have no counterpart in the ballad, but unnamed in the later chapters which share the narrative of the ballad, suggests that the opening is a later addition by the chapbook writer, which explains why nothing from these early chapters is in the play. This in itself is significant: when he did use sources, Shakespeare tended to begin by sticking to them quite closely, then to drift away from them; the complete absence of correspondence between the early part of the play and the early part of the prose narrative suggests that the prose narrative was not a Shakespearean source.

Fourth, one detail in the chapbook has no parallel in the play or the early editions of the ballad but does seem to be based on the misprint of 'clad' as 'glad' in later seventeenth-century texts of the ballad; this would make the chapbook a late seventeenth- or eighteenth-century invention. Its vocabulary supports this dating, for several words are not otherwise recorded before the eighteenth century – for example, *OED*'s first citation of 'outborders' (used in chap. 5) is 1769 (the

---

1 'Titus Andronicus' Complaint', stanza 25 (spelling modernized). The earliest surviving printed text of the ballad is in Richard Johnson's *The Golden Garland of Princely Pleasures and Delicate Delights* (1620); it is also included in the *Roxburghe* and *Shirburn* collections of ballads.

earliest record of the chapbook is a publisher's catalogue of 1764).

Fifth, in the chapbook, Lavinia is betrothed to 'the Emperor's only son by a former wife', whereas in the play and the ballad her partner is the emperor's brother; the reason for this difference is that the ballad-writer refers to Lavinia's betrothed as the emperor's son, but he means the emperor whose death has occurred immediately before the beginning of the play, and since he does not name that emperor (as Shakespeare does not) the chapbook writer has muddled him up with the new emperor (Saturninus) and made his Bassianus-figure a member of the wrong generation. As MacDonald Jackson says (*ShS*, 250), this 'furnishes a nice illustration of the process by which the ballad, enigmatically echoing [or, better, *compressing*] the play, beguiles the prose-writer along a false trail'.

A number of important consequences follow from the conclusion that the prose history is not a source. For instance, it means we can discount the view, subscribed to by nearly all editors and critics, that the play is set much later in Roman history than Shakespeare's subsequent Roman plays are – the chapbook is set in the time of Theodosius (late fourth century AD) but the play is nowhere near so specific about its temporal location. I suggested earlier, following G. K. Hunter, that in fact it sweeps through the whole history of Rome. More importantly, the removal of the chapbook from discussions of sources means that *Titus* can be seen as one of Shakespeare's 'sourceless' plays, like *A Midsummer Night's Dream*. I proceed on this basis, though there is always the possibility that it drew on some other lost prose narrative or that Shakespeare was reworking a lost old play, as seems to have been the case with *Hamlet*. We do not, however, need to posit lost sources: I shall try to show how Shakespeare could have invented the play out of his reading and the theatrical repertoire of the early 1590s.

The most successful plays in that repertoire were Kyd's *Spanish Tragedy* and Marlowe's *Jew of Malta*, so the first thing

Shakespeare would have done in order to produce a hit of his own was copy some of their most celebrated effects. I have already discussed the revenge structure in relation to Kyd's play, but there are many more local points of contact. Each action begins at the end of a war, with a parade of prisoners, prominent among whom is the enemy monarch's son; a spectacular processional entry of victors and prisoners occurs at a similar point in each opening scene. The life of the chief prisoner is spared, leading to amorous intrigue and eventual dire consequences. Public disputation occurs over a point of honour; love is a means of vengeance. Lying on the ground serves as physical embodiment of a character's low fortune. A *locus amoenus* (bower, forest glade) is established, then darkened and violated. A dramatically crucial and highly emotional *anagnorisis* takes place in the form of a linguistically charged soliloquy: Hieronimo's gradual recognition of his murdered son, Marcus' recognition of his raped and mutilated niece. Following this pivotal moment, there is a gradual movement from the expression of grief to the enactment of revenge. Props serve an emblematic function (letters seem to fall from the sky; Kyd has a Boy with a box, Shakespeare a Clown with a basket). Assumed madness and theatre are the revenger's two means of speaking and acting in public. The moment when the protagonist assumes his madness and his role as revenger is signalled by a substitution of laughter for speech: 'Ha, ha, ha!' (*Sp. Trag.*, 3.11.30). Even amidst his anger and his passion for revenge, the protagonist sympathizes momentarily with a lesser being (Senex Bazulto in Kyd; more radically, the fly in Shakespeare). The body becomes a 'map of woe' (*Tit* 3.2.12, adapting *Sp. Trag.*, 3.10.91). Metaphor is literalized: we have seen the process in Shakespeare; in Kyd, Hieronimo seeks for justice by digging with his dagger in the ground, and when revenge seems delayed the character called Revenge falls asleep. The language is formalized and symmetrical, studded with classical tags. There is a fascination with speech and silence, with tongues removed and acts of inscription. I include in my appendix three passages which should show how Shakespeare learnt from Kyd's rhetoric.

Where Kyd gave Shakespeare a model for the passion and the revenge of Titus, Marlowe gave him ideas for his villains. The remark which begins innocuously but has a stinging aside in the tail, the tendency to pun and stab in the same breath, the sheer delight in villainy: these are learnt from *The Jew of Malta* (which also exerts a structural influence on *Titus* in its movement towards an invitation to a feast at which there is an ambush and a spectacular revenge). Aaron's catalogue of misdeeds (5.1.124–44) is modelled on the exchange between Barabas and Ithamore in which they outdo each other in outrageous ill-doing (reprinted in my appendix). But the Marlovian villain is also a kind of hero, an extreme embodiment of the Renaissance self-made man. An outsider, he aspires to unimaginable heights before he tumbles to his fall; the theatre-audience delights in his energy and inventiveness, especially when he confides in them through soliloquy or aside. Morally, we know that we should condemn him, but dramatically we are mesmerized by him, especially when his language soars. Aaron's first soliloquy (which occupies the same structural position as Edmund's in *Lear*) is in just this mode. 'Now climbeth Tamora Olympus' top ... Then, Aaron, ... mount aloft with thy imperial mistress' (1.1.500–23) has the distinct smack of Faustus' heights:

> Learned Faustus...
> Did mount him up to scale Olympus top,
> Where, sitting in a chariot burning bright
> Drawn by the strength of yoked dragons' necks,
> He views the clouds, the planets, and the stars...
> (*Dr Faustus*, 1st Chorus)

Aaron's speech has been described as in all probability the

first great villain's soliloquy in Shakespeare (Serpieri, 200). Whatever the exact chronology of the early plays, there is no doubt that a direct line passes from Marlowe through Aaron to Richard III, Iago and Edmund.

The villainous but witty Moor is developed not only from the Marlovian figures, but also from Peele's Muly Mahamet in *The Battle of Alcazar*, another popular play of the early 1590s.[1] Indeed, Shakespeare draws not just on Kyd and Marlowe, but on a considerable cross-section of the repertoire. A lost drama performed by Strange's in 1592, known as both *Four Plays in One* and *The Second Part of the Seven Deadly Sins*, included a dramatization of the rape of Philomel with its climactic bloody banquet; Tereus was the exemplar of Lechery. Many plays included a spectacular processional entry at or near the beginning, such as this in Peele's *Edward I* (published 1593):

> *The Trumpets sound, and enter the traine, viz. his maimed Souldiers with headpeeces and Garlands on them, every man with his red Crosse on his coate: the Ancient borne in a Chaire, his Garland and his plumes on his headpeece, his Ensigne in his hand. Enter after them* Gloucester *and* Mortimer *bareheaded, and others as many as may be.*
>
> (1.40 SD)

Titus is also typical of the drama of its time in its use of stage space to dramatize the disputes which initiate the action. The technique of entry through opposite doors occurs in the opening stage direction of Shakespeare's own *First Part of the Contention* (subsequently known as *King Henry VI Part 2*):

> *Enter at one doore, King* Henry *the sixt, and* Humphrey *Duke of* Gloster, *the Duke of* Sommerset, *the Duke of* Buckingham, *Cardinall* Bewford, *and others.*

---

1   Vengeful, scheming Moors were also a staple of Italian novellas of the sixteenth century (see Bullough, 6.14–15, for an example in Bandello).

> *Enter at the other doore, the Duke of* Yorke, *and the*
> *Marquesse of* Suffolke, *and Queene* Margaret, *and the*
> *Earle of* Salisbury *and* Warwicke.
>
> (1594 edn, sig. A2^r)

(As with Tamora, Margaret, the royal woman from the defeated nation, is passed from conqueror to ruler; the structural similarity extends to the way in which a large public opening scene ends with a schemer in soliloquy.)

The use of the upper stage to represent the Roman Capitol may be borrowed from the opening scene of Lodge's *Wounds of Civil War* (performed 1588?, published 1594), in which, as in *Titus*, the action begins with the tribunes and senators aloft, while rival claimants (Marius and Sulla) and their followers clash on the main stage below. Lodge's play also works with the contrast between the city of Rome and the country outside it, and it parallels *Titus* in linking the description of place to the state of mind of the describer:

> This melancholy desert where we meet
> Resembleth well young Marius' restless thoughts.
> Here dreadful silence, solitary caves,
> No chirping birds with solace singing sweetly
> Are harboured for delight; but from the oak,
> Leaveless and sapless through decaying age,
> The screech-owl chants her fatal boding lays.
> Within my breast, care, danger, sorrow dwells,
> Hope and revenge sit hammering in my heart,
> The baleful babes of angry Nemesis
> Disperse their furious fires upon my soul.
>
> (3.4.55–65)

Onstage mutilation, with accompanying dialogue of macabre playfulness, was also a feature of the drama of the early 1590s. I include in my appendix a precedent for the hand-chopping scene in *The First part of the Tragical Reign of Selimus, sometime*

Emperor of the Turks (performed 1592?, published 1594 without dramatist's name, but often attributed to Greene). I have reprinted this at some length because both its jokes ('Which hand is this? right? or left? canst thou tell?') and its impassioned formal rhetoric ('witnesse these handlesse armes, / Witnesse these empty lodges of mine eyes...') seem to me very close to *Titus*. That the chopping off of the hands is immediately preceded by the following exchange reinforces one's sense of the association between *Titus* and *Lear*:

AGA

> Ah let me never live to see that day.

ACOMAT

> Yes thou shalt live, but never see that day,
> Wanting the tapers that should give thee light:
> > *Puls out his eyes.*
> > > (*Selimus*, lines 1412–15)

The best way of thinking about the origins of *Titus Andronicus* is not so much in terms of 'sources', but rather in the terms suggested by Titus as his justification for killing Lavinia: he describes the action of Virginius in killing his daughter because of her rape as 'A pattern, precedent, and lively warrant / For me, most wretched, to perform the like' (5.3.43–4). I believe that the play was composed out of a series of *precedents* in the dramatic repertoire of the period and a series of *patterns* in Shakespeare's reading of the classics. Aeneas, Hecuba, Virginius, Coriolanus and Seneca's Hippolytus are among those patterns, but the two most significant are the two exemplary classical stories of rape.

The patterning process is spelt out in what is possibly the most literary moment in the whole of Shakespeare, when Lavinia 'quotes the leaves' of a copy of Ovid's *Metamorphoses*, turning up the story of the rape of Philomel.[1] Titus replies:

---

1 Imogen's bedtime reading in *Cymbeline* is the same story, one of many links between *Titus* and that late play (see Thompson).

Lavinia, wert thou thus surprised, sweet girl,
Ravished and wronged as Philomela was,
Forced in the ruthless, vast and gloomy woods?
[*Lavinia nods.*] See, see!
Ay, such a place there is where we did hunt –
O, had we never, never hunted there! –
Patterned by that the poet here describes,
By nature made for murders and for rapes.

                                                        (4.1.51–8)

And his revenge is patterned just as explicitly: 'For worse than
Philomel you used my daughter, / And worse than Progne I
will be revenged' (5.2.194–5). It was in the *Metamorphoses*,
schoolroom reading for Shakespeare himself as well as Young
Lucius, that the dramatist read of how the Thracian tyrant
Tereus married Progne, but then burned with desire for her
sister Philomel, raped her in a gloomy wood, cut out her
tongue to prevent her from telling who did the deed, but then
had his identity revealed through her sewing a picture of the
scene in a sampler; and how the two sisters then took a terrible
revenge by killing Itys, son of Tereus and Progne, and dishing
him up in a pie at his father's table. Having 'swallowed downe
the selfe same flesh that of his bowels bred', Tereus asks for
his son and Progne replies, 'the thing thou askest for, thou
hast within': the pattern is followed closely in the final scene
of the play. Just how close the structure of the play is to the
Philomel story becomes clear if we compare *Titus* to an
explicit dramatization of that story, the Latin tragedy *Philomela*,
performed at St John's College, Oxford, on 29 December 1607:
there is an identical movement from initial public action to
violation in a dark wood to revelation of the terrible deed to
formal lamentation to plotting of revenge to climactic banquet.

    But the patterning is also an overgoing: as Marcus has
realized in his monologue in 2.3 (realized perhaps without
realizing that he's realized it), it is because Philomel was able

to reveal her rapist's identity by means of her 'tedious sampler' that the 'craftier Tereus' has forestalled this method of disclosure, 'hath cut those pretty fingers off, / That could have better sewed than Philomel'. Not only does a reading of Ovid replace Progne's act of reading in Ovid, but also, in a dazzling rhetorical *contaminatio* of sources, Shakespeare has then added a new method of disclosure, writing on the ground, from a different story in Ovid, that of Io, who is raped by Jupiter, turned into a heifer and only able to reveal her identity by scratching her hoof on the sand.[1]

Shakespeare grafted on to the Philomel pattern from classical mythology the Lucrece pattern from classical history (available to him in both Livy's *History of Rome* and Ovid's *Fasti*). *Titus* was published just a few months before his narrative poem, *The Rape of Lucrece*, which tells of how Tarquin's rape of Lucrece eventually led to the expulsion of the tyrannical Roman kings and the establishment of the republic. As we have seen, the man who led the people in their uprising was Lucius Junius Brutus. This is the role that Lucius fulfils in the play. Again, the patterning is explicit: the exemplary chastity of Lavinia is compared to that of Lucrece; Lucius goes into exile at the end of the first half of the play saying that he will return 'And make proud Saturnine and his empress / Beg at the gates like Tarquin and his queen' (3.1.298–9); Junius Brutus is explicitly invoked as an avenger for the rape (4.1.91).[2] To assist the reader in tracing these patterns, I have included in my appendix both the Philomel story (in the translation which Shakespeare read) and the 'Argument' prefixed to *Lucrece* which summarizes the narrative of that rape and its political consequences.

---

1   For a more detailed account of Ovidian patterning, see Bate, *Ovid*, 101–17.
2   There is a similar pattern in the precedent (also from Livy) which *Titus* cites as justification for killing his daughter: Virginia was sexually dishonoured by Appius Claudius, one of the decemviri, so Virginius her father killed her; there was then a popular uprising against the decemviri, and a change in the political and legal structure of Rome.

Names and casting

If the story of the play is invented, not based on a specific previous narrative, we need to find origins for the names it uses. Bassianus was the name of the third-century emperor now better known as Caracalla, who vied with his brother over the succession, one of them appealing to primogeniture, the other to the people; in Herodian's *History* (available to Shakespeare in Smyth's translation), a tribune called Saturninus was sent to assassinate Bassianus.[1] Titus was a common Roman name, and may have been inspired by the Titus who conquered Jerusalem on behalf of his father, the emperor Vespasian. Andronicus was one of the names of a late emperor from Byzantium; there are stories of his reign that involve hand-chopping and shooting arrows with messages on them,[2] but there is no obvious source in which Shakespeare would have read about the late, eastern empire. It may be, then, that the hero's family name comes from the story which is widely known as Androcles and the lion, but which in the *Familiar Epistles* of Antony of Guevara (available to Shakespeare in Hellowes' translation of 1584) was Andronicus and the lion. The story tells of how the emperor Titus returned from successful wars in Germany and celebrated by sending assorted criminals to fight with wild beasts; a fugitive slave called Andronicus was thrown to a cruel lion 'in the chase', but the lion lay down and embraced him instead of tearing him to pieces – Andronicus is brought before Titus, and tells him that it was the same lion which he had once helped by removing a thorn from its foot and curing its festering wound. The interplay of violence and kindness in Rome and its surrounding hunting-places is curiously redolent of the play: might this be the source of the central character's pair of names, and perhaps

1 This was first noted by Hunter in his excellent essay, 'Sources and Meanings'.
2 Samuel Bernard's academic Latin drama of 1618 concerning this emperor, *Andronicus Comnenus*, is actually influenced by Shakespeare's play, particularly in the character of Salmanazar, the villainous Moor (Bernard, 27–8).

93

even one reason why several early references to the play speak erroneously of 'Titus and Andronicus'?

I have already considered the Virgilian resonances of the name Lavinia, and those (associated with both Lucrece and British history) of Lucius. A Publius is paired with Junius Brutus in the Argument to *Lucrece*; several other Roman names in the play (Marcus, Martius, Quintus, Caius, Emillius, Sempronius) are clustered together in the life of Scipio Africanus in Plutarch, that favourite Shakespearean source; Demetrius (a Roman name given to a Goth) probably also comes from Plutarch; a Mutius in Livy proved his loyalty to the Roman code of honour by thrusting his hand into a fire.[1] Tamora may suggest Tomyris, a Scythian queen famous for her cruelty and, more specifically, for her spectacular revenge when Cyrus slew her only son. Aaron may be Roman as well as biblical: a man called 'Arron' assisted the Gauls when they marched into Italy (Plutarch, 149). Waith (Oxf[1], 87) cites a poem quoted in Puttenham which refers to how 'the Roman prince did daunt / Wild Africans and the lawless Alarbes', suggesting Alarbus; although wise and just, the Greek Chiron was a centaur, half-man, half-beast (centaurs are associated with violence at 5.2.203).

An absolute minimum company size of between twenty-five and twenty-seven (depending on the minimum-acceptable number of 'followers' for Saturninus and Bassianus) is necessary for the first scene. The major speaking parts can be divided between fourteen actors (originally eleven adults and three boys for Tamora, Lavinia, Young Lucius; or, if the Nurse was played by a boy, ten adults and four boys, though this would require the Clown to double in a named straight role), leaving small parts such as Messenger and 2 Goth to be played by those among the minimum-required eleven to thirteen 'extras'. Actors playing the following roles are not available for doubling:

---

1 Valentine is an odd-name-out among the Romans, but it is a Shakespearean favourite, also occurring in *TGV* and *TN*.

Titus, Aaron, Marcus, Saturninus, Lucius, Demetrius, Chiron, Tamora, Lavinia. The Clown is a specialist role, though he could also play, say, the Captain, the Messenger and perhaps the Nurse. Several dramatically striking doubling possibilities are available with other roles: Bassianus with 1 Goth (who helps to rid Rome of those who have destroyed Bassianus) or Emillius or Roman Lord (who help to restore order), Mutius with Young Lucius (Titus' youngest son and his grandson), Quintus and Martius[1] with Caius and Sempronius/Valentine (the same actors would thus represent sons who are killed and kinsmen who participate in the revenge for that killing).[2]

The largest parts, with numbers of lines in parenthesis, are: Titus (709), Aaron (353), Marcus (313), Tamora (256), Saturninus (208), Lucius (181), Demetrius (95), Bassianus (62), Lavinia (59), Chiron (50), Young Lucius (44).[3] Titus' part, twice the size of any other, is among the more demanding tragic roles in Shakespeare.

ESTABLISHING THE TEXT

Shakespeare wrote his plays as scripts for performance, not as texts for publication. He had no conception of a scholarly

1 In the first act, Shakespeare does not name Titus' two middle sons. Indeed, from the point of view of the theatre audience they *never* receive names: they are referred to throughout the dialogue as brothers or sons, and in the entry directions they are always 'Titus two sonnes'. They are only named in the SPs in the pit scene. Shakespeare obviously gave them names at this point so as to differentiate between them in his own mind and perhaps to begin developing them as characters, but he did not carry through that development – they serve their dramatic purpose better as an anonymous pair. The only named sons are the martyred youngest, Mutius, and the redeeming eldest, Lucius. In order to remind the reader of this I have retained Qq,F's '2 SON' and '3 SON' in the first act SPs and in later stage directions, but to help actors in the pit scene I have used the names there in the SPs. Quintus is probably the second son and Martius the third: Quintus initiates their dialogue, implying that he is older, and his name suggests that he was the fifth of Titus' twenty-five sons, and, given that Lucius is older still, this makes it likely that Martius is younger – it would be most unlikely for three of the eldest five to be among the only four survivors out of the twenty-five who have fought in ten years' campaigns.
2 Speculative casting charts are given by Waith (Oxf[1], 217) and King (22–3).
3 These figures include the added fly-killing scene.

THE
MOST LA-
mentable Romaine
Tragedie of Titus Andronicus:

As it was Plaide by the Right Ho-
nourable the Earle of *Darbie*, Earle of *Pembrooke*,
and Earle of *Suffex* their Seruants.

LONDON,
Printed by Iohn Danter, and are
to be fold by *Edward White* & *Thomas Millington*,
at the little North doore of Paules at the
figne of the Gunne.
1594.

14 The earliest printed Shakespearean play: title-page of the 1594 First
Quarto

edition of his works, though his reception of classical literary texts, which was so important to the composition of *Titus Andronicus*, owed a good deal to the practice of scholarly editing that was one of the great achievements of Renaissance humanism. The modern editor of Shakespeare is faced with a different set of problems from, say, Raphael Regius, the late fifteenth-century editor of Ovid. But problems they are: on numerous individual occasions, judgements have to be made about whether the text as it was first published represents what Shakespeare wrote or how a busy sixteenth-century printer misrepresented what he wrote; more generally, one has to deal with the differences between performance and reading, and between late sixteenth-century and late twentieth-century English. The Arden edition's approach to some of these problems is outlined in the general editors' preface; in this final section of the introduction, I shall examine some of them that are peculiar to *Titus Andronicus*.

Many of Shakespeare's plays were not published at all in his lifetime; they remained in the hands of the players until the handsome posthumous collected edition of 1623 known as the First Folio. Others – particularly the most popular ones – were published in his lifetime in a smaller format, which might be thought of as roughly equivalent to a modern cheap paperback, known as a Quarto. With some plays (notoriously, *Hamlet* and *King Lear*) the nature of the printer's copy for the quartos and the relationship between quarto and folio texts have been fiercely debated. It is a mark of the popularity of *Titus* that it went through three quarto editions in Shakespeare's life. Fortunately for the editor, the relationship between the early editions is basically a direct line of descent: the first quarto (Q1) was printed from Shakespeare's working manuscript, the second quarto (Q2) was printed from the first quarto (making some corrections and introducing some new errors), the third quarto (Q3) was printed from the second quarto (making some corrections and introducing some new errors), and the first folio (F) text of the play was printed from the third quarto (making some corrections and introducing some new errors). The folio also added more extensive stage directions and included the fly-killing scene (3.2) which had not appeared in any of the quartos.

A responsible modern edition of *Titus Andronicus* has to be based on Q1, which represents something unusually close to a play as Shakespeare wrote it and as it was first performed. I argued in the previous section that the play was written (or perhaps revised) by Shakespeare in late 1593, performed in that form for the first time in early 1594, then entered on the Stationers' Register and published as Q1 within a matter of weeks. At the same time, there are good reasons for believing that the folio stage directions reflect early seventeenth-century theatrical practice and that the fly-killing scene is authentic, so a text should also incorporate them. My text is, however, the first to draw attention to the different status of the fly-killing scene by printing it in a different typeface. The scene is moving, funny and pointed, but it does alter the rhythm of the play as originally written (the 1991 Cambridge production gained pace by cutting it).

The wording of the title-page of Q1 (Fig. 14) was discussed in the previous section. Why do we suppose that its text was printed from Shakespeare's working manuscript (known as 'foul papers', to suggest blottings and corrections of the sort that mar what seems to be the only surviving dramatic manuscript in Shakespeare's hand, the crowd scene in the collaborative play, *Sir Thomas More*)? Three features in particular suggest foul paper origin: imprecise entry directions, inconsistent speech prefixes and false starts. The processional entry of the victorious Titus in the first scene lists the characters who are supposed to come on, together with two men bearing a coffin, and then ends '*and others as many as can be*'. That is the kind of direction which a writer puts when he isn't sure exactly what the company size will be. Again, when Saturninus and Bassianus

leave the main stage to go up to the gallery at 1.1.66, the Q1
direction is '*They goe vp into the Senate house*': this is a literary
kind of direction, characteristic of foul paper texts; as Stanley
Wells elegantly puts it, 'Shakespeare was thinking in terms of
his fiction, not of his stage' (*Re-Editing*, 87). The Q1 speech
prefix for the chief Roman in the play is variously 'Saturninus',
'Saturnine', 'Emperour', 'King'; on one leaf the speech prefix
for the chief Goth is 'Queene' instead of 'Tamora'; her lover
and servant is sometimes 'Aron', sometimes 'Moore'; in one
entry direction Titus becomes simply 'Andronicus', in another
Marcus is 'olde Marcus'. Playhouse manuscripts, known as
'promptbooks', tended to iron out this kind of inconsistency –
indeed they sometimes have a different irregularity, whereby
actors' names creep into stage directions.

The third piece of evidence that Q1 was almost certainly set
from foul papers, not a promptbook, is the most interesting.
Sometimes Shakespeare seems to have begun a passage,
changed his mind and gone straight on to a revised version
without crossing out the first version sufficiently clearly for it
to be apparent to the printer who later worked from the
manuscript that it was a 'false start'. The best example is in
the first quarto text of Biron's long speech near the end of
Love's Labour's Lost, 4.3. Three passages in Q1 *Titus* may come
into this category, though none of them is as clear-cut a case
as that in *Love's Labour's*.

Possible false starts

(i) 1.1.35–8
Q1 prints

                              and at this day,
          To the Monument of that *Andronicy*
          Done sacrifice of expiation,
          And slaine the Noblest prisoner of the *Gothes*,

99

The alert Q2 corrector seems to have noticed that these lines apparently contradict the subsequent action: 'the noblest prisoner of the Goths', Tamora's son Alarbus, has not yet been slain. Q2 therefore omits these lines. I mark their questionable status with wavy brackets, but do not cut them, since they are defensible. 'At this day' could mean 'on the day corresponding to this': i.e., on each of Titus' five returns to Rome, his first action was to slay a prisoner. The lines would then be an anticipation of the slaying of Alarbus, not an inconsistency with it. This interpretation could be strengthened by emending 'at this day' to 'as this day', or (Jackson conj.) 'at this door' ('here at the entrance to the tomb of the Andronici').

(ii) 3.1.36
Q1 prints:

TITUS
>   Why tis no matter man, if they did heare
>   They would not marke me, if they did marke,
>   They would not pittie me, yet pleade I must,
>   And bootlesse vnto them.
>   Therefore I tell my sorrowes to the stones,

The text here is defensible: 'my pleas have no effect on them; I'm impelled to plead, and since it's useless to do so to them I'm addressing the stones'. But 'And bootless unto them' is grammatically awkward and forms a half-line interrupting the flow of the speech. Dover Wilson viewed it as a false start intended for deletion (Cam[1], 125). 'They would not pity me; yet plead I must, / Therefore I tell my sorrows to the stones' certainly flows much better. Stanley Wells cut the half-line from his Oxford text, arguing that 'Perhaps Shakespeare intended to write e.g. "And bootlesse vnto them bewaile my griefs", but abandoned the line on realizing the need to return to an explanation of why Titus should "recount [his] sorrowes to a stone"' (*TxC*, 211). In my text I put the half-line in wavy brackets to indicate a possible false start. I am not so confident

100

as to cut it altogether: after all, both grammatical disintegration and blockage of the measured flow of the pentameters are singularly appropriate to the content of the speech.

(iii) 4.3.94–107

Titus' lines 'Tell mee, can you deliuer an Oration to the Emperour with a grace' (4.3.97–8 in my text) and 'Sirra, can you with a grace deliuer vp a Supplication?' (4.3.106) have a similarity which invites the suspicion that the Q1 text includes two different versions of the business in question, especially as the Clown gives contradictory answers. The following are therefore likely to be alternative responses to the Clown saying that he is on his way to seek justice:

> MARCUS   Why sir, that is as fit as can bee to serue
>   for your Oration, and let him deliuer the pidgeons
>   to the Emperour from you.
> TITUS   Tell mee, can you deliuer an Oration to the
>   Emperour with a grace.
> CLOWNE   Nay truelie sir, I could neuer say grace in
>   all my life.
>
> > (4.3.94–100 in my text)

and

> TITUS
>   Sirra come hither, make no more adoo,
>   But giue your pidgeons to the Emperour,
>   By mee thou shalt haue iustice at his hands,
>   Hold, hold, meane while here's money for thy
>   charges,
>   Giue me pen and ink.
>   Sirra, can you with a grace deliuer vp a Sup-
>   plication?
> CLOWNE
>   I sir
>
> > (4.3.101–7 in my text)

Since it is printed first, since it involves Marcus speaking prose for the only time in the play, and since the joke about the Clown not being able to say grace leads to an impasse in the action, it seems likely that 94–100 is the 'false start'. The lines 94–100 are detachable, whereas 101–7 flow forward into the subsequent writing business. In Dover Wilson's words, 'if 94–100 be omitted, the text gains, since a suggestion by Marcus thus becomes a sudden idea of Titus', inspired by encountering a fellow-seeker for justice' (Cam[1], 143). Maxwell suggested that the original idea of using the Clown could come from Marcus and then be picked up by Titus, so one should merely cut 97–100, the joke which blocks the action. But this leaves Marcus both speaking prose and bearing ultimate responsibility for the Clown's death: it fits the pattern of the tragedy much better if Titus alone should be responsible for that.

Waith proposed a different cut. He noted the inconsistency between reference to an 'Oration' and a 'Supplication', and therefore removed from his Oxford text the sequence from 'Sirra, can you with a grace deliuer vp a Supplication?' to 'I warrant you sir, let me alone' (106–13 in my text; see Oxf[1], 211–12). This has the advantage of removing the 'Supplication', keeping consistent reference to an 'Oration', and retaining the joke about saying grace, but it has the major problem of suggesting that the 'false start' comes after the 'revised version', which seems implausible.

An alternative explanation of the presence of both 'Oration' and 'Supplication' is that there shouldn't be a cut at all. The Clown takes some persuading; he says he certainly couldn't do anything so grand as 'deliver' (i.e. speak) an oration (the nearest he could imagine to it is saying grace aloud before dinner and he can't even do that), but he can 'deliver' (i.e. hand over) a supplication. The Warner production worked well here without a cut.

I incline to the view that 94–100 is a false start, so I mark these lines off with wavy brackets. But since there are arguments in defence of them I do not follow the example of Stanley Wells' Oxford text and remove them from the text altogether – I would like to see readers and directors trying out the alternatives and deciding for themselves.

The killing of Alarbus and Mutius

There is another piece of evidence which definitely supports the view that Q1 is based on foul papers and possibly supports Q2's cutting of 1.1.35–8. The grand processional entry at 1.1.72 includes, according to Q1, 'Tamora *the Queene of Gothes and her two sonnes* Chiron *and* Demetrius'. Alarbus is not mentioned, as he certainly would have been if the printer's copy had been based on a theatrical manuscript (although Alarbus is a mute, it would have been essential to include the actor's entry cue). This suggests that Shakespeare's original intention was not to stage the sacrifice of Alarbus; perhaps it was merely to be implied by 1.1.35–8. We may assume that when Shakespeare added the incident, he didn't go back to alter the entry direction.

The sequence from Lucius' 'Giue vs the prowdest prisoner of the *Gothes*' (1.1.99, note the echo of 'the Noblest prisoner of the *Gothes*') to Titus' 'Make this his latest farewell to their soules' (1.1.152) is self-contained and interrupts the burial of Titus' sons. Dover Wilson suggested (Cam[1], xxxv) that Titus' burial speeches at 93–8 and 153–9 originally ran together (not an entirely convincing point, since the 'store'/'more' couplet at 97–8 suggests the rounding off of a speech). That the staging of the sacrifice is an afterthought would certainly account for the omission of Alarbus from the entry. It might suggest that Shakespeare forgot to go back and cross out 35–8. Nevertheless, if the slaying of Alarbus was an addition, it was almost certainly made during the composition of the first scene, for later in that scene Tamora refers back to it ('And make them know what 'tis to let a queen / Kneel in the streets and beg for grace in vain', 1.1.459–60) and throughout the play her revenges are predicated upon it.

The first scene includes the killing of both Tamora's oldest son and Titus' youngest son. They are suggestively parallel actions, in that they are both undertaken out of an obsession with honour as opposed to human kindness. Titus has to suffer for both deeds, as Lear has to suffer for banishing both Cordelia and Kent. If the killing of Alarbus was an addition, might that of Mutius have been one too?

Dover Wilson noted that the burial of Mutius also seems to be a self-contained incident which interrupts the flow of another sequence of thoughts (Cam[1], xxxvi). At 1.1.343–5, Titus remarks,

> I am not bid to wait vpon this bride,
> *Titus* when wert thou wont to walke alone,
> Dishonoured thus and challenged of wrongs.

This would lead naturally into an entry for Marcus and his exchange with his brother beginning, 'My Lord to step out of these dririe dumps' (396–402). The entrance of Titus' sons in the stage direction after 345, and the business of supplicating for Mutius' burial looks very much like a parallel addition to the Alarbus sequence at 99–152.

If this is right, it may explain the somewhat confusing staging when Mutius is killed. I reproduce overleaf the original Q1 text of the relevant page in parallel with my edited version of it (Fig. 15). But I have also marked the lines pertaining to the death of Mutius, which may be an addition. Imagine a first draft of the passage that lacked the passages marked < >: without Mutius' first two lines, Titus would reply more immediately to Saturninus' 'Surprised? By whom?', and without the killing Saturninus' 'No, Titus, no, the emperor needs her not' would be an instant reply, instead of a very delayed one, to 'Follow, my lord, and I'll soon bring her back'. Furthermore, Saturninus and the Goths might not have gone aloft at this point; in this draft, they could have stayed on the main stage until 342 (see also commentary at 1.1.331–2).

But the onstage slaying of Mutius, like the offstage sacrifice of Alarbus, must have been introduced at a fairly early point in the compositional process, since it becomes a point of reference later in the scene. And a staging must be imagined for the abduction of Lavinia and going aloft of Saturninus and the Goths. I reconstruct this moment differently from the way in which previous editors have done: the keys to my reconstruction are the stage directions I have inserted after lines 279, 292 and especially 293. My reasons for adopting them and for rejecting previous editors' stagings are explained in the appropriate commentary notes.[1]

Stage directions

My new stage directions in the Mutius sequence are characteristic of this edition's completely different approach from its predecessor's. Maxwell's dismissal of the play's stage qualities led him to 'sweep away almost the whole paraphernalia of later editorial stage directions and return to Q1' (Ard², xvii). My admiration for the play's stage qualities has led me to include very full stage directions to help the reader visualize it in action. In doing this, I have given more than usual authority to the early 'acting editions' of Menius and Ravenscroft.

---

1 Of previous editors, Stanley Wells is the one who has thought most seriously about this sequence: see his discussion and reconstruction in *Re-Editing*, 95–103; I am indebted to his analysis of the problems, but his conclusions differ from mine and necessitate a cut and the shifting of a line.

The moſt Lamentable *Tragedie*

Lauinia you are not diſpleaſde with this.

  Lauinia. Not I my Lord, ſith true Nobilitie,
VVarrants theſe words in Princely curteſie.

  Saturnine. Thanks ſweete *Lauinia*, Romans let vs goe,
Raunſomles here we ſet our priſoners free,
Proclaime our Honours Lords with Trumpe and Drum.

  Baſſianus. Lord *Titus* by your leaue, this maid is mine.

  Titus. How ſir, are you in earneſt then my Lord?

  Baſcianus. I Noble *Titus* and reſolude withall,
To doo my ſelfe this reaſon and this right.

  Marcus. Suum cuiqum is our Romane iuſtce,
This Prince in iuſtice ceazeth but his owne.

  Lucius. And that he will, and ſhall if *Lucius* liue.

  Titus. Traitors auaunt, where is the Emperours gard?
Treaſon my Lord, *Lauinia* is ſurprizde.

  Saturnine. Surprizde, by whom?

  Baſcianus. By him that iuſtly may,
Beare his betrothde from all the world away.

  Mutius. Brothers, helpe to conuay her hence away,
And with my ſword Ile keepe this doore ſafe.

  Titus. Follow my Lord, and Ile ſoone bring her backe.

  Mutius. My Lord you paſſe not here.

  Titus. What villaine boy, barſt me my way in Rome?

  Mutius. Helpe *Lucius*, helpe.

  Lucius. My Lord you are vniuſt, and more than ſo,
In wrongfull quarrell you haue ſlaine your ſonne.

  Titus. Nor thou, nor he, are any ſonnes of mine,
My ſonnes would neuer ſo diſhonour me,
Traitor reſtore *Lauinia* to the Emperour.

  Lucius. Dead if you will, but not to be his wife,
That is anothers lawfull promiſt loue.

    Enter aloft the Emperour with Tamora *and her two*
       ſonnes and Aron *the moore.*

  Emperour. No *Titus*, no, the Emperour needes her not,
Nor her, nor thee, nor any of thy ſtocke:

                            Ile

15 The killing of Mutius in Q1 and in edited text

Lavinia, you are not displeased with this?

LAVINIA   Not I, my lord, sith true nobility   275
    Warrants these words in princely courtesy.

SATURNINUS   Thanks, sweet Lavinia. Romans, let us go.
    Ransomless here we set our prisoners free;
    Proclaim our honours, lords, with trump and drum.
                      [*Sound drums and trumpets.*
          Tamora, Chiron, Demetrius and Aaron are released.]

BASSIANUS   [*seizing Lavinia*]   Lord Titus, by your leave, this maid is
    mine.   280

TITUS   How, sir? Are you in earnest then, my lord?

BASSIANUS   Ay, noble Titus, and resolved withal
    To do myself this reason and this right.

MARCUS   *Suum cuique* is our Roman justice:
    This prince in justice seizeth but his own.   285

LUCIUS   [*joining Bassianus*]   And that he will, and shall, if Lucius live.

TITUS   Traitors, avaunt! Where is the emperor's guard?
    Treason, my lord – Lavinia is surprised.

SATURNINUS   Surprised? By whom?

BASSIANUS   By him that justly may
    Bear his betrothed from all the world away.   290

<MUTIUS   Brothers, help to convey her hence away,>
    <And with my sword I'll keep this door safe.>
                  [*Bassianus, Marcus and Titus' sons
                     bear Lavinia out of one door.]

TITUS   Follow, my lord, and I'll soon bring her back.
          <[*Saturninus does not follow, but exit at the other door*>
              <*with Tamora, her two sons and Aaron the Moor.*]>

<MUTIUS   My lord, you pass not here.>

<TITUS   What, villain boy, barr'st me my way in Rome?>   295
                         <[*He kills him.*]>

<MUTIUS   Help, Lucius, help!>

<LUCIUS   [*returning*]   My lord, you are unjust, and more than so:>
    <In wrongful quarrel you have slain your son.>

<TITUS   Nor thou, nor he, are any sons of mine:>
    <My sons would never so dishonour me.>   300
    <Traitor, restore Lavinia to the emperor.>

<LUCIUS   Dead if you will, but not to be his wife>
    <That is another's lawful promised love.>   <[*Exit*]>
             <*Enter aloft the Emperor with* TAMORA>
             <*and her two sons and* AARON *the Moor.*>

SATURNINUS   <[*aloft*]>   No, Titus, no, the emperor needs her not,
    Nor her, nor thee, nor any of thy stock.   305

The stage directions are especially interesting in the quarto and folio editions because those in Q1 seem to reflect authorial intention in the process of composition, while those in F seem to reflect playhouse practice (e.g. a large number of additional trumpet 'Flourishes', presumably from offstage or the gallery). At the same time, there are many implied stage directions in the dialogue. A modern editor is faced with the conflicting demands of illustrating three different things: Shakespeare's compositional practice in the matter of stage directions, the practice of the (probably Jacobean) theatre that is reflected in F, and the pragmatics of staging in the imagination of the reader or in the actual productions of directors and actors using the edition. I have tried to answer to these demands by retaining wherever practicable the Q1 wording of stage directions, incorporating flourishes of various kinds from F (occurrences indicated in the textual notes, but not placed in square brackets in the SDs themselves), and adding (in square brackets) what seem to me to be incontrovertible directions implied by the dialogue.

We have seen that the staging of the first act is especially complicated, so I have been more explicit with directions than have many previous editors (for instance, '[*aloft*]' is given for all speeches spoken by characters in the gallery). Throughout, I have tried to assist the reader in a mental staging of the play, but not to clutter the text with enumerations of every gesture; thus I have indicated all major movements, such as kneelings and risings (of which there are many, and which are crucial for the play's supplications and oaths), but have not felt it necessary to precede, say, 'Why lifts she up her arms in sequence thus?' (4.1.37) with the SD '[*Lavinia raises one arm, then the other*]'. The commentary frequently addresses points of staging.

Punctuation, spelling, lineation

A quick comparison of the photograph of the page from Q1

and my edited text opposite it will reveal an obvious feature of a modernized edition: its spelling and punctuation are very different from those of the original. It will also raise the question of lineation.

I have completely modernized the punctuation whilst taking into account where possible the practice of the early texts (Q2 and F often provide much more help than Q1). Of modern editions, I have found Stanley Wells' Oxford text especially useful because its punctuation is so light – editions of the generation of Arden 2 are cluttered with unnecessary commas. I have frequently used colons to suggest logical sequences of thought, gradations and accumulations of phrase upon phrase that are characteristic of the play's rhetorical mode of composition; conversely, dashes are used for breaks in that sequence, interjections, shifts in trains of thought, breakdowns of communication. Thus Marcus interprets Lavinia's raised hands to mean that more than one person raped her, but then breaks off, realizing that his interpretation of her sign cannot be verified: 'Ay, more there was – / Or else to heaven she heaves them for revenge' (4.1.39–40).

I have also been thoroughgoing in modernization of spelling, and would accordingly urge the more advanced student to work with a facsimile of Q1 as well as my text. For the benefit of readers without access to facsimiles, I have used the textual notes to draw attention to some of the more notable instances of the difference between Elizabethan and modern spelling, such as their 'haystalks' for our 'haystacks' (5.1.133). Entries of this sort record the original edition and then give the original form in italic parenthesis.

It is very hard to decide on the limits of modernization. Shakespeare used both 'sith' and 'since' as contracted forms of the old word 'sithence'; only 'since' has survived, so does modernizing mean changing his 'sith' to 'since'? I think not, because, for example, 'sith true nobility' (1.1.275, in the Mutius sequence) sounds very different from 'since true nobility'. On the other hand, there are some occasions on which the folio provides precedents for modernization which I have felt able to follow (e.g. 'wore' for Q1's 'ware' at 1.1.6 and 'more' for Q1's 'mo' at 5.3.17). In Elizabethan English, 'and' sometimes means 'if' ('and if' also means 'if'); some editors distinguish this usage of 'and' from the normal one by 'modernizing' these occurrences to 'an' (e.g. at 2.3.9, 'An 'twere my cause, I should go hang myself'). But 'an' meaning 'if' doesn't strike me as modern English, so I have retained 'and' but included a commentary note where the sense may not be readily apparent.

Save when the Clown is on stage, the whole of *Titus* is written in verse. Sometimes, however, one character speaks a half-line and another character then speaks. Traditionally, editors join up these half-lines wherever they can, in order to keep the verse flowing. My view is that half-lines spoken by different characters should only be joined together (indicated by the second line beginning in the mid-line position where the first one ends) if, when combined, they are strong metrically and the context suggests that the second character is in some sense completing the line. This means that my text has more half-lines than is the case in most recent editions of the play, with consequent slight variations of line-number. Thus in the Mutius sequence, 'Surprised, by whom? / By him that justly may' (1.1.288–9) is made up into a single line, whereas 'My lord, you pass not here' (1.1.294) and 'Help, Lucius, help!' (1.1.296) are left as half-lines. Every editor since Alexander Pope has relineated here in order to avoid half-lines and create two pentameters:

MUTIUS
    My lord, you pass not here.
TITUS
                                What, villain boy,
    Barr'st me my way in Rome?
MUTIUS
                                  Help, Lucius, help!

This has the effect of breaking up Titus' growling 'What, villain boy, barr'st me my way in Rome?' (1.1.295) – dramatically, it is surely right for Titus to deliver a single solid line while Mutius interjects in urgently attenuated half-lines.

Transmission and emendation: Q2 and after

Playtexts were not given high priority in the Elizabethan printing house. They were quick, cheap, fill-in jobs. That is why many of them are riddled with compositorial errors. John Danter, however, printed a good many of them in 1593–4, and his compositors produced a text of *Titus* with far fewer blunders than most (though the punctuation is not well thought out).[1] It is a strikingly well laid out text, with full, centred entry directions and a scrupulous treatment of exits (see note on 5.1.165).[2] But blunders there are, ranging from literals too small to be worth mentioning in my textual notes,[3] to howlers arising from the compositor's small Latin, to a missing line at 4.3.32, to substantive cruxes and missing speech prefixes. The process of correction and conjectural emendation began with Q2 and has continued through to this edition. The textual notes at the foot of each page of my text derive from collation of every significant previous edition of the play. They serve two main functions: to indicate the origin of all emendations

1 Scholars differ as to whether Q1 was set up in print by one compositor or two: Haggard argues on the basis of analysis of damaged type that it was set from one case by a single compositor, while for Jackson (*ShS*, 248) variant spellings suggest that sheets F–K were set by a different compositor from A–E. Two compositors working simultaneously would have been likely if Danter was seeking to get the play into print quickly, while it was fresh from its success on stage in early 1594. The formal collation of Q1 is A–K⁴, with A1, presumably blank, missing from the only extant copy.
2 In an unpublished paper William Long has argued from the quality of Q1's SDs that it may not be set from foul papers, but there is no positive evidence of an intervening transcript. If, as I believe, the play was prepared as a major new work for Henslowe's 1593–4 season, then Shakespeare may well have prepared his manuscript with unusual care.
3 e.g. 'Frocd' for 'Forcd' at 4.1.53 – for a list of such misprints and obscurities, see Howard-Hill, 13.

of and additions to the text of the first quarto, and to give some sense of the process of textual transmission in the four hundred years between the publication of that quarto and this edition. The form in which the textual notes are presented is described in the general editors' preface. My commentary discusses all the major textual problems and emendations; indicating significant departures from Q1, deriving either from the editorial tradition (e.g. George Steevens' marvellous suggestion that Q1's '*Muliteus*' at 4.2.154 should be emended to 'Muly lives') or my own conjecture (note especially 'gride' at 2.2.260 and the suggestion of a missing speech prefix for Marcus at 5.3.87).

Editors have not only attempted to get rid of obvious misprints and change readings that seem not to make sense in Q1, they have also made changes in order to improve the metre. I have indulged in this practice when there seems to me reasonable evidence to support it (see, for example, my defence of Ravenscroft's 'Arm, arm' at 4.4.61), but have been more sparing than some editors, since I believe that Shakespeare did not always write regular pentameters – in the commentary I draw attention to what I take to be certain dramatically effective headless lines and hexameters.[1]

One of the play's most impressive editors was the corrector of Q2. That text was published with a title-page still beginning *The most lamentable Romaine Tragedie of Titus Andronicus*, but differing from Q1 in details of both acting and printing: 'As it hath sundry times beene playde by the Right Honourable the Earle of Pembrooke, the Earle of Darbie, the Earle of Sussex, and the Lorde Chamberlaine theyr Seruants. AT LONDON, Printed by I. R. for Edward White and are to bee solde at his shoppe, at the little North doore of Paules, at the signe of the Gun. 1600.' The order of the names of the first three companies seems to have

---

1 Wright (116–42) argues for the acceptability of many lines that are a full foot short.

been altered simply to improve the typographic layout; I have already discussed the addition of 'sundry times' and the Chamberlain's Servants. The change in 'publisher' was the result of John Danter's presses being seized by the authorities in 1597 because he had been producing supposedly seditious pamphlets; he died by the end of 1599.[1]

Q2 was set by two compositors in the printing-house of James Roberts.[2] It has greatly improved punctuation and makes some corrections which suggest a real attentiveness to the text. Some notable changes in addition to the cutting of 1.1.35–8 include 'chance' for 'change' at 1.1.268, 'try experiments' for 'trie thy experimens' at 2.2.69, 'embrewed heere' for 'bereaud in blood' at 2.2.222, 'Piramus' for 'Priamus' at 2.2.231, 'in' for 'like' at 3.1.126, 'Tut' for 'But' at 5.1.141 and the insertion of 'gracious' at 5.3.26. These are, however, the changes of a careful printer, not the result of consultation of an independent manuscript. We know this because there are some alterations of whole lines in the final scene. In a remarkable piece of scholarly detective-work, Joseph S. G. Bolton demonstrated in 1929 that these were the result of Q2 being set from a copy of Q1 in which the bottom of the final two leaves (sigs K3–4)

---

1 His widow, who took over the business for a time, assigned rights in some of his copies, but not apparently *Titus* – there was no Stationers' Register entry prior to the 1600 edition. An entry of 19 April 1602 assigns 'A booke called Titus and Andronicus' from Thomas Millington to Thomas Pavier, and yet Edward White published editions in both 1600 and 1611. Waith accounts for this apparent anomaly by suggesting that the 1602 entry (and others later in the seventeenth century) may refer not to the play but to the supposed 'History' preserved in the eighteenth-century chapbook (Oxf[1], 213–15). This hypothesis is unnecessary: Q1 was 'to be sold by *Edward White* & *Thomas Millington*', so it seems reasonable to suppose that this gave White his authority to have the editions of 1600 and 1611 printed for him, while Millington assigned his share to Pavier (who was a close associate of William and Isaac Jaggard, the Folio printers). It must be remembered that entry in the Stationers' Registers did not constitute anything like so binding a claim to the legal rights in a book as post-1709 Copyright does.
2 See Cantrell & Williams for an exemplary analysis of its typesetting. Two copies are extant, one at the Huntington Library in California, the other in Edinburgh University Library; the Huntington copy has some press corrections (listed by Adams, 19).

had been torn away, so the printer had to make up the missing lines.[1] If there had been an independent manuscript to check against, this would not have been necessary. The tear on the final sheet included the middle of the last line of the play, the final '*Exeunt*' and the line which reads '*Finis the Tragedie of Titus Andronicus*'. The editor of Q2 had no way of knowing that Q1's 'And being dead let birds on her take pittie' was the last line of the text. He therefore gave the play an extra four lines (see textual notes at 5.3.199), depriving it of its powerful close on a rhyme of pity with pity.

This change was received into the editorial tradition and remained there well into the twentieth century. It is a mark of Q1's popularity that this flimsy little playbook was virtually read into disintegration: Ravenscroft and the eighteenth-century editors of the play knew only the sequence of texts that ran from Q2 through the folios. But then in 1904 a single copy of Q1 turned up in Sweden; it is now among the most prized possessions of the Folger Shakespeare Library.[2] But even after the copy of Q1 was discovered some editions (e.g. Yale and Temple) continued to print Q2's patched-up ending instead of Shakespeare's original. The Brook production used Ridley's Temple text and thus gave the play its false ending.

A third quarto appeared in 1611, printed by Edward Allde for Edward White. Its title-page removed the names of the old acting companies (and the word 'Roman'), making space for larger print and mentioning only the leading company of the day, 'the Kings Maiesties Seruants' (as the Chamberlain's had by then become). Q3 was set up from a copy of Q2, reproducing

---

1 Other alterations suggest that there was also slight damage at the top of sig.I4 and the bottom of sig.K2.

2 An early owner of the copy seems to have read the play with unusual attention, inking in a number of alterations by hand (most notably, an attempt to correct the phrase 'bereaud in blood' – see t.n. for 2.2.222). For full lists of difficult readings and MS emendations, see Adams, 40–1, and Allen & Muir, 889–90. In the bottom margin of one page (sig.G1ʳ), the early reader copied the last line of the page, 'I say my Lord that if I were' (ink faded; reading clear under ultra-violet light), perhaps to test a pen.

its page arrangement, catchwords and signatures. Its alterations are not of great substance, though one or two of them are useful (e.g. explicit stage directions are introduced for Titus' killing of Mutius and Lavinia, where in Q1–2 they are merely implied by the dialogue).

The text in the 1623 First Folio was set from Q3. It made a handful of corrections and emendations (the best being 'giue it action' for 'giue that accord' at 5.2.18), but also introduced a large number of new errors. Five individual lines were inadvertently dropped, an odd phrase 'What booke?' crept in at 4.1.36, and many speech prefixes were changed (sometimes due to misunderstanding of the action: see, e.g., note on 5.3.72–5). The folio text is poor in quality because it was mostly set by 'Compositor E', the least accurate of the men working on Shakespeare's *Comedies, Histories, & Tragedies* (he was probably an apprentice).[1]

But the changes to stage directions are purposeful and seem to have the authority of the playhouse; in addition, the folio's division of the play into five acts seems to reflect the introduction of act-breaks in the Jacobean theatre. Bolton, who undertook the first full collation of all the early editions, noted that seventeen stage directions were altered and nineteen new ones added ('Text', 771). Some of these change Q1's literary direction '*Sound trumpets*' to the technical theatrical prompt, '*Flourish*'; others are additional prompts for a '*Flourish*' or, in one case, '*Hoboyes*'. An added direction such as '*A Table brought in*' (5.3.25) looks very much like a stage-manager's note. Scholars therefore agree that F was set from Q3 but that either an annotator of Q3 or the printer of F had access to a theatrical promptbook. It is because the folio directions reflect early staging practice that I have incorporated most of them in my text without the square brackets which I put around editorial stage directions. The question then arises as to the nature of

---

1   *Titus* occupies sigs cc4^r–ee2^v; Compositor E seems to have set all but the first and last pages, attributable to Compositor B, and possibly dd3^v (see *TxC*, 154).

this promptbook copy for the folio text. It could have been an independent manuscript, but Sir Walter Greg argued that it was a marked-up copy of Q2.[1] If he is right, it would have reflected post-1600 theatrical practice, something consistent with the marking of act-divisions.

One passage reveals how complicated the process of textual transmission can be. I have already quoted the Q1 text where Titus is pleading to the tribunes for his sons' lives (3.1.34–7), apropos of the possibility that 'And bootlesse vnto them' represents a false start. Q2 made one small emendation to these lines, improving the rhythm of the second one by adding 'or':

> Why tis no matter man, if they did heare
> They would not marke me, or if they did marke,
> They would not pitty me, yet pleade I must,
> And bootlesse vnto them.
> Therefore I tell my sorrows to the stones,

Q3 omitted the third line, presumably due to inadvertent eyeskip, then tried to make sense of the result by changing 'And bootlesse' to 'All bootlesse', but also repeated 'bootles[s]' in the following line:

> Why tis no matter man, if they did heare
> They would not marke me, or if they did marke,
> All bootlesse vnto them.
> Therefore I tell my sorrowes bootles to the stones,

F produced the following:

> Why 'tis no matter man, if they did heare
> They would not marke me: oh if they did heare,
> They would not pitty me.
> Therefore I tell my sorrowes bootles to the stones.

---

1 See Greg, 203–9. There is a comparable case of a marked-up quarto of *A Looking Glass for London and England* serving as a promptbook (see reproductions in Baskervill).

Since 'bootles' was retained in the last line, the previous half-line was dropped, but something was needed between 'if they did heare' and 'Therefore I tell', so at this point the compositor or annotator presumably looked to his other copy and set what he saw immediately above 'bootlesse vnto them': 'They would not pitty me'. In support of his argument that the prompt copy was a marked-up Q2, Greg noted that the spelling here is Q2's 'pitty' (Q1 reads 'pittie') and that 'or' in the previous line (misprinted by F as 'oh') was in Q2 but would not have been in a manuscript.[1] But this is not sufficient evidence to be decisive.

Whether or not F had recourse to a manuscript that was independent from the quartos, the one complete line it adds to a quarto scene must be viewed as conjectural rather than authoritatively Shakespearean. That line is 'Yes, and will Nobly him remunerate' (1.1.403). Someone thought that Titus' question, 'Is shee not then beholding to the man, / That brought[her for this high good turne so farre[?]', demanded an answer, so made one up. I print the line (following most editors in assigning it to Marcus) because I cannot be sure that it is not Shakespearean, but indicate its questionable status by putting it in a different typeface. Directors should ask themselves whether its inclusion is dramatically necessary, or whether the answer to Titus' question is supplied visually by the entrance that immediately follows it in the quarto text.

The killing of the fly (3.2)

The first folio text includes one complete, self-contained scene that had not previously been printed. It has all the marks of an addition to the action, like the celebrated added mad scenes in Kyd's *Spanish Tragedy*. Its inclusion requires a group of

---

1 In support of the alternative view that the promptbook was a MS, Waith suggested that 'or' was in Shakespeare's foul papers and 'might have stood in a lost press-corrected state of Q1, via which it found its way into the text of Q2' (Oxf[1], 42).

characters to go offstage and come straight back, something that Shakespeare nearly always avoided.

The printing clearly indicates that different copy was being used from that which furnished the rest of the play. As may be seen from the extract reproduced here (Fig. 16), Titus' lines are given the speech prefix '*An.*': this never occurs in the quarto text. There are also a number of errors which suggest misreading of a manuscript (e.g. in the extract here: 'complaynet' for 'complainer' and the omission of the copulative in 'Mine eyes cloi'd'); the lineation is also highly irregular. Greg suggested that the scene would conveniently have filled a single leaf of foolscap, which could easily have been appended to a promptbook; he also pointed out that it must have been added to the play before the division into acts was made, for otherwise the third act would have been exceptionally short (Greg, 204–5).

If *Titus* was originally written in 1591 or 1592, Henslowe's 'ne' in January 1594 could mean 'newly revised, with an added mad scene', but this is unlikely in view of the absence of the scene from the quarto entered in February 1594. It is noteworthy that the scene does the same kind of work as the *Spanish Tragedy* additions in providing additional testimony to (and witty performance of) the protagonist's madness, and that those additions date from around 1600. They were first printed in the 1602 edition of *The Spanish Tragedy*; if they are Jonson's, they date from 1601–2, but some scholars date them to 1597 – perhaps the fly-killing belongs to the same broad period. The authorship of the scene has been questioned, but its consistency of style with the rest, notably its self-conscious play on 'hands' and the problem of expressing emotion, leaves little doubt that it is by Shakespeare. Line 5.1.142 perhaps gave him the germ of it: Aaron's willingness to do dreadful things as readily as he would kill a fly is flipped around so that he becomes the fly; the added scene thus gives Titus an occasion to express his vindictiveness against Aaron, whereas elsewhere he always identifies Tamora as his chief antagonist.

Speechlesse complaynet, I will learne thy thought:
In thy dumb action, will I be as perfect
As begging Hermits in their holy prayers,
Thou shalt not sighe nor hold thy stumps to heauen,
Nor winke, nor nod, nor kneele, nor make a signe,
But I (of these) will wrest an Alphabet,
And by still practice, learne to know thy meaning.

Boy. Good grandsire leaue these bitter deepe laments,
Make my Aunt merry, with some pleasing tale.

Mar. Alas, the tender boy in passion mou'd,
Doth weepe to see his grandsires heauinesse.

An. Peace tender Sapling, thou art made of teares,
And teares will quickly melt thy life away.

Marcus strikes the dish with a knife.
What doest thou strike at *Marcus* with knife.

Mar. At that that I haue kil'd my Lord, a Flys

An. Out on the murderour: thou kil'st my hart,
Mine eyes cloi'd with view of Tirranie:
A deed of death done on the Innocent
Becoms not *Titus* broher: get thee gone,
I see thou art not for my company.

Mar. Alas (my Lord) I haue but kild a flie.

An. But? How: if that Flie had a father and mother?
How would he hang his slender gilded wings
And buz lamenting doings in the ayer,
Poore harmelesse Fly,
That with his pretty buzing melody,
Came heere to make vs merry,
And thou hast kil'd him.

Mar. Pardon me sir,
It was a blacke illfauour'd Fly,
Like to the Empresse Moore, therefore I kild him.

An. O,o,o,
Then pardon me for reprehending thee,
For thou hast done a Charitable deed:
Giue me thy knife, I will insult on him,
Flattering my selfes, as if it were the Moore,
Come hither purposely to poyson me.
There's for thy selfe, and thats for *Tamira*: Ah sirra,
Yet I thinke we are not brought so low,
But that betweene vs, we can kill a Fly,
That comes in likenesse of a Cole-blacke Moore.

Mar. Alas poore man, griefe ha's so wrought on him,
He takes false shadowes, for true substances.

An. Come, take away: *Lauinia* goe with me,
Ile to thy closset, and goe read with thee
Sad stories, chanced in the times of old.
Come boy, and goe with me, thy sight is young,
And thou shalt read, when mine begin to dazell. *Exeunt*

16 The killing of the fly in F

A comparison of the photographic extract with my text will give the reader an indication of how the editor has to intervene more heavily in this scene than in the rest of the play. I shall end this introduction by considering the options available with one line, that which appears in the folio as

AN. But? How: if that Flie had a father and mother?

Having changed the speech prefix to TITUS, the editor then has to decide whether this is an acceptable line of verse and whether it is punctuated correctly. Rhythmically, it is very awkward; that awkwardness could be put down to Titus' madness (as could the fragmented half-lines later in the speech), but it seems to me that the best way of helping the reader or actor is to give the question the stress of incredulity or reproach it requires by placing it on a separate line (in inverted commas, since Titus is quoting Marcus' word) and to assume that the punctuation after 'How' is erroneous. One would then have

TITUS 'But'?
How if that fly had a father and mother?
(3.2.60–1)

The metre remains awkward, so one must then consider whether the printer missed something in the manuscript (as he seems to have done a few lines above, where F2 sensibly emended 'knife' to 'thy knife' and 'cloi'd' to 'are cloi'd'). I think that he did, so I emend to the rhetorically and metrically stronger 'a father and a mother' (a conjecture anticipated by Craig in his 1892 edition).

But one must also consider the subsequent lines: 'How would he hang his slender gilded wings / And buz lamenting doings in the ayer'. Who is 'he'? Not the fly which has been swatted, but the father, who is Titus' surrogate. Some editors therefore seek consistency of number by removing the mother: both the single-volume and *Complete Works* Oxford texts have 'How if that fly had a father, brother?' This follows an ingenious conjecture first made by Ritson over two hundred years ago: one has to suppose that Shakespeare intended 'brother' as an address to Marcus and that the printer changed it to 'mother' because 'father and mother' is a more natural combination.

But 'father, brother' to 'father and mother' is a substantial change: is it not high-handed for editors to erase the mother on the basis of such a large conjecture about the printer's incompetence? Might not Titus in his madness momentarily imagine that the fly had two lamenting parents, then remember that his own wife is dead and subsume the traditional maternal function of lamentation into his own paternal role? It is a good thing that Jane Howell, who directed the fine television production, was not using an edition which adopted Ritson's emendation, for she found the play's 'depth of passion and philosophy' in that cry, 'How if that fly had a father and mother?' (BBC, 31). *Hysterica passio* was also known as 'the mother': it is the climbing sorrow which swells up in Lear's heart; it is the strong feeling that is at the core of tragedy. In becoming a mother as well as a father Titus becomes a human being.

But wait: the tragic empathy here is with a fly. Is this an extreme instance of the 'special providence in the fall of a sparrow' cited by Jesus and Hamlet? Or is it a glorious comic parody of tragic empathy? I suspect it is both, and in that lies the greatness of *Titus Andronicus*.

THE MOST LAMENTABLE ROMAN TRAGEDY OF

TITUS ANDRONICUS

ROMANS

SATURNINUS	*eldest son of the recently deceased Emperor of Rome, later Emperor*
BASSIANUS	*younger brother of Saturninus*
TITUS ANDRONICUS	*a Roman nobleman, general against the Goths* 5
MARCUS ANDRONICUS	*a Tribune of the people, brother of Titus*
LUCIUS QUINTUS MARTIUS MUTIUS	*the surviving sons of Titus Andronicus (in descending order of age)* 10
LAVINIA	*only daughter of Titus Andronicus, betrothed to Bassianus*
YOUNG LUCIUS	*a Boy, son of Lucius* 15
PUBLIUS	*son of Marcus Andronicus*
SEMPRONIUS CAIUS VALENTINE	*kinsmen of the Andronici*
EMILLIUS	*a Roman* 20
A CAPTAIN	
A MESSENGER	
A NURSE	
A CLOWN	
OTHER ROMANS	*including Senators, Tribunes, Soldiers and Attendants* 25

GOTHS

TAMORA	*Queen of the Goths and later Empress of Rome by marriage to Saturninus* 30
ALARBUS DEMETRIUS CHIRON	*the sons of Tamora (in descending order of age)*
AARON	*a Moor in the service of Tamora, her lover* 35
OTHER GOTHS	*forming an army*

LIST OF ROLES Ravenscroft was the first to print such a list, headed 'The Persons' Names' and divided into Romans and Goths. For likely origins of the names, and discussion of company size and doubling, see introduction, pp. 93–5.

1 SATURNINUS probably intended to suggest a 'saturnine' temperament – under the influence of Saturn, 'sullen' and 'self-willed' (Lyly, *Woman in the Moon* [?1592], 1.1.144–9); compare Aaron at 2.2.31–6

3 BASSIANUS second 'a' probably pronounced as in 'name'

6 MARCUS ... *a Tribune* see 1.1.21

9–11 QUINTUS, MARTIUS only given names in speech prefixes (SPs) in 2.2 – see introduction, p. 95n.1

13 LAVINIA originally played by a boy actor

15 YOUNG LUCIUS So named in some entry directions in Qq,F, but SP for him is always *Puer* in Q1, *Boy* in F. I follow this practice, giving the name at entry, but BOY as SP to keep the reader in constant mind of the fact that this is a child – the dialogue frequently reminds the reader of the name Lucius; the SP, which in a written text stands in for the spectator's sight of the actor, reminds us that he is a Boy.

17–19 SEMPRONIUS, CAIUS, VALENTINE Sempronius and Caius are addressed as 'kinsmen' by Titus in 4.3; Caius and Valentine are in his house and at his call in 5.2. Shakespeare might have forgotten that he had used the name Sempronius, so Valentine might be the same character; they could easily be doubled.

20 EMILLIUS always spelt thus in Qq and F, and by Ravenscroft. Theobald emended to the commoner Roman spelling, Aemilius, but the emendation is the product of an eighteenth- and not a sixteenth-century notion of Roman proper names; 'Emillius' is perfectly plausible and scans well in all the lines in which it is used, so I have restored the original spelling. He is more senior than a common messenger, but it is not clear whether he is a senator or a tribune; Ravenscroft made him a Tribune, brought him on in the first act and gave him prominence at the end of the play.

23 NURSE possibly played by an adult male actor, rather than a boy, though 4.2.148 suggests the cry of an unbroken voice

24 CLOWN a specialist role for the company Clown

28 TAMORA originally played by a boy actor. Pronounced with stress on first syllable. Her sexual love (*amor*) and its object (the Moor) may be heard within her name.

34 AARON 'Aron' in Qq (and Ravenscroft), but eds since Rowe follow F's Aaron. The pun on 'air' at 4.2.171 supports this spelling in terms of pronunciation. An Elizabethan audience would have known that the biblical Aaron had an eloquent, persuasive tongue (Exodus, 4.10–16).

LIST OF ROLES *first included by Ravenscroft (adapted), Rowe*   TITLE] *The most Lamentable Romaine Tragedy of Titus Andronicus: As it was Plaide by the Right Honourable the Earle of Darbie, Earle of Pembrooke, and Earle of Sussex their Seruants Q1 head title; The most lamentable Tragedie of Titus Andronicus Q1 running head; The Lamentable Tragedy of Titus Andronicus F head title; The Tragedie of Titus Andronicus F running head; 'Romaine' first om. in Q3*

THE MOST
LAMENTABLE
ROMAN TRAGEDY OF
TITUS ANDRONICUS

1.1   *Flourish. Enter the Tribunes [including* MARCUS
ANDRONICUS] *and Senators aloft. And then enter [below]*
SATURNINUS *and his followers at one door, and* BASSIANUS
and his followers at the other, with drums and colours.

SATURNINUS
  Noble patricians, patrons of my right,
  Defend the justice of my cause with arms.
  And countrymen, my loving followers,

1.1 The setting is Rome; the gallery *aloft*
represents the Capitol/Senate House;
the tomb of the Andronici could have
been represented by the discovery-
space at the back of the stage or the
trap-door downstage, though some
eds suggest a free-standing structure
(but this would have to be removed
at the end of the scene). Eighteenth-
century eds introduced the convention of giving locations for the
scenes: examples given in t.n., but it
must be remembered that they impose
rigidity on the fluid space of the Elizabethan theatre.

0.1–4 *Flourish ... colours* Marcus is a
tribune so presumably enters aloft
among the Tribunes, then steps forward '*with the crown*' for his first
speech. F, however, has him entering
aloft after 17. Q1 has '*Drums and Trum-*

pets', meaning that there are drummers
among the followers on either side. F
has a fanfare ('*Flourish*') of trumpets
from offstage before the entry and
'*Drum & Colours*' in the entry direction. The most satisfactory direction is
to have the trumpets sounding offstage, as occurs frequently in the play,
and each faction accompanied by a
drummer and standard-bearer. The
doors were at either end of the tiring-
house; the rival brothers thus take up
confrontational positions on opposite
sides of the stage, with the powers of
arbitration between and above them in
the gallery.

1 **patrons** supporters, protectors, possibly also with technical Roman sense
of legal advocate

1–8 **Noble patricians ... indignity**
Saturninus' appeal is patriarchal: to

1.1] *no act and scene numbers in Q q*; *Actus Primus. Scaena Prima. F*   Location] *Rome Rowe;* Before
the Capitol *Theobald;* In it the tomb of the Andronici *Capell*   0.1 *Flourish] F*   0.1–4 *Enter ...*
colours] Q1 subst., except as indicated below   0.1*including* MARCUS ANDRONICUS] *this edn; among*
them MARCUS ANDRONICUS *Riv*   0.2 *aloft] Q1; aloft, as in the Senate / Rowe   below] Capell*   0.4
at the other] F   drums and colours] Drum & Colours F; Drums and Trumpets Q1, Q2; Drum Q3   1
SATURNINUS] *Q1 centred, as are all SPs up to and including Enter a Captaine; SP for this character*
variously SATURNINUS, SATURNINE, *sometimes abbreviated*

127

Plead my successive title with your swords.
I am his first-born son that was the last   5
That wore the imperial diadem of Rome:
Then let my father's honours live in me,
Nor wrong mine age with this indignity.

BASSIANUS

Romans, friends, followers, favourers of my right,
If ever Bassianus, Caesar's son,   10
Were gracious in the eyes of royal Rome,
Keep then this passage to the Capitol,
And suffer not dishonour to approach
The imperial seat, to virtue consecrate,
To justice, continence and nobility;   15
But let desert in pure election shine,
And, Romans, fight for freedom in your choice.

the patricians, to the principle of primogeniture and to his father's honour. Lines 3–4 are clearly addressed to his followers, but 1–2 may be addressed to the Senators (representatives of the patricians) above and implicitly not to the Tribunes (representatives of the plebeians).

4 **successive** hereditary. Compare 'successive line' (*Sp. Trag.*, 3.1.15).

5 **his first-born son** that first-born son of him who; it was common Elizabethan usage to have the possessive pronoun as antecedent

7 **honours** like *patrons*, a latinate term with a range of meanings: respect accorded to high rank; fame, good name, dignity

8 **mine age** my status as elder brother
indignity antithesis of *honours*; the insult of having his title questioned

9–17 **Romans ... choice** Bassianus appeals to the whole of Rome and bases his claim on *desert* according to the Roman virtues of justice, freedom, restraint (*continence*). 'Pure election' suggests a vote free from con-

sideration of primogeniture.

11 **gracious** acceptable, worthy of favour (also at 1.1.434, 531)

12 **keep** guard
Capitol the summit of the Capitoline hill in Rome, on which was the temple of Jupiter, guardian of the city. Elizabethan dramatists generally assumed that the Capitol was the site of the Senate House, here represented by the upper stage; the assumption is incorrect, though Herodian noted that during a crisis in the reign of the emperor Bassianus the Senate assembled 'not in the Coorte as thei were wonte before, but in the Temple of Jupiter Capitolyne, the whyche beynge buylded in the highest place of the Citie, the Romaines have in most estimacioun' (Herodian, 7.10.2).

14 **virtue** Latin *virtus*: worth, also manliness
consecrate consecrated

15 **continence** 'Continence is a vertue which keepeth the plesaunt appetite of man under the yoke of reason' (Elyot, 179).

5 am his] *Q1;* was the *F*   6 wore] *F;* ware *Qq*   14 seat, ... consecrate,] *Rowe (anticipated in Ravenscroft's adaptation);* seate to vertue, consecrate *Qq;* seate to Vertue: consecrate *F*

MARCUS ([*aloft*,] *with the crown*)
    Princes, that strive by factions and by friends
    Ambitiously for rule and empery,
    Know that the people of Rome, for whom we stand   20
    A special party, have by common voice
    In election for the Roman empery
    Chosen Andronicus, surnamed Pius
    For many good and great deserts to Rome.
    A nobler man, a braver warrior,   25
    Lives not this day within the city walls.
    He by the senate is accited home
    From weary wars against the barbarous Goths,
    That with his sons, a terror to our foes,
    Hath yoked a nation strong, trained up in arms.   30
    Ten years are spent since first he undertook
    This cause of Rome and chastised with arms
    Our enemies' pride; five times he hath returned
    Bleeding to Rome, bearing his valiant sons
    In coffins from the field {and at this day   35

19 **empery** status of emperor
21 **a special party** i.e. as elected Tribune. Originally Tribunes were magistrates of free plebeian birth, but later men of noble birth (the Andronici are manifestly a patrician family) could qualify (as Cicero's enemy Clodius did, through being adopted into a plebeian family).
voice expressed opinion, hence vote (as frequently in *Cor*)
22 **In election** nominated (*Chosen*) as a candidate
23 **surnamed** three syllables: 'sur-nam-ed'. In subsequent instances where the past participle 'ed' is sounded as a separate syllable *contrary to normal modern practice*, this is indicated in the commentary by means of a grave

accent ('surnamèd') – see general editors' preface, p. x.
Pius embodying the virtues of the legendary founder of Rome, Virgil's 'Pius Aeneas': 'Religious; devoute; godly; mercifull; benigne; that beareth reverent love towarde his countrei and parentes; Naturall to his kinsefolke' (Cooper).
24 **deserts** actions deserving reward
27 **accited** summoned
28 **Goths** see introduction (pp. 18–21)
30 **yoked** conquered, brought under imperial subjection
32 **chastised** chastisèd
35–8 **and at ... the Goths** On the status of these lines, see introduction, pp. 99–100.

18 *aloft*] *this edn (and for all subsequent speeches spoken from upper stage)* *with the crown*] *Marcus Andronicus with the Crowne Q1 (centred); Enter Marcus Andronicus aloft with the Crowne F* 23 Pius] *Q1*; Pious *F* 35–8 and at this day ... of the Goths] *Q1; not in Q2–3, F* 35 day] *Q1;* door (*Jackson, ShS*)

To the monument of the Andronici
Done sacrifice of expiation,
And slain the noblest prisoner of the Goths}.
And now at last, laden with honour's spoils,
Returns the good Andronicus to Rome,   40
Renowned Titus, flourishing in arms.
Let us entreat, by honour of his name
Whom worthily you would have now succeed,
And in the Capitol and senate's right,
Whom you pretend to honour and adore,   45
That you withdraw you and abate your strength,
Dismiss your followers and, as suitors should,
Plead your deserts in peace and humbleness.

SATURNINUS
How fair the tribune speaks to calm my thoughts.

BASSIANUS
Marcus Andronicus, so I do affy   50
In thy uprightness and integrity,
And so I love and honour thee and thine,
Thy noble brother Titus and his sons,

36 *the Andronici 'that *Andronicy*' in
   Q1: 'The MS presumably had "y"',
   which could easily be misread as "y'"
   by a compositor who did not realize
   (note his spelling of it) that *Andronici*
   was plural' (Ard²).
37 expiation The suffix '-ion' was frequently pronounced as two syllables.
41 Renowned Renownèd
   flourishing at the height of fame or
   excellence
42–3 of his name ... succeed To whom
   does 'his' refer? The sentence is
   addressed to Saturninus and Bassianus, so it cannot be Titus' name,
   since they do not want him to
   succeed. It could be the brothers
   themselves: 'by the honour of the
   candidate – yourself – whom you
   intend to succeed worthily to the
   empery' (both flattering them for and

exhorting them to worthiness). The
alternative is Capell's emendation,
'succeeded': Marcus would then be
entreating by the honour of the name
of the late emperor, the candidates'
father, whom they would certainly
want to be worthily succeeded. By
appealing to the late emperor, the
Capitol (a synecdoche for Rome
itself) and the Senate, Marcus is able
to appease even the ambitious Saturninus. 'Succeeded' makes this sense
clear at the cost of rendering the line
hypermetric: Riv, following Stoll, gets
round this problem by suggesting that
'succeed' might originally have been
intended as a contracted form of the
past participle, but comparable cases
are hard to find.
45 pretend claim
50 affy trust, rely upon

36 the Andronici] *Red Letter;* that *Andronicy Q1*   43 worthily] *Q1;* (worthily) *F*   succeed] *Q1;*
succeeded *Capell*

130

And her to whom my thoughts are humbled all,
Gracious Lavinia, Rome's rich ornament,   55
That I will here dismiss my loving friends
And to my fortune's and the people's favour
Commit my cause in balance to be weighed.

Exeunt [his] Soldiers.

SATURNINUS
Friends that have been thus forward in my right,
I thank you all and here dismiss you all,   60
And to the love and favour of my country
Commit myself, my person and the cause.

[Exeunt his Soldiers.]

Rome, be as just and gracious unto me
As I am confident and kind to thee.
Open the gates and let me in.   65

BASSIANUS
Tribunes, and me, a poor competitor.

Flourish. They go up into the Senate House.

Enter a Captain.

57 **fortune's** could be 'to my fortunes',
   but Q1 omits apostrophes for pos-
   sessives (e.g. 'Romes rich ornament'
   at 55) and 'my fortune's favour' seems
   to be implied
63–5 **Rome ... let me in** The first
   two lines are addressed to the city
   in abstract, the third to those aloft,
   imagined to be in the Senate House.
   'Open the gates' perhaps indicates a
   symbolic shift in the meaning of the
   doors at the back of the stage: when
   the followers exit through them, they
   are merely leaving the public arena,
   but with the ensuing exit of Saturninus and Bassianus the doors
   become the gates to the Senate House.
   The last line is a foot short.
64 **confident and kind** trustful and well

disposed, because possessed of natural, familial affection
66 **Tribunes** suggests that Saturninus
   has addressed the Senators above,
   whereas Bassianus appealed to the
   Tribunes
   competitor fellow-candidate (Latin
   for 'co-petitioner' – Wells, *Re-Editing*,
   87), rival
66.1 *Flourish* F has this trumpet-sound
   to cover the exit and ascent. Many
   eds (inc. Ard[2], Oxf[1]) have a re-
   entrance aloft for Saturninus, Bassianus, Tribunes etc. at 172, but it is
   more likely that the candidates would
   appear immediately on ascending the
   gallery and remain there with the
   Tribunes and Senators, watching
   Titus' procession below.

57 fortune's] *Delius;* fortunes *Qq;* Fortunes *F*   58.1] *this edn; Exit Soldiers Q1; Exeunt the*
Followers of Bassianus / Capell   62.1] *this edn; Exeunt the Followers of Saturninus / Capell*   66.1]
Flourish F

CAPTAIN

Romans, make way: the good Andronicus,
Patron of virtue, Rome's best champion,
Successful in the battles that he fights,
With honour and with fortune is returned   70
From where he circumscribed with his sword
And brought to yoke the enemies of Rome.

Sound drums and trumpets, and then enter two of TITUS' *Sons,*
and then two men bearing a coffin covered with black, then two
other Sons, *then* TITUS ANDRONICUS, *and then* [, *as prisoners,*]
TAMORA, *the Queen of Goths, and her* [*three*] *sons,* [ALARBUS,]
CHIRON *and* DEMETRIUS, *with* AARON *the Moor, and others*
as many as can be. Then set down the coffin and TITUS *speaks.*

TITUS

Hail, Rome, victorious in thy mourning weeds!
Lo, as the bark that hath discharged his freight
Returns with precious lading to the bay   75

67 **Romans, make way** The main stage is empty at this point: the Captain perhaps addresses the theatre audience as *Romans* (Hunter, 'Flatcaps', 18–20).

68 **Patron** In sixteenth-century English, this spelling was used for both senses now differentiated as 'patron' and 'pattern'.

71 **circumscribed** circumscribèd. confined

72.1–6 *Sound drums ... speaks* The drummers who exit with the followers of Saturninus and Bassianus might re-enter among the *as many as can be* as part of Titus' procession. Qq, F mention only two sons, Chiron and Demetrius, for Tamora – on the omission of Alarbus, see introduction, p. 103. Oxf, prompted by F's plural at 152SD, has 'coffins', since Titus

is burying more than one son, but Elizabethan staging was often more emblematic than literal. The Warner production had a single wide multiple coffin; its entry procession was simple but stunning, with Titus sitting on a ladder held horizontally by his sons, the prisoners' heads stuck between the rungs.

74 **his freight** modernization of Q1's 'fraught'. Some eds emend to 'her' for consistency with 76; the compositor could have misread MS 'hir'.

75–7 **precious ... boughs** As the boat has picked up valuable fresh cargo in return for what was discharged, so Titus has gained a victor's headgear (*laurel boughs*, which the actor presumably wears) in return for his deeds.

71 where] *Q1;* whence *F*   72.1–6] *Q1 subst., except as indicated below*   72.3 TITUS ANDRONICUS] *Oxf, Oxf¹ add 'in a chariot' as prisoners*] *this edn; and other Goths, prisoners / Cam*   72.4 *three sons, Alarbus*] *Rowe subst.; her two sonnes Chiron and Demetrius Qq, F*   72.5 AARON] *F (thus throughout in SDs and dialogue, but Aron in SPs); Aron Qq (throughout; sometimes Moore in SPs)*   72.6 *Then set*] *Q1; They set F*   74 his] *Q1; her F4*   freight] *Rowe; fraught Q1*

From whence at first she weighed her anchorage,
Cometh Andronicus, bound with laurel boughs,
To resalute his country with his tears,
Tears of true joy for his return to Rome.
Thou great defender of this Capitol,   80
Stand gracious to the rites that we intend.
Romans, of five-and-twenty valiant sons,
Half of the number that King Priam had,
Behold the poor remains, alive and dead:
These that survive, let Rome reward with love;   85
These that I bring unto their latest home,
With burial amongst their ancestors.
Here Goths have given me leave to sheathe my sword.
Titus, unkind and careless of thine own,
Why suffer'st thou thy sons unburied yet   90
To hover on the dreadful shore of Styx?
Make way to lay them by their brethren.

They open the tomb.

There greet in silence, as the dead are wont,
And sleep in peace, slain in your country's wars.
O sacred receptacle of my joys,   95
Sweet cell of virtue and nobility,

80 **Thou** Jupiter Capitolinus
81 **gracious** disposed to show grace
83 **King Priam** King of Troy during the Trojan war, during which nearly all his fifty sons were killed. The first of the play's many linkings of Rome and Troy.
89 **unkind** lacking in consideration due to family (kind)
careless of insufficiently solicitous for
91 **Styx** river boundary of the classical underworld, which could only be crossed by the shade when the body was properly buried. See Virgil, *Aeneid*, trans. Phaer, 6.352–3: 'Nor from these fearfull bankes nor ryvers hoarce they passage get: / Till under earth in graves their bodies bones at

rest are set'.
92 **brethren** pronunciation as three syllables indicated by Q3's spelling: 'bretheren'. On subsequent occasions where early edns assist pronunciation, spelling and edn are given in commentary.
92.1 *open the tomb* probably by opening the discovery space or the trap-door
95 **receptacle** repository, from Latin *receptaculum*, 'shelter', 'place of refuge'. Also used for a tomb at *RJ* 4.3.39. Olivier (correctly) stressed it 'réceptácle' – 'Here was panache,' observed Evelyn Waugh in his review of the Brook production (Waugh, 300).
96 **cell** like a monastic room, but *store* in the next line shifts the metaphor towards a storage closet

81 rites] *F;* rights *Qq*

How many sons hast thou of mine in store
That thou wilt never render to me more!

LUCIUS

Give us the proudest prisoner of the Goths,
That we may hew his limbs and on a pile   100
Ad manes fratrum sacrifice his flesh
Before this earthly prison of their bones,
That so the shadows be not unappeased,
Nor we disturbed with prodigies on earth.

TITUS

I give him you, the noblest that survives,   105
The eldest son of this distressed queen.

TAMORA   [*kneeling*]

Stay, Roman brethren, gracious conqueror,
Victorious Titus, rue the tears I shed,
A mother's tears in passion for her son!
And if thy sons were ever dear to thee,   110
O, think my son to be as dear to me.
Sufficeth not that we are brought to Rome
To beautify thy triumphs, and return

99–152 LUCIUS ... **souls** The killing of Alarbus is probably an insertion made between first draft and first performance (see introduction, pp. 103–4). Lucius, the first to speak, is the eldest of the four surviving sons of Titus: it is in response to his demand that Titus symmetrically offers to sacrifice 'the eldest son' of Tamora.

101 *Ad manes fratrum* Latin: 'to the shades of our brothers'

102 **earthly** 'earthy' (Qq) and 'earthly' (F) were interchangeable in Elizabethan usage; F's variant makes clearer to the modern reader the primary sense of pertaining to earth as opposed to heaven

104 **disturbed ... earth** Ill-omened signs and events on earth were often

associated with unappeased ghosts, as in *Ham* and *JC*. But in *Titus* the human will to revenge outweighs gods and ghosts (who are conspicuously absent), so proper burial does not bring peace.

105 **I give him you** Capell adds SD 'Giving them Alarbus.'

106 **distressed** distressèd

107 *kneeling* implied by 1.1.459–60. See the Peacham drawing (introduction, p. 39); Chiron and Demetrius may kneel too.

109 **passion** grief; in Shakespearean usage, the word has a wide penumbra of meanings associated with strong emotion

113 **triumphs, and return** Since Tamora has not been to Rome before,

97 hast thou of mine] *Q1*; of mine has thou *Q3*, F   101 manes] *F3*; manus *Qq*, F   102 earthly] F; earthy *Qq*   107 SD] *Oxf*; *kneeling with her sons* / *Oxf¹*   111 son] *Q1*; sonnes F

Captive to thee and to thy Roman yoke?
But must my sons be slaughtered in the streets   115
For valiant doings in their country's cause?
O, if to fight for king and commonweal
Were piety in thine, it is in these.
Andronicus, stain not thy tomb with blood.
Wilt thou draw near the nature of the gods?   120
Draw near them then in being merciful.
Sweet mercy is nobility's true badge:
Thrice noble Titus, spare my first-born son.

TITUS

Patient yourself, madam, and pardon me.
These are their brethren whom your Goths beheld   125
Alive and dead, and for their brethren slain,
Religiously they ask a sacrifice.
To this your son is marked, and die he must,
T'appease their groaning shadows that are gone.

LUCIUS

Away with him, and make a fire straight,   130
And with our swords upon a pile of wood
Let's hew his limbs till they be clean consumed.

                    Exeunt Titus' sons with Alarbus.

TAMORA   [*rising*]
O cruel, irreligious piety!

Theobald removed the comma, reading 'triumphs and return' as a hendiadys for 'triumphant return', but the obvious sense is that Titus returns with the Goths as captives. *Triumph* was the technical term for the procession into Rome of a victorious general.

120–1 **Wilt … merciful** proverbial (Tilley, M898)

124 **Patient yourself** calm down

125 **their brethren whom** the brothers of those whom

127 **Religiously … sacrifice** Rome prided itself on not allowing human sacrifice; this is a first sign that the city is becoming barbaric in its practices; it renders *religiously* (intended to suggest 'out of piety to the dead') ironic.

130 **fire** two syllables
    straight straightaway

132 **Let's … consumed** The image seems to suggest that chopping and burning are to take place simultaneously.

133 **irreligious piety** echoing back 118 and 127 in a telling oxymoron

125 their] *Q1;* the *F*   your] *Q1;* you *Q2–3, F*   132.1 *Exeunt*] *Q1 (Exit)*   133 SD] *Oxf; rising with her sons / Oxf¹*

135

CHIRON
  Was never Scýthia half so barbarous!
DEMETRIUS
  Oppose not Scythia to ambitious Rome.   135
  Alarbus goes to rest and we survive
  To tremble under Titus' threatening look.
  Then, madam, stand resolved, but hope withal
  The self-same gods that armed the queen of Troy
  With opportunity of sharp revenge   140
  Upon the Thracian tyrant in his tent
  May favour Tamora, the queen of Goths
  (When Goths were Goths and Tamora was queen),
  To quit the bloody wrongs upon her foes.

                Enter the Sons *of Andronicus again.*

LUCIUS
  See, lord and father, how we have performed   145

134 **Scythia** ancient region extending over much of Europe and Asiatic Russia, inhabited by a nomadic people viewed as barbaric, renowned in the drama as the origin of Marlowe's Tamburlaine

135 **Oppose ... Rome** Rome liked to contrast (*oppose*) itself to barbarian nations; Demetrius doubly inverts the comparison, making Rome both presumptuous (*ambitious*) and ultra-barbaric.

137 **threatening** 'threatning' (Q1)

138 **stand resolved** possibly a cue for Demetrius to help Tamora to rise, but it is more likely that she gets off her knees at 133
  withal as well, moreover

139–41 **queen of Troy ... in his tent** Hecuba, wife of Priam, took revenge for the death of her son Polydorus by blinding his murderer, the Thracian tyrant Polymestor (Ovid, *Met.*, 13.640–78). Jones (104) argues that the tent is a detail derived from Eur-

ipides' *Hecuba* and that Shakespeare therefore knew a Latin translation of that tragedy. But there it is 'her tent' (emended thus by Theobald). It is more likely that Shakespeare's memory conjured a tent out of Golding's phrase 'desyrde his presence too thentent' at this point in his trans. of Ovid (13.661), or that it fused the story with the biblical one of Jael (Judges, 4.17–22).

140 **sharp** severe, merciless; adjective applied to revenge on numerous occasions in the drama of the period

144 **quit** repay
  the see t.n. for plausible emendations

144.1 **Enter ... again** Capell usefully adds 'with their swords bloody', thus cuing 'See'. The BBC production emphasized the ritual: 'Titus' sons return, their faces daubed with ritual markings and holding out hands covered in blood. Lucius throws entrails on to the altar fire.'

134 never ... barbarous!] neuer ... barbarous. *Q1*; euer ... barbarous? *Q2–3, F*   135 not] *Q1*; me *F*   137 look] *Q1*; lookes *F*   144 the] *Q1*; her *Rowe*; these *(Capell)*

Our Roman rites: Alarbus' limbs are lopped
And entrails feed the sacrificing fire,
Whose smoke like incense doth perfume the sky.
Remaineth nought but to inter our brethren
And with loud 'larums welcome them to Rome.   150

TITUS

Let it be so, and let Andronicus
Make this his latest farewell to their souls.
        Sound trumpets, and lay the coffin in the tomb.
In peace and honour rest you here, my sons;
Rome's readiest champions, repose you here in rest,
Secure from worldly chances and mishaps.   155
Here lurks no treason, here no envy swells,
Here grow no damned drugs, here are no storms,
No noise, but silence and eternal sleep:
In peace and honour rest you here, my sons.

Enter LAVINIA.

LAVINIA

In peace and honour, live Lord Titus long: 160
My noble lord and father, live in fame!

---

146 **lopped** technical term from forestry, for cutting off side-branches – compare *hew* (100, 132), the verb used for chopping down trees with an axe

147 **entrails** 'his entrails': the possessive is carried forward although the verb form varies

148 **perfume** stress on second syllable

150 **'larums** trumpet calls

152.1 *Sound trumpets* F has '*Flourish. Then Sound Trumpets*'. This is probably an unnecessary duplication, 'but a "Flourish" could include drums and horns, so two soundings may be intended' (*TxC*, 210).
  coffin The preparer of F noted that there was more than one son, so has '*coffins*', but this does not necessarily

reflect the original staging.

153–9 **In peace ... sons** Collier has Titus kneeling here, but he must be standing by 164. For these lines on the peace of the grave as an echo of Seneca and an anticipation of *Mac*, see introduction, pp. 30–1.

154 **readiest** most expert, ready to act

157 **damned** damnèd
  drugs poisonous plants. The verb 'grow' counts against Q3's emendation to 'grudges'.

159.1 *Enter Lavinia* Cam[1] places the entry a line earlier, so she hears the words which she echoes.

161 **live** let him live: optative not imperative

---

146 rites] *F2;* right(e)s *Qq, F*   152.1] *Q1; Flourish. Then Sound ... F*   coffin] *Q1; Coffins F*   157
drugs] *Q1;* grudg(g)es *Q3, F*   160 LAVINIA] *indicated in Q1 by centred Enter Lauinia*

Lo, at this tomb my tributary tears
I render for my brethren's obsequies,
[*kneeling*] And at thy feet I kneel with tears of joy
Shed on this earth for thy return to Rome.   165
O bless me here with thy victorious hand,
Whose fortunes Rome's best citizens applaud.

TITUS

Kind Rome, that hast thus lovingly reserved
The cordial of mine age to glad my heart.
Lavinia live, outlive thy father's days   170
And fame's eternal date, for virtue's praise.

[*Lavinia rises.*]

[*Enter* MARCUS *below.*]

MARCUS

Long live Lord Titus, my beloved brother,

162 **tributary** paid as a tribute, but perhaps also suggesting the tears as 'tributary rivers' (*Cym* 4.2.36) joining the ocean of grief for the dead Andronici and thus establishing a bond of aquatic imagery between Titus and Lavinia, which prepares for 3.1.222–30. Very literal in BBC: 'Lavinia gives Titus a phial of her tears. He sprinkles them on the altar.'

163 **obsequies** An early MS hand in the Folger copy of Q1 emends to 'exequies', the correct classical Latin word for 'funeral rites'; 'obsequies' is a corrupt medieval Latin form, which in Elizabethan usage often meant 'commemorative rites performed at the grave'.

168 **reserved** kept in store

169 **cordial** medicine or nourishment which invigorates the heart and stimulates the circulation; a comforting drink. Establishes a link between Lavinia and the *heart* of

Titus (compare Lear and *Cord*elia).

171 **fame's ... praise** i.e. 'in view of your exemplary virtue, may you live even longer than fame, which is supposed to live for ever'

171.2 ***Enter Marcus below*** Recent eds, guided by the Folio SD at 237, keep Marcus aloft for this sequence. But it is much more logical for him to come down, greet his brother on behalf of the people and offer him the palliament. Lines 184–9 demand that a robe be offered, but only Bevington acts on this, and since he still has Marcus aloft he is forced to bring on an Attendant with it. Marcus clearly says that the palliament is sent 'by me' and he is not going to throw it down from the balcony. As often, Ravenscroft understood the staging better than later eds have done: he has 'Enter Marcus' at this exact point.

172 **beloved** belovèd

164 SD] *Bevington* 165 this] *Q1;* the *Q2–3, F* 167 fortunes] *Q1;* Fortune *F* 168 reserved] *Q1;* preserv'd *Hanmer* 171.1] *Bevington subst.* 171.2] *this edn;* Enter Marcus / *Ravenscroft;* Enter, below, Marcus Andronicus and Tribunes; re-enter Saturninus and Bassianus, attended / *Dyce; Marcus Andronicus speaks from above where he is accompanied by Saturninus, Bassianus, other Tribunes, etc. / Bevington*

Gracious triumpher in the eyes of Rome!
TITUS
Thanks, gentle tribune, noble brother Marcus.
MARCUS
And welcome, nephews, from successful wars,   175
You that survive and you that sleep in fame.
Fair lords, your fortunes are alike in all
That in your country's service drew your swords;
But safer triumph is this funeral pomp
That hath aspired to Solon's happiness   180
And triumphs over chance in honour's bed.
Titus Andronicus, the people of Rome,
Whose friend in justice thou hast ever been,
Send thee by me, their tribune and their trust,
This palliament of white and spotless hue,   185
And name thee in election for the empire
With these our late-deceased emperor's sons.
Be *candidatus* then and put it on,
And help to set a head on headless Rome.   [*Offers robe.*]
TITUS
A better head her glorious body fits   190
Than his that shakes for age and feebleness.

---

173 **triumpher** stress: triúmpher
176 **you that sleep** Having greeted his living nephews, Marcus turns to his dead ones. An address to the tomb of the Andronici comes more easily if Marcus is on the main stage, not aloft.
179–81 **safer triumph … honour's bed** A military triumph will be short-lived; no man, as the ancient Greek philosopher and lawgiver Solon observed, may be counted securely happy until he is dead. Plutarch (p. 103) emphasized Solon's wisdom and cited his famous saying: 'But when the goddes have continued a mans good fortune to his end, then we thinke that man happy and blessed,

and never before'.
184 **trust** the representative in whom their trust is placed
185 **palliament** candidate's gown, from Latin *pallium*, cloak, and *paludamentum*, garment worn by a general; word probably coined by Peele in *The Honour of the Garter* (see introduction, p. 82)
186 **in election for** as a candidate for
187 **deceased emperor's** five syllables: de-ceas-èd emp-ror's
188 *candidatus* Latin: literally 'clad in a white robe'
189 **head … headless** introduces the important image of the *body* of the state

177 alike] *Q1;* all alike *F*   189 SD] *this edn; A white cloak is brought to Titus / Bevington*

What, should I don this robe and trouble you?
Be chosen with proclamations today,
Tomorrow yield up rule, resign my life
And set abroad new business for you all?   195
Rome, I have been thy soldier forty years,
And led my country's strength successfully,
And buried one-and-twenty valiant sons,
Knighted in field, slain manfully in arms
In right and service of their noble country: 200
Give me a staff of honour for mine age,
But not a sceptre to control the world.
Upright he held it, lords, that held it last.

MARCUS
Titus, thou shalt obtain and ask the empery.

SATURNINUS [*aloft*]
Proud and ambitious tribune, canst thou tell?   205

TITUS
Patience, prince Saturninus.

SATURNINUS [*aloft*]
Romans, do me right.
Patricians, draw your swords and sheathe them not
Till Saturninus be Rome's emperor.
Andronicus, would thou were shipped to hell   210
Rather than rob me of the people's hearts.

LUCIUS
Proud Saturnine, interrupter of the good

192 ***What, should** Theobald introduced punctuation; other eds have
interpreted Q1's 'What should' as
'Why should'

195 **set abroad** probably a variant form
of 'set abroach', a common expression
meaning 'set on foot, initiate' (F3
emended thus)

199 **Knighted** The medieval custom of
knighting – raising in honourable
military rank – was often retrospectively applied to classical personages.

200 **right** in support of the just claims

204 **obtain and ask** obtain if you ask

206–7 **Patience ... right** could be run
into one line, but it would be hypermetric; two half-lines are preferable

212–13 **Proud ... to thee** Lucius, as
eldest son and knowing his father's
dedication to old values, assumes that
Titus will favour primogeniture and
support the claim of Saturninus.

212 **interrupter** probably stressed: int-
rúpt-er

192 What, should] *Theobald subst.;* What should *Q1*   195 abroad] *Q1;* abroach *F3*   210 were]
Q1; wert *Q3, F*

That noble-minded Titus means to thee.

TITUS

Content thee, prince, I will restore to thee
The people's hearts, and wean them from
    themselves. 215

BASSIANUS   *[aloft]*

Andronicus, I do not flatter thee,
But honour thee, and will do till I die.
My faction if thou strengthen with thy friends,
I will most thankful be, and thanks to men
Of noble minds is honourable meed. 220

TITUS

People of Rome, and people's tribunes here,
I ask your voices and your suffrages.
Will ye bestow them friendly on Andronicus?

TRIBUNES   *[aloft]*

To gratify the good Andronicus
And gratulate his safe return to Rome, 225
The people will accept whom he admits.

TITUS

Tribunes, I thank you, and this suit I make,
That you create our emperor's eldest son,
Lord Saturnine, whose virtues will, I hope,

---

215 **wean ... themselves** reconcile
them to not getting their own way
(*OED* wean, *v.* 2); the popular will is
not for Saturninus
220 **meed** reward
221 **here** could imply that the other
Tribunes have descended to the main
stage with Marcus at 171, but it is
more likely that Titus gestures
upwards to the gallery, where they
have remained with the candidates
222 **voices ... suffrages** synonyms for
'votes'
223 **friendly** on amicable terms (often
used for treaties and legal arrangements); until the late seven-

teenth century the adverbial form was
this, not 'friendlily'
225 **gratulate** express joy at
228 **son,** Oxf omits comma, implying
that Titus is saying that Saturninus
should be created 'Lord', but in
Marcus' next speech it is clear that
he is 'Lord Saturnine' already (as
Titus is sometimes 'Lord Titus') and
that what he is being created is
emperor – the 'create' sentence collapses in a series of epithets and is
then revived in the last two lines of
the speech, hence my dash at the end
of 231. Q1 puts the string of epithets
between colons.

227 suit] *Rowe;* sute *Q1–3;* sure *F*   228 our] *Q1;* your *Q2–3, F*

Reflect on Rome as Titan's rays on earth,   230
And ripen justice in this commonweal –
Then if you will elect by my advice,
Crown him and say, 'Long live our emperor!'

MARCUS

With voices and applause of every sort,
Patricians and plebeians, we create   235
Lord Saturninus Rome's great emperor,
And say, 'Long live our emperor Saturnine!'

A long flourish till they come down.

SATURNINUS

Titus Andronicus, for thy favours done
To us in our election this day,
I give thee thanks in part of thy deserts,   240
And will with deeds requite thy gentleness.
And for an onset, Titus, to advance
Thy name and honourable family,
Lavinia will I make my empress,
Rome's royal mistress, mistress of my heart,   245

230 **Reflect** shine
   Titan's Titan was used generally for the god of the sun; more specifically, he was of the race of Titans and elder brother to Saturn, perhaps thus playing on Saturninus, as at 4.3.57.

231 **ripen justice** Astraea, goddess of justice, is associated with the golden age of Saturn, Saturn with Titan and hence the sun that ripens fruit. But ironically Saturninus will not bring the golden age: see 4.3.4.

234 **applause** acclamation. Foxe, *Acts and Monuments*, translates Latin 'cum applausu populi' as 'with the rejoycing triumph of the people' (1587 edn, 3.828).
   of every sort from every rank (patrician and plebeian)

237.1 *they come down* This Folio SD brings Saturninus and Bassianus,

Tribunes and Senators down, clearing the upper stage for the subsequent reversal where Saturninus and the released Goths ascend. During Marcus' speech, or possibly after the descent, Saturninus is crowned as emperor. Oxf has the SD 'Marcus invests Saturninus in the white palliament, and hands him a sceptre', but the palliament seems to be the robe of a *candidatus*, not the emperor; the crown, held by Marcus in his first speech, perhaps a laurel band, is as likely as a sceptre.

239 **election** four syllables

240 **in … deserts** as part-payment of the reward you deserve. The *deeds* that will constitute the rest of the payment are far from *gentle*.

242 **onset** beginning

244 **empress** 'Emperess' (F4)

230 Titan's] Tytans *Q2;* Tytus *Q1*   237.1] *F*

And in the sacred Pantheon her espouse.
Tell me, Andronicus, doth this motion please thee?

TITUS

    It doth, my worthy lord, and in this match
    I hold me highly honoured of your grace,
    And here in sight of Rome to Saturnine,   250
    King and commander of our commonweal,
    The wide world's emperor, do I consecrate
    My sword, my chariot and my prisoners,
    Presents well worthy Rome's imperious lord:
    Receive them then, the tribute that I owe,   255
    Mine honour's ensigns humbled at thy feet.
    [Titus' sword and prisoners are handed over to Saturninus.]

SATURNINUS

    Thanks, noble Titus, father of my life.
    How proud I am of thee and of thy gifts,
    Rome shall record, and when I do forget
    The least of these unspeakable deserts,   260
    Romans forget your fealty to me.

246 **Pantheon** circular temple dedicated to all the gods. Q1 has 'Pathan', and 'Tytus' for 'Titan's' at 230, above; the errors are a result of a combination of the compositor's lack of Latin and the MS convention of writing 'n' in the form of an easily overlooked stroke above the preceding vowel.

247 **motion** proposal

253 **chariot** Does this imply that, like Marlowe's Tamburlaine and Peele's Moor in *Alcazar*, Titus has initially entered in a chariot? Oxf and Oxf[1] assume that it does, but who or what would be available to pull it? The Goth prisoners could, but if that were the intention the entry SD would surely have said so. And when would it have been removed? Given these complications, my SD at 256 has the sword and prisoner handed over but leaves the chariot in the imagination, though it would be interesting to see a production which included it.

254 **imperious** imperial; emended thus in Q2, but an acceptable alternative form

256 **ensigns** emblems, tokens

256.1 *sword ... Saturninus* Ravenscroft saw the need for an SD here and had '*Presents his Captives to the Emperor*'.

259–61 **when ... fealty** The parallel construction seems to invite dramatic irony. *Unspeakable*: inexpressible. *Fealty*, the feudal tenant's obligation of loyalty to his lord, is another retrospectively applied medieval term.

246 Pantheon] *F2*; Pathan *Qq, F* 254 imperious] *Q1*; Imperiall *Q2–3, F* 256 thy] *Q1*; my *F* 256.1] *this edn*; Presents his captives to the Emperor / *Ravenscroft*; Lays tributes at Saturninus' feet / *Bevington*

TITUS   [*to Tamora*]

Now, madam, are you prisoner to an emperor,
To him that for your honour and your state
Will use you nobly and your followers.

SATURNINUS

A goodly lady, trust me, of the hue   265
That I would choose were I to choose anew.

[*to Tamora*]

Clear up, fair queen, that cloudy countenance:
Though chance of war hath wrought this change of
    cheer,
Thou com'st not to be made a scorn in Rome;
Princely shall be thy usage every way.   270
Rest on my word, and let not discontent
Daunt all your hopes; madam, he comforts you
Can make you greater than the queen of Goths.
Lavinia, you are not displeased with this?

LAVINIA

Not I, my lord, sith true nobility   275
Warrants these words in princely courtesy.

SATURNINUS

Thanks, sweet Lavinia. Romans, let us go.
Ransomless here we set our prisoners free;
Proclaim our honours, lords, with trump and drum.

---

263 **for** because of
   state high rank
264 **use** treat, but may subliminally
   anticipate the carnal relationship
   (*OED v.* 10b: have sex with); ironically, it is Tamora and her followers
   who will in several senses 'use' Saturninus
265–6 **A goodly ... anew** The couplet
   form suggests a self-contained aside,
   but it would not be out of character

for Saturninus to speak these lines
publicly.
268 **chance of war** proverbial phrase
   (Tilley, C223). Q1 misprinted as
   'change', probably under the influence of the latter part of the line.
   cheer countenance
272 **he comforts** he who comforts
275 **sith** since
276 **Warrants** guarantees, authenticates

---

262 SD] *Johnson*   you] *Q1;* your *F*   263 your honour] *Q1;* you honour *F*   267 SD] *Rowe²*   268
chance] *Q2;* change *Q1*   273 you] *Q1;* your *F*   279.1–2] *this edn; Flourish. Saturninus addresses
Tamora / Capell; Flourish. Saturninus courts Tamora in dumb show / Dyce, following SD of Rowe
at 283; Flourish. Exeunt Saturninus, Tamora, Demetrius, Chiron, and Aaron the Moor / Oxf, which
accordingly cuts 288–90 and moves 293 to follow 303SD*

[*Sound drums and trumpets.*
Tamora, Chiron, Demetrius and Aaron are released.]

BASSIANUS   [*seizing Lavinia*]

Lord Titus, by your leave, this maid is mine.   280

TITUS

How, sir? Are you in earnest then, my lord?

BASSIANUS

Ay, noble Titus, and resolved withal
To do myself this reason and this right.

MARCUS

Suum cuique is our Roman justice:
This prince in justice seizeth but his own.   285

LUCIUS   [*joining Bassianus*]

And that he will, and shall, if Lucius live.

TITUS

Traitors, avaunt! Where is the emperor's guard?
Treason, my lord – Lavinia is surprised.

SATURNINUS

Surprised? By whom?

BASSIANUS   By him that justly may

Bear his betrothed from all the world away.   290

279.1–2 *Sound . . . released* Oxf has Saturninus and the Goths exiting at this point (they reappear above at 303). 'Let us go' does imply that Saturninus intends to exit, but why would he leave Lavinia behind when he still intends to marry her and why would he be accompanied by all the Goths when he has just ordered them to be released from his custody? He says 'Romans, let us go', not 'Goths, let us go'. It is surely his latter two lines, not his first one, that carry the implied SD. On Tamora's release, Saturninus, in accordance with his promise at 270, shows courtesy to her (compare Rowe's SD here, 'Saturninus courts Tamora in dumb show'). Meanwhile, on the other side of the stage, Bassianus initiates his claim.

283 **reason** 'that treatment which may with reason be expected' (*OED sb.*[1] 15)
284 *suum cuique* Latin: 'to each his own'. Grammar corrected by F2.
285 **prince** retrospectively applied medieval/Renaissance title
    seizeth technical legal term for taking possession of property
286 **and shall** compare Tamburlaine's emphatic 'will and shall' (*Pt 1*, 3.3.41)
287 **Where . . .** Where indeed? Perhaps busy releasing the Goths.
288 **surprised** suddenly and unexpectedly assaulted and captured
289 **Surprised?** Presumably Saturninus has not noticed the seizure because he has been overseeing the release of the Goths and then showing courtesy to Tamora. On the split-stage effect, see introduction, p. 38.

280 SD] *Rowe; Bassianus Seizes Lavinia from the Emperour / Ravenscroft*   284 *cuique*] *F2; cuiqum Q1; cuiquam Q3, F*   286 SD] *this edn*

MUTIUS

Brothers, help to convey her hence away,
And with my sword I'll keep this door safe.

> [*Bassianus, Marcus and Titus' sons*
> *bear Lavinia out of one door.*]

TITUS

Follow, my lord, and I'll soon bring her back.

> [*Saturninus does not follow, but exit at the other door*
> *with Tamora, her two sons and Aaron the Moor.*]

MUTIUS

My lord, you pass not here.

TITUS

What, villain boy, barr'st me my way in Rome? 295

> *He kills him.*

MUTIUS

Help, Lucius, help!

LUCIUS [*returning*]

My lord, you are unjust, and more than so:
In wrongful quarrel you have slain your son.

TITUS

Nor thou, nor he, are any sons of mine:

291–303.2 MUTIUS ... *Moor* The killing of Titus' youngest son, Mutius, like that of Alarbus, is probably an insertion made between first draft and first performance (see introduction, pp. 104–7).

292.1–2 *Bassianus ... door* It may be assumed that Bassianus, Marcus and 2 and 3 Sons exit, since they have later re-entries. Lucius and Mutius are at the rear of the party, the latter stationing himself between Titus and the door. Lucius may have just exited when Mutius calls for him to help, or he may be exiting and turn back.

293.1–2 *Saturninus ... Moor* Saturninus and the family of Goths reappear aloft at 303. When do they exit from below? In my view, Oxf is premature at 279, since Saturninus has not yet rejected Lavinia, whereas other eds, following Cam, propose a clumsy exit during the scuffle in which Mutius is killed. My SD – its timing anticipated by Ravenscroft – gives them slightly longer to get upstairs and enacts a decisive moment for Saturninus' switch from Titus' family to Tamora's, marked by another symmetrical use of the doors at either end of the stage.

295.1 *He kills him* Q3's SD: Titus stabs Mutius, who cries out for Lucius and then dies.

292.1–2] *this edn; Exeunt Marcus, Lucius, Mutius, Bassianus and followers with Lavinia / Ravenscroft; Exit [Bassianus], bearing off Lavinia; Marcus, and Titus' Sons, guarding them; Mutius last / Capell (after 290)* 293.1–2] *this edn; Exeunt Emp &c. / Ravenscroft; most edns follow Cam in placing the exit 'During the fray' after 296* 295.1] *Q3* 297 SD] *this edn; Re-enter Lucius / Capell*

My sons would never so dishonour me.   300
Traitor, restore Lavinia to the emperor.

LUCIUS

Dead if you will, but not to be his wife
That is another's lawful promised love.   [*Exit.*]

Enter aloft the Emperor *with* TAMORA
and her two sons and AARON *the Moor.*

SATURNINUS   [*aloft*]

No, Titus, no, the emperor needs her not,
Nor her, nor thee, nor any of thy stock.   305
I'll trust by leisure him that mocks me once,
Thee never, nor thy traitorous haughty sons,
Confederates all thus to dishonour me.
Was none in Rome to make a stale
But Saturnine? Full well, Andronicus,   310
Agree these deeds with that proud brag of thine
That saidst I begged the empire at thy hands.

TITUS

O monstrous! What reproachful words are these?

SATURNINUS   [*aloft*]

But go thy ways, go give that changing piece

---

304 **No, Titus, no** From above, Saturninus now replies belatedly to Titus' 'Follow, my lord', his negative reply having already been indicated by his exit at 293. The stage-action unfolds very rapidly here; the belatedness of the reply is also accounted for if the killing of Mutius is an insertion not in the first draft: if 294–303 is removed, it becomes an immediate reply.

306 **by leisure** barely (i.e. I will not be quick to)

309 **stale** (1) laughing-stock; more specifically, lover whose devotion is turned to ridicule for the amusement of a rival; (2) person made use of as a tool for inducing some result, as a cover for some sinister design (used for decoy-birds and prostitutes used as decoy by thieves). Compare 'Had he none else to make a stale but me?' (*3H6* 3.3.260), which perhaps supports F2's attempt (see t.n.) to make the line into a pentameter.

314 **piece** person, woman (*OED sb.* 9b), but with *changing* suggests loose coin or fickle piece of flesh (*sb.* 3c,d): Saturninus views woman as sexual commodity.

303 *Exit*] Capell; *Exit with Mutius' body* / Oxf 304 SATURNINUS] EMPEROR *Q1* (SP *for* SATURNINUS *hereafter sometimes* EMPEROUR, KING) 309 Was none] *Qq, F*; Was there none els *F2*

147

To him that flourished for her with his sword.   315
A valiant son-in-law thou shalt enjoy,
One fit to bandy with thy lawless sons,
To ruffle in the commonwealth of Rome.

TITUS

These words are razors to my wounded heart.

SATURNINUS   [*aloft*]

And therefore, lovely Tamora, queen of Goths,   320
That like the stately Phoebe 'mongst her nymphs
Dost overshine the gallant'st dames of Rome,
If thou be pleased with this my sudden choice,
Behold, I choose thee, Tamora, for my bride,
And will create thee empress of Rome.   325
Speak, queen of Goths, dost thou applaud my
    choice?
And here I swear by all the Roman gods,
Sith priest and holy water are so near,
And tapers burn so bright, and everything
In readiness for Hymenaeus stand,   330
I will not resalute the streets of Rome,
Or climb my palace, till from forth this place

---

315 **flourished** brandished his sword to win her, perhaps with phallic innuendo

317 **bandy** brawl

318 **ruffle** fight, as *bandy*, but perhaps with a hint of 'make a stir' or 'hector'

319 **razors** the sharpest of the play's many metaphors of violence inscribed upon or within the body

321 **Phoebe** Diana, goddess of hunting and chastity; compare 2.2.57ff., where the irony of applying the latter characteristic to Tamora becomes fully apparent. Printed '*Thebe*' by the unclassical Q1 compositor.

322 **overshine** Ritson noted that this word suggests that the passage is influenced by Phaer's trans. of Virgil's *Aeneid*: 'Most like unto *Diana* bright when shee to hunt goth out ... /

Whom thousands of the ladie *Nimphes* await to do her will. / Shee on her armes her quiver beres, and all them overshines' (*Aen.*, 1.474–7).

gallant'st finest-looking (same sense at 1.1.405); pronunciation suggested by Q1's 'gallanst'

325 **empress** 'Emperesse' (Q1)

328 **priest and holy water** a back-projection of Christian on to Roman religion

330 **Hymenaeus** Roman god of marriage

331–2 **resalute ... climb** Contra the SD at 303, this sounds as if Saturninus is currently at street-level (as does 338), which he may have been in the first draft before the Mutius incident was inserted.

321 Phoebe] *F2;* Thebe *Qq, F*

I lead espoused my bride along with me.

TAMORA   [*aloft*]

And here in sight of heaven to Rome I swear,

If Saturnine advance the queen of Goths,   335

She will a handmaid be to his desires,

A loving nurse, a mother to his youth.

SATURNINUS   [*aloft*]

Ascend, fair queen, Pantheon. Lords, accompany

Your noble emperor and his lovely bride,

Sent by the heavens for prince Saturnine,   340

Whose wisdom hath her fortune conquered.

There shall we consummate our spousal rites.

Exeunt omnes [except Titus].

TITUS

I am not bid to wait upon this bride.

Titus, when wert thou wont to walk alone,

Dishonoured thus and challenged of wrongs?   345

Enter MARCUS *and* TITUS' [*three remaining*] Sons.

337 **mother to his youth** Undoing Saturninus' address to Titus as 'father of my life' (257), Tamora takes over as dominator of the emperor. She simultaneously feeds desire and offers nurture, as Venus attempts to with Adonis in Shakespeare's poem.

338 **Ascend ... accompany** The Q1 compositor failed to understand that Pantheon is a building and punctuated as if it were an epithet going with 'Lords'. The awkward rhythm led F to divide the line (see t.n.), but if 'Pantheon' is pronounced as two syllables (as at 246) and 'accompany' is syncopated (as at *TS* 1.2.106) the line can just be salvaged. Elizabethan writings on Rome often referred to Pantheon without the definite article (e.g. Livy, trans. Holland, pp. 1392–4).

341 **Whose ... conquered** 'who has wisely overcome her misfortune (by accepting Saturninus)' – but ironically reminds us of his lack of wisdom in asking her. Syllabic ending: conquerèd.

342 **There** in the Pantheon

343 **I ... bride** In the Warner production, Brian Cox suggested Titus' genuine (and hence comic) perplexity at not being invited (*bid*).

344 **alone** Titus is alone save for the body of Mutius (unless, as Oxf assumes, it was dragged off by Lucius at 303 and brought back at 345 – Ravenscroft has 'Mutius Born in Dead' at the sons' re-entry).

345 **challenged** challengèd; accused

345.1–395.1 **and Titus' three ... but** *Marcus and Titus* probably part of the Mutius insertion (see intro-

338 queen, Pantheon. Lords, accompany] *Pope subst.*; Queene: Panthean Lords accompany *Q1*; Qeene, / Panthean Lords, accompany *F*; the Pantheon *(Walker)*   342.1 except Titus] Manet Titus Andronicus / Theobald   345.1 three remaining] this edn; Enter Marcus, Lucius, Martius, Quintus, Mutius Born in Dead / Ravenscroft; Enter Marcus and Titus' sons ... carrying Mutius' body / Oxf

MARCUS

  O Titus, see! O see what thou hast done!

  In a bad quarrel slain a virtuous son.

TITUS

  No, foolish tribune, no. No son of mine,

  Nor thou, nor these, confederates in the deed

  That hath dishonoured all our family –   350

  Unworthy brother and unworthy sons.

LUCIUS

  But let us give him burial as becomes;

  Give Mutius burial with our brethren.

TITUS

  Traitors, away! He rests not in this tomb.

  This monument five hundred years hath stood,   355

  Which I have sumptuously re-edified.

  Here none but soldiers and Rome's servitors

  Repose in fame; none basely slain in brawls.

  Bury him where you can, he comes not here.

MARCUS

  My lord, this is impiety in you;   360

  My nephew Mutius' deeds do plead for him,

  He must be buried with his brethren.

2 & 3 SONS

  And shall, or him we will accompany.

---

duction, pp. 103–7). In the original draft, 343–5 and 396–402 would have fitted together well, with Titus alone and then joined solely by Marcus, his remaining Sons returning with Bassianus and Lavinia at 403SD.

352 **becomes** is fitting

353 **brethren** 'bretheren' (Q1)

362 **buried** probably pronounced 'bur-yed' (two syllables)

   brethren 'bretheren' (Q3)

363 2 & 3 SONS Q1 has 'Titus two sonnes

speakes': the form of the verb and the later SP '2. Sonne', meaning '2nd Son', together with the fact that Titus replies in the singular, led Bolton ('Notes') to conjecture that this should be spoken by the 2nd Son alone. But it is better staging for the two sons to work together, as they do later in the play, and this is supported by '*we* will accompany'. Titus then challenges one of them to speak alone, and in the next line one of them does.

---

355 hundred] *Q1 (*hundreth*)*   363 2 & 3 SONS] *this edn; Titus two sonnes speakes Qq, F (centred);*
QUINTUS / *Ravenscroft, Rowe;* QUINT. MART. *Capell;* MART. *Ard² (Bolton)*

TITUS
  And shall? What villain was it spake that word?
2 SON
  He that would vouch it in any place but here.   365
TITUS
  What, would you bury him in my despite?
MARCUS
  No, noble Titus, but entreat of thee
  To pardon Mutius and to bury him.
TITUS
  Marcus, even thou hast struck upon my crest,
  And with these boys mine honour thou hast wounded.   370
  My foes I do repute you every one,
  So trouble me no more, but get you gone.
3 SON
  He is not with himself, let us withdraw.
2 SON
  Not I, till Mutius' bones be buried.

                        The brother and the sons kneel.
MARCUS
  Brother, for in that name doth nature plead –   375
2 SON
  Father, and in that name doth nature speak –
TITUS
  Speak thou no more, if all the rest will speed.
MARCUS
  Renowned Titus, more than half my soul –

---

364 **And shall?** Like Coriolanus, Titus
  does not like to hear the emphatic
  shall coming from a lesser mouth than
  his own (*Cor* 3.1.86–92).
365 2 SON Q1 does not specify which son
  speaks, but '2. Sonne' is the more
  vigorous in his insistence on Mutius'
  burial, and indeed 377 shows that

Titus is especially annoyed with him,
so he is the likelier candidate.
vouch maintain, assert. Pronunciation could be elided: 'vouch't'.
369 **crest** of a helmet
374 **buried** buri̇ed
377 **speed** have success
378 **Renowned** Renownèd

365 2 SON] *this edn; Titus sonne speakes Q q,* F *(centred);* MARTIUS *Ravenscroft;* QUIN. *Rowe*   vouch]
Q1; vouch'd F   369 struck] *Q1* (stroke)   373 3 SON] *Q1;* 1 SONNE *F;* LUC. *Rowe;* QUI. *Capell;*
MART. *Malone*   with] *Q1; not in* F   374 2 SON] *Q1;* QUINTUS *Ravenscroft, Rowe;* MART.
Capell   376 2 SON] *Q1;* LUCIUS *Ravenscroft;* QUINTUS *Rowe;* MART. *Capell*   378 Renowned]
Q1 (Renowmed)

LUCIUS
Dear father, soul and substance of us all –
MARCUS
Suffer thy brother Marcus to inter   380
His noble nephew here in virtue's nest,
That died in honour and Lavinia's cause.
Thou art a Roman, be not barbarous.
The Greeks upon advice did bury Ajax
That slew himself, and wise Laertes' son   385
Did graciously plead for his funerals:
Let not young Mutius then, that was thy joy,
Be barred his entrance here.
TITUS   Rise, Marcus, rise. [*They rise.*]
The dismall'st day is this that e'er I saw:
To be dishonoured by my sons in Rome!   390
Well, bury him, and bury me the next.
                                                They put him in the tomb.

LUCIUS
There lie thy bones, sweet Mutius, with thy friends',
Till we with trophies do adorn thy tomb.

384–6 **Greeks ... funerals** an incident
in the Trojan war, probably known to
Shakespeare from a school commentary on Horace. The Greek
general Ajax was angry because the
armour of the dead Achilles was given
to Ulysses, not to himself; in a fit of
madness he slew sheep, thinking they
were Greek generals; he then killed
himself for shame. The wise Ulysses
('Laertes' son') persuaded the Greeks
that Ajax nevertheless deserved a
proper burial. Plural form of *funerals*
as French 'funerailles'.
384 **advice** deliberation
387 **young ... joy** 'Young' Mutius may
helpfully be imagined as the last of
Titus' twenty-five sons, since youngest sons, such as the biblical Benjamin, are traditionally their father's *joy*.

391.1 *They ... tomb* Oxf has Lucius
dragging the body of Mutius off at
303 and the family bringing it back
at 346 (see Wells, *Re-Editing*, 103).
But just under 100 lines is not an
excessive time for an actor to lie still,
and the image of Titus alone on the
main stage, save for the son whom he
has slain, is a strong one.
392 **friends'** i.e. 'friends' (brothers'/
kindred's) bones', though the possessive is not marked in Qq,F (see
note to 1.1.57) and cannot really be
pronounced by an actor
393 **trophies** memorial to a military
victory, hung with arms taken from
the enemy – thus indicating the
martial memorializing of Mutius previously denied by Titus

385 wise] *Q1; not in F*   388 SD] *Bevington*

MARCUS & TITUS' SONS   [*kneeling*]

No man shed tears for noble Mutius:
He lives in fame that died in virtue's cause.   395
                    Exeunt all but Marcus and Titus.

MARCUS

My lord – to step out of these dreary dumps –
How comes it that the subtle queen of Goths
Is of a sudden thus advanced in Rome?

TITUS

I know not, Marcus, but I know it is –
Whether by device or no, the heavens can tell.   400
Is she not then beholden to the man
That brought her for this high good turn so far?

MARCUS

Yes – and will nobly him remunerate.   *Flourish.*

Enter the Emperor, TAMORA ⎱ ⎰ *Enter at the other door*
and her two sons, with the ⎬ ⎨ BASSIANUS *and* LAVINIA,
Moor at one door. ⎭ ⎩ *with* [*Titus' three* Sons].

394 MARCUS ... *kneeling* Q1 has '*they
all kneele and say*'. I assume that
Titus' command in 391 means that
he does not participate here; in the
Warner production, however, he did,
but he spoke a little more slowly than
the others, so that 'in virtue's cause'
emerged as his hollow echo after the
others had completed the recitation.
396 **dreary dumps** melancholy mood.
'Dump' was a technical term in music
for a mournful tune.
399 **it is** it is so
400 **Whether** could be pronounced as
monosyllable   (sometimes   spelt
'where')
device scheming
401 **beholden** indebted, under obli-

gation. Spelt 'beholding' in the early
texts.
403 *MARCUS ... **remunerate** Added in
F, presumably because the preparer
of the text thought that an answer
was needed to Titus' question, but not
strictly necessary. See introduction, p.
117. F has no SP, but the worldly-
wise, ironic tone and the fact that
it is a reply suggest that Marcus is
intended.
403.3 *with ... Sons* 'with others' in Qq,
F, but for symmetry Titus' three
sons should support Bassianus and
Lavinia, as Tamora's two sons and
Aaron support her and Saturninus.
The MS might have had 'the others',
meaning 'the other sons'. In the orig-

394 SP&SD] *they all kneele and say, Qq, F (centred)*   395.1] *Q1 (Exit); all but Titus and Marcus
stand aside / Kittredge*   396 dreary] *Q1;* sudden *F*   401 beholden] *Q1 (*beholding*)*   403] *F
continues to* TITUS; *Dyce (Malone) assigns to* MARCUS; *line not in Qq*   Flourish] *F*   403.3 *Titus'
three sons*] *this edn; Others Qq, F; Lucius, Quintus, and Martius Oxf*

SATURNINUS

So, Bassianus, you have played your prize.

God give you joy, sir, of your gallant bride.   405

BASSIANUS

And you of yours, my lord. I say no more,

Nor wish no less, and so I take my leave.

SATURNINUS

Traitor, if Rome have law or we have power,

Thou and thy faction shall repent this rape.

BASSIANUS

'Rape' call you it, my lord, to seize my own,   410

My true betrothed love, and now my wife?

But let the laws of Rome determine all;

Meanwhile am I possessed of that is mine.

SATURNINUS

'Tis good, sir. You are very short with us.

But if we live we'll be as sharp with you.   415

BASSIANUS

My lord, what I have done, as best I may,

Answer I must, and shall do with my life.

Only thus much I give your grace to know:

By all the duties that I owe to Rome,

This noble gentleman, Lord Titus here,   420

Is in opinion and in honour wronged,

That in the rescue of Lavinia

With his own hand did slay his youngest son

In zeal to you, and highly moved to wrath

inal draft this would have been the sons' first entry after their exit with Bassianus and Lavinia; with the inserted Mutius material, it is a re-entry – having had their youngest brother buried, they go off at 395SD to fetch their sister and new brother-in-law.

404 **played your prize** won your bout (technical term from fencing)

405 **God ... joy** a catch-phrase used in sales, especially of livestock

409 **rape** applied to the act of carrying away a woman by force, not necessarily to forcible sexual intercourse

411 **betrothed** betrothèd

413 **that** that which (common Elizabethan usage)

414 **'Tis good** very well

421 **opinion** reputation: a key idea in several of Shakespeare's honour-obsessed plays

413 am I] *Q1;* I am *Q3, F*

To be controlled in that he frankly gave.   425
Receive him then to favour, Saturnine,
That hath expressed himself in all his deeds
A father and a friend to thee and Rome.

TITUS
Prince Bassianus, leave to plead my deeds;
'Tis thou and those that have dishonoured me.   430
[*He kneels.*]
Rome and the righteous heavens be my judge
How I have loved and honoured Saturnine!

TAMORA   [*to Saturninus*]
My worthy lord, if ever Tamora
Were gracious in those princely eyes of thine,
Then hear me speak indifferently for all,   435
And at my suit, sweet, pardon what is past.

SATURNINUS
What, madam, be dishonoured openly,
And basely put it up without revenge?

TAMORA
Not so, my lord. The gods of Rome forfend
I should be author to dishonour you.   440
But on mine honour dare I undertake
For good Lord Titus' innocence in all,
Whose fury not dissembled speaks his griefs.
Then at my suit look graciously on him;
Lose not so noble a friend on vain suppose,   445
Nor with sour looks afflict his gentle heart.

---

425 **controlled** checked, thwarted
   frankly freely, unconditionally
429 **leave to plead** i.e. 'leave off pleading on behalf of'
430 **those** i.e. Titus' sons and brother
431 *He kneels* He is told to rise at 464;
   this seems the obvious place to kneel;
   that he should be kneeling at 460
   when Tamora remembers how she
   was made to kneel is typical of the
   pattern of the scene.
435 **indifferently** impartially

438 **put it up** submit to it (metaphor
   from sheathing a sword)
440 **be author to** be instigator of an
   action which (*OED* 1. d)
441 **undertake** vouch
443 **Whose ... griefs** i.e. his genuine
   fury proves the truth of his grief.
   Grief and anger over *her* dead son mo-
   tivate Tamora's aside: the speech as a
   whole presents a typically complex
   mix of true and *dissembled* emotions.
445 **vain suppose** needless supposition

431 SD] *Bevington subst.*   433 SD] *Oxf¹*

[*aside to Saturninus*]
My lord, be ruled by me, be won at last,
Dissemble all your griefs and discontents.
You are but newly planted in your throne;
Lest then the people, and patricians too,   450
Upon a just survey take Titus' part,
And so supplant you for ingratitude,
Which Rome reputes to be a heinous sin,
Yield at entreats – and then let me alone:
I'll find a day to massacre them all,   455
And raze their faction and their family,
The cruel father and his traitorous sons
To whom I sued for my dear son's life,
And make them know what 'tis to let a queen
Kneel in the streets and beg for grace in vain.   460
[*aloud*]
Come, come, sweet emperor – come, Andronicus –
Take up this good old man, and cheer the heart
That dies in tempest of thy angry frown.

SATURNINUS

Rise, Titus, rise: my empress hath prevailed.

TITUS   [*rising*]

I thank your majesty and her, my lord;   465
These words, these looks, infuse new life in me.

TAMORA

Titus, I am incorporate in Rome,
A Roman now adopted happily,

---

451 **survey** stress on second syllable
454 **let me alone** leave it to me (with sinister implication)
456 **raze** Waith (Oxf[1]) suggests that 'The Q1 spelling "race" suggests both "raze" and the obsolete "arace", to root out'.
458 **sued** suèd
462 **Take up** bid to rise
462–3 **heart … dies** 'This kills my heart' was proverbial
467 **incorporate** formally admitted, by

legal procedure
468 **adopted** legal term originating in mid-sixteenth century for voluntary taking of someone into a relationship as heir, friend, citizen, etc. Latin *adoptio* was, ironically in this context, the term 'designating the successor to the Principate' (Wirszubski, 157).
happily (1) fortunately, (2) opportunely

447 SD] *Rowe; line indented in Q1, perhaps to indicate aside*   452 you] *Q1; vs Q3, F*   456 raze]
*Q1 (*race)*   461 SD] *Hanmer*   465 SD] *Oxf[1]*

And must advise the emperor for his good.
This day all quarrels die, Andronicus;   470
And let it be mine honour, good my lord,
That I have reconciled your friends and you.
For you, Prince Bassianus, I have passed
My word and promise to the emperor
That you will be more mild and tractable.   475
And fear not, lords, and you, Lavinia:
By my advice, all humbled on your knees,
You shall ask pardon of his majesty.   [*Titus' sons kneel.*]

LUCIUS
We do, and vow to heaven and to his highness
That what we did was mildly as we might,   480
Tendering our sister's honour and our own.

MARCUS   [*kneeling*]
That on mine honour here do I protest.

SATURNINUS
Away, and talk not; trouble us no more.

TAMORA
Nay, nay, sweet emperor, we must all be friends;
The tribune and his nephews kneel for grace;   485
I will not be denied: sweet heart, look back.

SATURNINUS
Marcus, for thy sake, and thy brother's here,
And at my lovely Tamora's entreats,
I do remit these young men's heinous faults.
                        [*Marcus and Titus' sons*] *stand up.*

---

470 die optative, i.e. 'let, them die', like
lie at 392
478 *Titus' sons kneel* Bassianus and
Lavinia may kneel too.
479 *LUCIUS See t.n.: Rowe's suggestion
makes the best dramatic sense of the
various ways of supplying Q1's
missing SP.

480–1 mildly … Tendering 'done as
mildly as we could, whilst having
regard for'; 'Tendring' (Q1)
489.1 *stand up* In Q1 this phrase is the
beginning of the next line spoken by
Saturninus, but as such it badly
breaks the rhythm of the passage. 'I
do remit' together with a gesture

478 SD] *this edn; Marcus, Lavinia, and Titus' sons kneel / Yale (after Collier MS); Bassianus,
Lavinia, Lucius, Quintus, and Martius kneel / Oxf*   479 LUCIUS] *Rowe; Q1 continues to* TAMORA*;
Q2 indents without SP;* ALL *Q3;* SON *F;* MARTIUS *Ravenscroft*   480 mildly] *Q2;* mild ie *Q1*   482
SD] *Oxf*   do I] *Q1;* I doe *Q2–3,* F   489.1] *this edn, after Pope;* Stand up: *Lauinia though you
left me like a Churle Qq,* F

Lavinia, though you left me like a churl,   490
I found a friend, and sure as death I swore
I would not part a bachelor from the priest.
Come, if the emperor's court can feast two brides,
You are my guest, Lavinia, and your friends.
This day shall be a love-day, Tamora.   495

TITUS

Tomorrow, and it please your majesty
To hunt the panther and the hart with me,
With horn and hound we'll give your grace *bonjour*.

SATURNINUS

Be it so, Titus, and gramercy too.
            Sound trumpets. Exeunt all except the Moor.

[2.1]

AARON

Now climbeth Tamora Olympus' top,   500
Safe out of fortune's shot, and sits aloft,

would imply the order to stand up: I therefore agree with Dyce's conjecture (anticipated by Pope, in that he omitted the phrase) that this is a stage direction mistakenly printed as speech (compare 4.1.45 and 5.1.165). For an SD phrased as an imperative, compare '*Stab him*' (2.2.116).

490 **like a churl** ungenerously (a *churl* is someone niggardly in money-matters)

491 **friend** (1) patron, who is generous, unlike the *churl*; (2) paramour, who marries a *bachelor*

495 **love-day** day appropriate for amicable settling of dispute, with play on day devoted to love-making

496 **and** if

499 **gramercy** thanks ('*grand merci*', picking up on Frenchified courtliness of *bonjour*).

499.1 *Exeunt ... Moor* Q1's '*manet Moore*' makes it quite clear that the scene continues, with the hitherto silent Moor now speaking. But F introduced an act division, which all eds have followed. Johnson saw the folly of this ('This scene ought to continue the first Act'), but did not adjust his text accordingly. For convenience of reference, I include in square brackets the scene and line numbers established by the editorial tradition.

500 **Olympus'** Mount Olympus was the abode of the Greek gods. On the Marlovian language here, see introduction, p. 87.

501 **Safe ... shot** Compare 'Maior sum quam cui possit fortuna nocere' (*Met.*, 6.198): 'I am too great for fortune to harm'. Dramatically ironic both in Ovid and when quoted by Marlowe's Mortimer (*Edward II*, 5.4.69).

491 swore] *Q1*; sware *F*   499.1] *Exeunt.* / *Sound trumpets, manet* Moore. *Q1*; *Exeunt.* / *Actus Secunda.* / *Flourish. Enter Aaron alone. F*

Secure of thunder's crack or lightning flash,
Advanced above pale envy's threatening reach.
As when the golden sun salutes the morn
And, having gilt the ocean with his beams,   505
Gallops the zodiac in his glistering coach
And overlooks the highest-peering hills,
So Tamora.
Upon her wit doth earthly honour wait,   [10]
And virtue stoops and trembles at her frown.   510
Then, Aaron, arm thy heart and fit thy thoughts
To mount aloft with thy imperial mistress,
And mount her pitch whom thou in triumph long
Hast prisoner held, fettered in amorous chains
And faster bound to Aaron's charming eyes   515
Than is Prometheus tied to Caucasus.
Away with slavish weeds and servile thoughts!
I will be bright, and shine in pearl and gold
To wait upon this new-made empress.   [20]

502 **of** from
503 **threatening** 'threatning' (Q1)
    * reach. The grammatically necessary
    full stop is from F, whereas Q1 con-
    tinues the sentence to 508, its looser
    punctuation suggesting something of
    Aaron's boundless energy.
506 **Gallops ... coach** Imagery of this
    sort was popularized by Peele and
    Marlowe: 'Gallops the Zodiack in his
    fierie wayne' (Peele, *Anglorum Feriae*,
    24); 'Gallop apace, bright Phoebus,
    through the sky' (Marlowe, *Edward II*,
    4.3.44).
507 **overlooks** looks down on (compare
    overshine at 1.1.322, also applied to
    Tamora)
    highest-peering Normally the sun
    peers down on the hill (as at *1H4*
    5.1.1), but here the epithet is trans-
    ferred and even the highest hill peers
    up, emphasizing Tamora's rise (the
    social sense of 'peer' is also relevant).
510 **virtue stoops** A bald statement of
    Tamora's power to pervert justice.

513 **mount her pitch** rise to the highest
    point of her flight (from falconry).
    Idiom not used elsewhere in Shake-
    speare; repetition of verb from pre-
    vious line 'raises suspicion' (*TxC*, 211,
    where Gary Taylor proposes 'fly her
    pitch' on the analogy of *1H6* 2.4.11).
    Possibly imitated in *Ironside*: 'to
    mount a lofty pitch' (480).
514 **prisoner ... chains** Compare the
    image of amorous ensnarement in *VA*:
    'Leading him prisoner in a red rose
    chain' (110).
515 **charming** spell-casting
516 **Prometheus ... Caucasus** In pun-
    ishment for his theft of fire from the
    gods, Prometheus was chained to a
    rock in the Caucasus mountains,
    where he had his liver perpetually
    gnawed by an eagle. The language
    again resembles Peele: 'To tie
    Prometheus' limbs to Caucasus'
    (*Edward I* [1593], 4.21).
519 **empress** 'Emperesse' (Q1)

503 above] *Q1;* about *F*   517 servile] *Q1;* idle *Q3, F*

To wait, said I? – to wanton with this queen,   520
This goddess, this Semiramis, this nymph,
This siren that will charm Rome's Saturnine
And see his shipwreck and his commonweal's.
Hallo, what storm is this?

Enter CHIRON *and* DEMETRIUS, *braving.*

DEMETRIUS
Chiron, thy years want wit, thy wits want edge   525
And manners to intrude where I am graced
And may, for aught thou knowest, affected be.
CHIRON
Demetrius, thou dost overween in all,
And so in this, to bear me down with braves.   [30]
'Tis not the difference of a year or two   530
Makes me less gracious, or thee more fortunate:
I am as able and as fit as thou
To serve, and to deserve my mistress' grace,
And that my sword upon thee shall approve,
And plead my passions for Lavinia's love.   535
AARON   [*aside*]
Clubs, clubs! These lovers will not keep the peace.
DEMETRIUS
Why, boy, although our mother, unadvised,
Gave you a dancing-rapier by your side,

520 **queen** proximity to *wanton* suggests
possible pun on 'quean', whore
521 **Semiramis** Assyrian queen famed
for beauty and cruelty
522 **siren** legendary bewitching sea-
nymph who lures sailors to shipwreck
525 **want** It was common Elizabethan
usage to have 'wants' with a plural,
where one would expect 'want'; in
this instance, in view of the Q and F
variants (see t.n.), it seems reasonable
to modernize to 'want', as Cam[1] does.
527 **knowest** F elides to 'know'st'

affected loved
528 **overween** be presumptuous
529 **bear me down** maintain your point
against me in the argument
braves bravado, swaggering (as at
524 SD)
534 **approve** prove
536 **Clubs** 'The cry raised at a London
brawl for the watch to come and
separate the combatants with clubs'
(Ard[2])
538 **dancing-rapier** sword worn only
for ornament when dancing

521 nymph] *Q1;* Queene *Q3, F*   523 shipwreck] *Q1* (shipwracke)   525 years want] *F2;* yeares
wants *Q1*   wits want] *Cam[1]*; wits wants *Q1;* wit wants *Q2–3, F*   536 SD] *Dyce*

Are you so desperate grown to threat your friends? [40]
Go to, have your lath glued within your sheath 540
Till you know better how to handle it.

CHIRON
Meanwhile, sir, with the little skill I have,
Full well shalt thou perceive how much I dare.

DEMETRIUS
Ay boy, grow ye so brave? *They draw.*

AARON   Why, how now, lords?
So near the emperor's palace dare ye draw 545
And maintain such a quarrel openly?
Full well I wot the ground of all this grudge.
I would not for a million of gold
The cause were known to them it most concerns, [50]
Nor would your noble mother for much more 550
Be so dishonoured in the court of Rome.
For shame, put up.

DEMETRIUS   Not I, till I have sheathed
My rapier in his bosom, and withal
Thrust those reproachful speeches down his throat
That he hath breathed in my dishonour here. 555

CHIRON
For that I am prepared and full resolved,
Foul-spoken coward, that thunderest with thy tongue,
And with thy weapon nothing dar'st perform.

AARON
Away, I say. [60]
Now, by the gods that warlike Goths adore, 560
This petty brabble will undo us all.

---

539 **friends** blood relations
540 **lath** stage sword made of wood
545 **near ... draw** In Elizabethan England, it was illegal to draw weapons in public places.
546 **maintain** stress on first syllable
553 **withal** in addition
557 **thunderest** 'thundrest' (Q1)
561 **brabble** brawl, quarrel

544 AARON] *Q1; Dyce adds SD: coming forward*   545 ye] *Q1;* you *Q2–3, F*   554 those] *Q1;* these *Q3, F*   559 Away, I say] *Capell adds SD: beating down their swords*   561 petty] *Q1;* pretty *F*

161

Why, lords, and think you not how dangerous
It is to jet upon a prince's right?
What, is Lavinia then become so loose,
Or Bassianus so degenerate,   565
That for her love such quarrels may be broached
Without controlment, justice, or revenge?
Young lords, beware – and should the empress know
This discord's ground, the music would not please.   [70]

CHIRON
I care not, I, knew she and all the world: 570
I love Lavinia more than all the world.

DEMETRIUS
Youngling, learn thou to make some meaner choice;
Lavinia is thine elder brother's hope.

AARON
Why, are ye mad? Or know ye not in Rome
How furious and impatient they be,   575
And cannot brook competitors in love?
I tell you, lords, you do but plot your deaths
By this device.

CHIRON
Aaron, a thousand deaths would I propose   [80]
T'achieve her whom I love.

AARON   T'achieve her how?   580

DEMETRIUS
Why makes thou it so strange?

---

563 **jet** encroach – *OED*'s first usage in this sense (*v.*² 1.b)
567 **controlment** restraint (as at *KJ* 1.1.20)
569 **discord's ground** basis of this dispute, with play on musical sense of 'ground bass'
570 **knew she** if she knew
572 **meaner** socially inferior

575 **impatient** four syllables
576 **brook** tolerate
579 **propose** be ready to meet
580 ***T'achieve** 'To atchieue' both times in Q1, but the metre calls for elision
581 **makes ... strange** why do you find it so surprising? (*makes* is an alternative form of 'makest')

---

563 jet] *Q1;* set *F*   569 discord's] discords *Q1;* discord *F*   574 Why, are] *Theobald;* Why are *Qq, F*   580 T'achieve] *this edn (both occurrences);* To atchieue *Q1*   love] *Q1;* do love *Q3, F*   581 makes] *Q1;* mak'st *F*

She is a woman, therefore may be wooed;
She is a woman, therefore may be won;
She is Lavinia, therefore must be loved.
What, man, more water glideth by the mill   585
Than wots the miller of, and easy it is
Of a cut loaf to steal a shive, we know.
Though Bassianus be the emperor's brother,
Better than he have worn Vulcan's badge.   [90]
AARON [*aside*]
Ay, and as good as Saturninus may.   590
DEMETRIUS
Then why should he despair that knows to court it
With words, fair looks and liberality?
What, hast not thou full often struck a doe
And borne her cleanly by the keeper's nose?
AARON
Why then, it seems some certain snatch or so   595
Would serve your turns.
CHIRON   Ay, so the turn were served.
DEMETRIUS
Aaron, thou hast hit it.

582–3 **She ... won** proverbial (Tilley, W681), but also similar rhetorical repetition to that of Suffolk on Margaret (*1H6* 5.3.78–9) and Richard of Gloucester on Lady Anne (*R3* 1.2.227–8)

587 **shive** slice. Both this figure and that of the water by the mill are proverbial (Tilley, T34, W99). Demetrius means: 'once a woman is no longer a virgin, no one is to know how many times she's been had'. Chiron and Demetrius have an unusually high frequency of proverbial language: they talk in clichés.

589 **Vulcan's badge** cuckold's horns (Vulcan was cuckolded when his wife Venus slept with Mars). Metre suggests pronunciation may be either 'wor-en' or 'Vul-can-us'.

591 **court it** play the courtier

593–4 **struck ... nose** killed a deer and smuggled it away without the gamekeeper noticing

595 **snatch** begins as a development of the hunting language, from the greyhound's sudden grab of its prey; develops into sexual play, from 'snack', equivalent to modern slang 'quickie'

596 **turns ... turn** continues the sporting/sexual wordplay: both the sudden turning of the hare when closely pursued by the greyhound and the sense of *Antony and Cleopatra*'s 'best turn i' th' bed' (2.5.59)

597 **hit** plays on shooting and having sex – 'hit it': 'to attain the sexual target of the pudend' (Partridge). Compare the sustained bawdy of the shooting match in *LLL* 4.1.118–30.

590 SD] *Theobald*   593 struck] *Q1 (*stroke*)*

AARON   Would you had hit it too,
Then should not we be tired with this ado.
Why, hark ye, hark ye, and are you such fools   [100]
To square for this? Would it offend you then   600
That both should speed?

CHIRON
Faith, not me.

DEMETRIUS   Nor me, so I were one.

AARON
For shame, be friends, and join for that you jar.
'Tis policy and stratagem must do
That you affect, and so must you resolve   605
That what you cannot as you would achieve,
You must perforce accomplish as you may.
Take this of me: Lucrece was not more chaste
Than this Lavinia, Bassianus' love.   [110]
A speedier course than lingering languishment   610
Must we pursue, and I have found the path.
My lords, a solemn hunting is in hand;
There will the lovely Roman ladies troop.
The forest walks are wide and spacious,
And many unfrequented plots there are,   615
Fitted by kind for rape and villainy.

598 **ado** fuss, but with further play on 'doing' for 'copulating' (as at 4.2.78)
600 **square for** quarrel over
601 **speed** succeed
602 **so** provided that
603 **that you jar** what you quarrel for ('A common type of ellipse' – Ard²)
604 **policy** cunning, calculation – a word beloved of Elizabethan stage Machiavels
605 **affect** aim at
606–7 **as you ... may** proverbial: 'men must do as they may, not as they would' (Tilley, M554)
608 **Lucrece** killed herself after being

raped by Tarquin in one of the play's patterning narratives – see introduction, p. 92
610 *****than** Rowe's emendation of Q1's 'this', a compositorial error probably resulting from the presence of 'Than this' in the previous line or MS abbreviations involving 'y' and superscripts
lingering languishment protracted love-sorrow; 'lingring' (Q1)
612 **solemn** ceremonial
615 **plots** spots, which the next line suggests are the natural place ('Fitted by kind') for fulfilling villainous *complots*

601] *Q1; not in F*   610 than] *Rowe; this Qq, F*

Single you thither then this dainty doe,
And strike her home by force, if not by words:
This way or not at all stand you in hope. [120]
Come, come, our empress, with her sacred wit 620
To villainy and vengeance consecrate,
Will we acquaint withal what we intend,
And she shall file our engines with advice
That will not suffer you to square yourselves,
But to your wishes' height advance you both. 625
The emperor's court is like the house of Fame,
The palace full of tongues, of eyes and ears;
The woods are ruthless, dreadful, deaf and dull:
There speak and strike, brave boys, and take your
    turns; [130]
There serve your lust, shadowed from heaven's eye, 630
And revel in Lavinia's treasury.

CHIRON
Thy counsel, lad, smells of no cowardice.

DEMETRIUS
Sit fas aut nefas, till I find the stream

617 **single** select an animal from the herd
dainty choice, pleasing to the palate
618 **strike her home** further hunting/sexual wordplay: 'strike' was the technical term for killing or wounding a deer with arrow or spear; 'strike home' means making an effective thrust with a weapon or tool
620 **sacred** recent eds gloss as 'devoted', i.e. 'consecrated to villainy', as the next line says; but this makes the word redundant, so there may also be a hint (not intended by Aaron?) of *OED a.* 6, 'accursed', as in Spenser's 'O sacred hunger of ambitious minds' (*Faerie Queene*, 5.12.1), a latinate usage based on Virgil's 'auri sacra fames' (*Aen.*, 3.57, 'sacred hunger for gold')

622 **acquaint withal** inform
623 **file our engines** sharpen our stratagems
624 **square yourselves** 'thwart yourselves, and each other, by quarrelling' (Ard²)
626 **house of Fame** associated in Ovid's *Metamorphoses* (12.46–69) with whispering gossip and echoing rumour (also known from Chaucer's poem of this title)
629 **turns** still sexually punning
633 *Sit fas aut nefas* Latin: 'be it right or wrong'. Perhaps adapts 'a verse in Horace' (see 4.2.22): 'cum fas atque nefas exiguo fine libidinum / discernunt avidi' – 'when, under the influence of ardent sexual desire, they scarcely distinguish between right and wrong' (*Odes*, 1.18.10–11). Also close

622 what] *Q1;* that *Q2–3, F*   627 and] *Q1;* of *Q3, F*   630 lust] *Q1;* lusts *F*   633 stream] *Q1;* streames *F*

To cool this heat, a charm to calm these fits,
Per Stygia, per manes vehor.   *Exeunt.*

2.1 [2.2]   *Enter* TITUS ANDRONICUS *and his three*
sons, and MARCUS, *making a noise with hounds and horns.*

TITUS
The hunt is up, the morn is bright and grey,
The fields are fragrant and the woods are green.
Uncouple here, and let us make a bay
And wake the emperor and his lovely bride,
And rouse the prince, and ring a hunter's peal,   5
That all the court may echo with the noise.

to Procne's confounding of right and
wrong in the Philomel story ('fasque
nefasque / confusura ruit' – Ovid,
Met.,   6.585–6;   Golding's   trans.,
6.746).
635 *Per . . . vehor* Latin: 'I am carried
through the Stygian regions, through
the realm of shades', i.e. 'I am in hell'
(Styx: see on 1.1.91). Adapted from
Seneca, *Hippolytus*, 1180: 'per Styga,
per amnes igneos amens sequar' ('I
[Phaedra] will madly follow you [Hip-
polytus] through Styx and through
fiery rivers'). F4 (see t.n.) assumed
that 'Stygia' was an error for Seneca's
'Styga' (the compositor's error,
Demetrius' or Shakespeare's?), but it
is an acceptable adjectival form and
the changes from 'amnes'/'amens' to
'manes' and 'sequar' to 'vehor'
suggest purposeful adaptation of the
original: 'Phaedra's expression of
frustrated love becomes here an
expression of personal abandonment
to evil. Styx flows within the human
soul' (Miola, 14).
2.1 'The division of the play into acts,
which was first made by the editors

in 1623, is improper. There is here
an interval of action, and here the
second act ought to have begun'
(Johnson). What should be scenes 2.1,
2.2, 2.3 are accordingly numbered 2.2,
2.3, 2.4 in the editorial tradition. This
short opening scene sets the atmosphere of the morning after the double
wedding-night.
0.1–2 *Enter . . . horns* Live animals were
not unknown on the Elizabethan
stage, but offstage sounds are likelier
here. The economical Warner production achieved the effect simply
through the actors whooping and
banging their spear-ends on the
ground.
1 **up** afoot
3 **Uncouple** to release hounds from
being fastened in couples, set them
free for the chase
bay deep prolonged bark of hunting
hounds
5 **peal** horn-blowing to rouse the
hounds
6 **court** Capell took this to refer to a
courtyard in front of a hunting lodge
in the forest (perhaps the lodge

634 these] *Q1;* their *Q3, F*   635 *Stygia*] *Q1; Styga F4*

2.1] *this edn; 2.2 in edns since Rowe*   Location] A forest *Rowe;* A Chace near Rome. Court before
a Lodge *Capell;* Rome. Before the Emperor's Palace *Pelican*   0.1–2 *and* MARCUS] *F (at end of
SD)*   1 morn] *Q3;* Moone *Q1–2*

Sons, let it be your charge, as it is ours,
To attend the emperor's person carefully.
I have been troubled in my sleep this night,
But dawning day new comfort hath inspired.   10

Here a cry of hounds, and wind horns in a peal; then enter
SATURNINUS, TAMORA, BASSIANUS, LAVINIA, CHIRON,
DEMETRIUS, *and their Attendants.*

Many good morrows to your majesty;
Madam, to you as many and as good.
I promised your grace a hunter's peal.
SATURNINUS
And you have rung it lustily, my lords,
Somewhat too early for new-married ladies.   15
BASSIANUS
Lavinia, how say you?
LAVINIA   I say no:
I have been broad awake two hours and more.
SATURNINUS
Come on then, horse and chariots let us have,
And to our sport. [*to Tamora*]
                     Madam, now shall ye see
Our Roman hunting.
MARCUS   I have dogs, my lord,   20
Will rouse the proudest panther in the chase
And climb the highest promontory top.

referred to at 2.2.254), but it could
equally mean the emperor's court –
the scene may be set in front of the
palace in Rome, rather than the
'forest' assumed by Rowe. The desire
to fix 'realistic' locations only begins
in the Restoration theatre.
8 **To attend** probably elided T'attend
10.1 *cry* deep barking in unison
13 **promised** promisèd
16 **say you** metre implies stress on first
word

21 **chase** land especially reserved for
royal hunting (as *park* at 3.1.89). The
Romans did hunt imported panthers
as well as deer in their chases or *silvae*
(Barton, 56–7). In the Androcles/
Androclus story, the emperor Titus
is said to have kept wild animals.
22 **promontory** from Latin, 'pro-
montorium', mountain-ridge, not
necessarily suggesting modern sense
of jutting into the sea

11 *Q1 repeats SP*   16–17 I ... more] *F; 1 line in Qq*   17 broad] *Q1; not in F*   19 SD] *Johnson*

TITUS
  And I have horse will follow where the game
  Makes way and runs like swallows o'er the plain.
DEMETRIUS   [*aside*]
  Chiron, we hunt not, we, with horse nor hound,   25
  But hope to pluck a dainty doe to ground.   *Exeunt.*

2.2 [2.3]   *Enter* AARON *alone* [*with a money-bag*].

AARON
  He that had wit would think that I had none,
  To bury so much gold under a tree
  And never after to inherit it.
  Let him that thinks of me so abjectly
  Know that this gold must coin a stratagem   5
  Which, cunningly effected, will beget
  A very excellent piece of villainy.
  And so repose, sweet gold, for their unrest
  That have their alms out of the empress' chest.

                              [*Hides the money-bag.*]

24 **runs** The swirling motion implied by the simile suggests that the verb applies to the scattering game, not to the pursuing horses.
2.2 Rowe continues the previous scene; eds since Capell number 2.3. The location is the forest; the trap-door which represents the pit would probably have been opened at the beginning of the scene. Waith (Oxf[1]) suggests that properties like Henslowe's 'bay tree' and 'moss banks' might have been brought on, but the staging need not be so realistic: the language does all the work necessary to convey the atmosphere of the forest.
3 **inherit** enjoy the possession of
4 **thinks … so abjectly** 'has such a low opinion of me'; *OED*'s earliest usage of the adverbial form
5 **coin** make, devise; figurative, from

stamping of metal to make money. Also used for begetting a child, an association which leads to the verb in the next line.
8 **repose … unrest** This juxtaposition is influenced by the rhetoric of Hieronimo's celebrated soliloquy: 'Thus therefore will I rest me in unrest' (*Sp. Trag.*, 3.13.29).
9 **alms … chest** a schemer's inversion of the idea of royal charity (*alms*) bringing comfort. Capell glosses as a metaphor: 'meaning – curses out of her bosom; for this villainous character can pun and stab at once' (*Notes*, 102).
9.1 *Hides the money-bag* Waith (Oxf[1]) assumes that a property 'elder tree' (see 272–3) has been brought on, but in a non-realistic staging a pillar could stand in for a tree.

24 runs] *Qq, F;* run *F2* like] *Q1;* likes *F*   25 SD] *Capell*   **2.2**] *this edn; 2.3 in edns since Capell* Location] A desart part of the Forest *Theobald*   0.1 *with a money-bag*] *this edn; with Money / Ravenscroft; with a bag of gold / Capell*   9.1] *this edn; Aron Digs a hole in the Earth with his Sword, & burys the bag of Money / Ravenscroft; Hides the gold / Malone*

Enter TAMORA *alone, to the Moor.*

TAMORA

My lovely Aaron, wherefore look'st thou sad   10
When everything doth make a gleeful boast?
The birds chant melody on every bush,
The snakes lies rolled in the cheerful sun,
The green leaves quiver with the cooling wind
And make a chequered shadow on the ground.   15
Under their sweet shade, Aaron, let us sit,
And whilst the babbling echo mocks the hounds,
Replying shrilly to the well-tuned horns
As if a double hunt were heard at once,
Let us sit down and mark their yellowing noise;   20
And after conflict such as was supposed
The wandering prince and Dido once enjoyed,
When with a happy storm they were surprised
And curtained with a counsel-keeping cave,

---

11 **boast** show
12–15 **birds ... ground** a formal
Ovidian-style description of a *locus
amoenus* ('pleasant place'), in which
the landscape reflects the state of
mind of the speaker; it is expanded
and inverted to create the opposite
mood at 93–104. Compare the pair of
apostrophes, first *in bono*, then *in
male*, at *Met.*, 13.929–50. A similar
passage in Seneca, *Hippolytus*, 508–
10, describes a Golden Age landscape,
an ironic resonance in view of 4.3.4.
For a close parallel in Lodge's *Wounds
of Civil War*, see introduction,
p. 89.
13 **snakes lies** an acceptable Elizabethan
inflection, producing a suitably snaky
sibilance. Q3 emends to 'snake', but
snakes are plural to the tune of a
thousand at 100, so I retain the plural here,
where it parallels the birds and trees.

Ravenscroft modernized the verb to
'lie'.
rolled rollèd
17 **babbling echo** In Ovid's *Metamorphoses*, Echo is the disembodied
form of a 'babling Nymph' (Golding's
trans., 3.443).
20 **yellowing** according to *OED* (*v.*²), a
Shakespearean coinage that extends
'yell' on the analogy of 'bell'-'bellow'.
Serpieri suggests that the effect is
synaesthetic.
22 **wandering** 'wandring' (Q1)
prince and Dido While on his sea-
wanderings after the fall of Troy,
Aeneas landed in Carthage and fell
in love with Queen Dido; when out
hunting, they were caught in a storm,
took refuge in a cave and made love
for the first time (Virgil, *Aen.*, 4.160–
72).
23 **happy** fortuitous
24 **counsel** secret

9.2 *alone*] *Q1; not in F*   13 snakes lies] *Q1;* snake lies *Q3, F;* snakes lie *Ravenscroft*   20 yellowing]
Q1; yelping *F*

We may, each wreathed in the other's arms,   25
Our pastimes done, possess a golden slumber,
Whiles hounds and horns and sweet melodious birds
Be unto us as is a nurse's song
Of lullaby to bring her babe asleep.

AARON

Madam, though Venus govern your desires,   30
Saturn is dominator over mine.
What signifies my deadly-standing eye,
My silence and my cloudy melancholy,
My fleece of woolly hair that now uncurls
Even as an adder when she doth unroll   35
To do some fatal execution?
No, madam, these are no venereal signs;
Vengeance is in my heart, death in my hand,
Blood and revenge are hammering in my head.
Hark, Tamora, the empress of my soul,   40
Which never hopes more heaven than rests in thee,
This is the day of doom for Bassianus,
His Philomel must lose her tongue today,
Thy sons make pillage of her chastity
And wash their hands in Bassianus' blood.   45
Seest thou this letter? Take it up, I pray thee,

                                        [*Gives letter.*]

25 **wreathed** wreathèd
26–9 **golden slumber ... asleep** dramatically ironic language of infancy and innocence
30 **Venus** the classical goddess associated with sexual desire (hence *venereal* at 37)
31 **dominator** technical term in astrology for the planet ruling a person's disposition. On *Saturn*, see 'List of Roles' under Saturninus.
32 **deadly-standing** death-dealing, like the stare of the mythical cockatrice (as at *R3* 4.1.54–5) or the petrifying Gorgon

39 **Blood ... head** a stock image: compare 'Blood and revenge did hammer in my head' (Giles Fletcher the elder, 'The Rising to the Crown of Richard the Third', 1593), 'A rash revenging hammer in thy brain' (Lodge, *Wounds of Civil War*, 2.1.84). *OED* cites under *v.* 4b, 'Of an idea: to present itself persistently to one's mind', but 2a, 'devise, contrive', is also relevant – Aaron plots even as he is agitated.
43 **Philomel** see introduction, pp. 90–2, and appendix, pp. 279–83

46.1] *Bevington*

And give the king this fatal-plotted scroll.
Now question me no more: we are espied.
Here comes a parcel of our hopeful booty,
Which dreads not yet their lives' destruction.   50

Enter BASSIANUS *and* LAVINIA.

TAMORA
Ah, my sweet Moor, sweeter to me than life!
AARON
No more, great empress: Bassianus comes.
Be cross with him, and I'll go fetch thy sons
To back thy quarrels, whatsoe'er they be.   [*Exit.*]
BASSIANUS
Who have we here? Rome's royal empress,   55
Unfurnished of her well-beseeming troop?
Or is it Dian, habited like her,
Who hath abandoned her holy groves
To see the general hunting in this forest?
TAMORA
Saucy controller of my private steps,   60

47 **fatal-plotted** contrived to deal death.
The sense of 'plot' as a contrivance
was very new at this time, but widely
used in the drama; the compound
is a Shakespearean coinage, though
compare 'fatal-boding' in Lodge,
Wounds, 3.4.61.
48 **we are espied** He has seen Bassianus
and Lavinia: they may therefore enter
a little before the moment indicated
in Q1.
49 **parcel** part
hopeful hoped-for: epithet transferred on to its object, as at *MM*
1.1.59
50 **dreads** has (fearful) anticipation of
52 **more** playing on 'Moor' in the previous line?
53 **cross** contrary, quarrelsome
54 **quarrels ... be** 'whatever quarrel you
can provoke'

55 **empress** 'Emperess' (Rowe[2]); also at
66
56 **well-beseeming** appropriate to her
rank
57 **Dian** the classical goddess associated
with hunting and chastity; the
opposite of Venus and thus ironic in
the light of 30
habited wearing hunting-dress
58 **abandoned** abandonèd
59 **general** participated in by all
60 **Saucy** insolent towards a superior
(she thus asserts her rank)
controller household official whose
duty was to manage and check expen-
diture (she thus down-grades Bassianus' rank). Previous eds gloss as
'censorious critic', but this misses the
point about rank (compare 'arrogant
controller', the adjective again suggesting presumption, at *2H6* 3.2.205).

54 quarrels] *Q1;* quarrell *Q3, F*   54 SD] *Rowe*   55 Who] *Q1;* Whom *F*   56 her] *Q1;* our *Q3,*
F   60 my] *Q1;* our *Q3, F*

Had I the power that some say Dian had,
Thy temples should be planted presently
With horns, as was Actaeon's, and the hounds
Should drive upon thy new-transformed limbs,
Unmannerly intruder as thou art. 65

LAVINIA
Under your patience, gentle empress,
'Tis thought you have a goodly gift in horning,
And to be doubted that your Moor and you
Are singled forth to try experiments.
Jove shield your husband from his hounds today: 70
'Tis pity they should take him for a stag.

BASSIANUS
Believe me, queen, your swart Cimmerian
Doth make your honour of his body's hue,
Spotted, detested and abominable.

61 **power** one syllable
61–4 **Dian ... limbs** In the *Meta-morphoses* Actaeon saw the naked Diana bathing; she punished him immediately (*presently*) by turning him to a hart and he was then hunted down (the meaning of *drive upon*) by his own hounds (3.160–304). Of all Ovid's myths, perhaps the most widely alluded to in the Renaissance, especially in contexts of cuckoldry (Actaeon's *horns*) and intrusion (his illicit gaze) – both relevant here (hence *horning* in 67), as is the idea of the hunter becoming hunted.
63 **the** possibly an error for 'thy' (*TxC*, 211)
64 **new-transformed** new-transformèd
65 **Unmannerly intruder** Completes the nexus of social terminology, suggesting a lack of 'manners' and the technical legal sense of one who 'intrudes' into the estate of, or usurps upon the rights of, another.

66 **Under your patience** by your leave
68 **doubted** suspected
69 **singled** see on 1.1.617
***try** 'try thy' in Q1, but Q2's omission of the pronoun greatly improves the metre. It is possible that, having set the first word, the Q1 compositor's eye lingered on it for a moment, misread it and set it again. Emendation also improves sense, which cannot stand the singular 'thy'.
70–1 **Jove ... stag** Lavinia transforms Tamora's image, making Saturninus into the Actaeon figure. *Jove* was the alternative name for Jupiter, supreme god in the Roman pantheon.
72 **swart** black. Capell's modernized spelling is good for the metre.
Cimmerian 'People inhabitynge the furthest parte of Europe ... by the farre distance of the sunne from it, that countrey is always very darke' (Cooper) – hence a term for the Moor.
74 **Spotted** morally stained, blemished

61 power] *Q1* (powre) 64 thy] *Q1; his Q3, F* 69 try experiments] *Q2;* trie thy experimens *Q1* 72 swart] *Capell;* swartie *Q1;* swarty *Q3;* swarth *F* Cimmerian] *F2 subst.;* Cymerion *Qq, F*

Why are you sequestered from all your train,   75
Dismounted from your snow-white goodly steed,
And wandered hither to an obscure plot,
Accompanied but with a barbarous Moor,
If foul desire had not conducted you?

LAVINIA

And being intercepted in your sport,   80
Great reason that my noble lord be rated
For sauciness. [*to Bassianus*] I pray you, let us hence,
And let her joy her raven-coloured love.
This valley fits the purpose passing well.

BASSIANUS

The king my brother shall have note of this.   85

LAVINIA

Ay, for these slips have made him noted long:
Good king, to be so mightily abused!

TAMORA

Why, I have patience to endure all this.

Enter CHIRON *and* DEMETRIUS.

DEMETRIUS

How now, dear sovereign and our gracious mother,

---

75 **sequestered** original pronunciation probably indicated by Q1's spelling: 'sequestred' (first syllable stressed)
81 **rated** berated
83 **joy** enjoy
85 ***note** 'notice' in the early texts, but Pope's emendation improves the metre and facilitates the verbal play in the next line
86 **slips** errors in moral conduct, perhaps also playing on 'slippings of the leash' and '(sexual) graftings'
noted long branded with disgrace, stigmatized (as at *JC* 4.3.2). But for how 'long' when 'he had been married

but one night' (Johnson)? Either there is an *Othello*-style double time scheme or this is a slip. Or there may be some textual corruption in this sequence: the SP for Tamora's next two speeches is QUEENE, for the only time in the play, which may suggest an early draft or revision. The possibility of corruption is supported by the variations in G1620 at this point: the empress is alone when Titus' daughter and her husband bait her, the baiting is extended, and the dalliance with the Moor occurs after the sons take away the girl to rape her.

78 but] *Q1; not in Q3, F*   82 SD] *Oxf¹*   85 note] *Pope;* notice *Q q, F*   88, 91 TAMORA] QUEENE in *Q1 (but elsewhere* TAMORA *or* TAM. *throughout)*   88 Why, I have] *Q1 (*Why I haue*);* Why haue I *F2*

173

Why doth your highness look so pale and wan?   90
TAMORA
Have I not reason, think you, to look pale?
These two have 'ticed me hither to this place:
A barren detested vale you see it is;
The trees, though summer, yet forlorn and lean,
O'ercome with moss and baleful mistletoe;   95
Here never shines the sun, here nothing breeds
Unless the nightly owl or fatal raven.
And when they showed me this abhorred pit,
They told me here at dead time of the night
A thousand fiends, a thousand hissing snakes,   100
Ten thousand swelling toads, as many urchins,
Would make such fearful and confused cries
As any mortal body hearing it
Should straight fall mad, or else die suddenly.
No sooner had they told this hellish tale,   105
But straight they told me they would bind me here
Unto the body of a dismal yew
And leave me to this miserable death.
And then they called me foul adulteress,
Lascivious Goth, and all the bitterest terms   110
That ever ear did hear to such effect.
And had you not by wondrous fortune come,
This vengeance on me had they executed.
Revenge it as you love your mother's life,
Or be ye not henceforth called my children.   115

---

92 **'ticed** enticed
95 **mistletoe** noted for being parasitic
97 **fatal** ominous, as the poetic raven usually is
98 **abhorred** abhorrèd
101 **urchins** goblins, elves (*OED* 1c). The plants and animals throughout this speech (e.g. *raven*, *toads* and *yew*) are associated with evil, foreboding and death. Contrast 2.2.12–15. In the

Warner production, Chiron and Demetrius offered lively impersonations of snakes, toads etc.
102 **confused** confusèd
110 **Lascivious Goth** 'Goth' was probably pronounced as 'goat', so there may be a pun on that proverbially lascivious creature, as at *AYL* 3.3.7–9.
115 **be ye not henceforth** Some eds emend for the sake of metre (see t.n.),

95 O'ercome] *Q2* (Orecome); Ouercome *Q1*   110 Lascivious] *Q1* (Lauicious)   115 be ye not henceforth] *Q1;* be not henceforth *Capell;* be ye not henceforward *Oxf*

DEMETRIUS

This is a witness that I am thy son.   *Stab him.*

CHIRON

And this for me, struck home to shew my strength.

[*He also stabs Bassianus, who dies.*]

LAVINIA

Ay, come, Semiramis, nay, barbarous Tamora,

For no name fits thy nature but thy own.

TAMORA

Give me the poniard. You shall know, my boys,   120

Your mother's hand shall right your mother's wrong.

DEMETRIUS

Stay, madam, here is more belongs to her:

First thrash the corn, then after burn the straw.

This minion stood upon her chastity,

Upon her nuptial vow, her loyalty,   125

And with that quaint hope braves your mightiness.

And shall she carry this unto her grave?

CHIRON

And if she do, I would I were an eunuch.

Drag hence her husband to some secret hole

And make his dead trunk pillow to our lust.   130

but the line may stand if 'b'ye' is elided to one syllable and chil-der-en expanded to three (compare *CE* 5.1.35). Compositorial misordering of 'my children called' is another possibility.

118 **Ay, come** Oxf precedes with the SD '*Tamora turns to Lavinia*'.
   Semiramis see on 1.1.521

120 **poniard** the dagger which Chiron has taken from Demetrius at 117

123 **thrash** 'to thrash in a woman's barn' was a slang idiom for having sex (Dent, B89.1)

124 **minion** hussy, jade

126 ***quaint** Q1 has 'painted hope', which is perhaps defensible on the grounds that Chiron and Demetrius would see chastity as something false, unreal (the word is turned on them by Aaron at 4.2.100). But it makes the metre very awkward, so I adopt Wells' emendation (Oxf, with its appropriately lewd pun on 'cunt'); it is easy to imagine 'q' in the MS becoming 'p' in print and a corrector then feeling it necessary to introduce the past participle ending. Another possibility is 'faint hope'.

129–30 **Drag ... lust** corresponds strikingly to the rape in Nashe's *Unfortunate Traveller* (see introduction, p. 77)

117.1] *Capell subst.*   118 Ay, come] *Hanmer;* I come *Qq, F*   120 the] *Q1;* thy *Q3, F*   126 quaint] *Oxf;* painted *Q1*

TAMORA

But when ye have the honey we desire,
Let not this wasp outlive, us both to sting.

CHIRON

I warrant you, madam, we will make that sure.
Come, mistress, now perforce we will enjoy
That nice-preserved honesty of yours.   135

LAVINIA

O Tamora, thou bearest a woman's face –

TAMORA

I will not hear her speak; away with her!

LAVINIA

Sweet lords, entreat her hear me but a word.

DEMETRIUS [*to Tamora*]

Listen, fair madam, let it be your glory
To see her tears, but be your heart to them   140
As unrelenting flint to drops of rain.

LAVINIA

When did the tiger's young ones teach the dam?
O, do not learn her wrath: she taught it thee.
The milk thou suckst from her did turn to marble;

---

131 **we desire** F2 emended to 'ye desire':
Tamora isn't going to share Lavinia's
sexual sweets. But she certainly wants
the honey to be extracted and 'we'
fits with 'us both' in the following
line ('both' meaning 'both myself and
you two'), so I retain the original
reading. 'Tamora is entering whole-
heartedly into her sons' plans, so that
the desire is hers as well as theirs'
(Ard²).

132 **outlive** live longer (ironically
echoing 1.1.170). This meaning,
together with Theobald's punctuation, makes sense of the line,
though Maxwell (Ard²) notes that
'*outlive* intransitively in the sense of

survive is unparalleled' and suggests
'o'erlive' as a possible alternative.

133 **warrant** monosyllabic: 'warr'nt'

135 **nice-preserved** nice-preservèd

136 **bearest** F elides to 'bear'st'

141 **As ... rain** inversion of the proverbial power of water to wear stone

142 **dam** mother

143 **learn** teach

144 **suckst** Ravenscroft and Rowe corrected the tense, but Shakespeare
cared more for the actor's tongue than
grammatical nicety, so both here and
at *1H6* 5.4.28 he wrote 'suckst' rather
than 'suckdst'. The idea of sucking
one's nature from one's mother's
breast was commonplace.

---

131 we desire] *Q1;* ye desire *F2*   132 outlive, us] *Theobald;* out liue us *Q1*   136 woman's] *Q1;*
woman *F*   139 SD] *Oxf¹*   144 suckst] *Q1;* suck'dst *Ravenscroft, Rowe²*

Even at thy teat thou hadst thy tyranny.   145
Yet every mother breeds not sons alike:
[*to Chiron*] Do thou entreat her show a woman's pity.
CHIRON
What, wouldst thou have me prove myself a bastard?
LAVINIA
'Tis true, the raven doth not hatch a lark.
Yet have I heard – O, could I find it now –   150
The lion, moved with pity, did endure
To have his princely paws pared all away.
Some say that ravens foster forlorn children
The whilst their own birds famish in their nests.
O be to me, though thy hard heart say no,   155
Nothing so kind, but something pitiful.
TAMORA
I know not what it means; away with her!
LAVINIA
O, let me teach thee for my father's sake,
That gave thee life when well he might have slain
    thee.
Be not obdurate, open thy deaf ears.   160
TAMORA
Hadst thou in person ne'er offended me,
Even for his sake am I pitiless.

146 **sons alike** identical sons
149 **raven ... lark** *raven* suggests not
    only (moral) blackness, as at 83 and
    97, but also 'ravening' (ravishing,
    devouring); the *lark* suggests bright-
    ness and, because of its high flight,
    heaven. A variation on the proverbial
    'an eagle does not hatch a dove'
    (Tilley, E2).
151–2 **lion ... paws pared** a proverbial
    fable (Tilley, L316), but with a hint
    of Androcles/Andronicus and the lion
    (see introduction, p. 93). *paws* sub-
    stitutes for claws.

153 **ravens foster** Although usually ill-
    omened, ravens sometimes have a
    positive emblematic significance as
    providential figures, in allusion to
    those which fed Elijah (1 Kings 17.4–
    6).
154 **birds** chicks
156 **Nothing ... pitiful** 'if not as kind
    as the fostering raven, then at least
    have some pity'
160 **obdurate** stress on second syllable
    ears Q1's spelling, 'yeares' (also at
    4.4.97), is phonetic (Cercignani, 362)

147 SD] *Warburton*   woman's] *Q1;* woman *Q2–3, F*   153 Some] *Q2;* So me *Q1*   160 ears] *Q3;*
yeares *Q1*

Remember, boys, I poured forth tears in vain
To save your brother from the sacrifice,
But fierce Andronicus would not relent.   165
Therefore away with her and use her as you will:
The worse to her, the better loved of me.

LAVINIA   [*clinging to Tamora*]
O Tamora, be called a gentle queen,
And with thine own hands kill me in this place.
For 'tis not life that I have begged so long;   170
Poor I was slain when Bassianus died.

TAMORA
What begg'st thou then, fond woman? Let me go!

LAVINIA
'Tis present death I beg, and one thing more
That womanhood denies my tongue to tell.
O, keep me from their worse-than-killing lust,   175
And tumble me into some loathsome pit
Where never man's eye may behold my body.
Do this, and be a charitable murderer.

TAMORA
So should I rob my sweet sons of their fee.
No, let them satisfy their lust on thee.   180

DEMETRIUS   [*to Lavinia*]
Away, for thou hast stayed us here too long.

LAVINIA
No grace? No womanhood? Ah, beastly creature,
The blot and enemy to our general name,

---

163 **Remember, boys** In the Warner
    production, Estelle Kohler's normally
    powerful voice quivered here, as
    Tamora recollected her dead son.
167 **The worse** 'you are' understood
172 **fond** foolish
173 **present** immediate
174 **womanhood** female modesty
176 **tumble** ironically for Lavinia, has
    sexual connotations (as at *AC* 1.4.17)

177 **man's eye** emphasizes the male eye:
    she will be ashamed to be seen, yet
    the men in the play will insist on
    displaying her
179 **fee** The monetary term reduces
    Lavinia to a commodity, like a whore
    (contrast her word *charitable*)
183 **our general name** the reputation
    of womankind

168 SD] *this edn; She tugs at Tamora's garments / Bevington (at 171); embracing Tamora's knees /*
Oxf¹   175 their] *Q2;* there *Q1*   180 satisfy] *Q1* (satisfie)   181 SD] *Oxf*

Confusion fall –
CHIRON   Nay then, I'll stop your mouth.
                    [*Grabs her, covering her mouth.*]
[*to Demetrius*] Bring thou her husband: 185
This is the hole where Aaron bid us hide him.
                    [*Demetrius throws Bassianus' body into the pit,*
                    he and Chiron then exeunt, dragging Lavinia.]
TAMORA
Farewell, my sons; see that you make her sure.
Ne'er let my heart know merry cheer indeed
Till all the Andronici be made away.
Now will I hence to seek my lovely Moor,   190
And let my spleenful sons this trull deflower.   *Exit.*

Enter AARON *with two of Titus' sons* [QUINTUS *and* MARTIUS].

AARON
Come on, my lords, the better foot before.
Straight will I bring you to the loathsome pit
Where I espied the panther fast asleep.

---

184 **Confusion fall** – Lavinia's final
words are interrupted, her speech cut
off, anticipating her subsequent fate.
My arrangement of the half-lines
conveys the idea of her speech being
taken from her. *Confusion* has many
relevant senses – discomfiture, ruin,
putting to shame, mental per-
turbation, throwing into disorder –
some of which rebound upon Lavinia,
others of which are ultimately fulfilled
upon Tamora.
186.1 *into the pit* through the stage's
trap-door
186.2 *dragging Lavinia* In the Deborah
Warner production, Chiron (Richard
McCabe) picked her up bodily,

obscenely stuffing one hand between
her legs; the sounds of the rape were
heard from offstage.
187 **make her sure** make sure of her (i.e.
ensure she cannot reveal anything)
189 **made away** killed
191 **spleenful** The spleen was regarded
as the seat of strong passions
trull deflower A trull is a whore,
whereas it is a virgin who is deflowered: it is characteristic of Tamora
to refer to Lavinia's virtue in this
oxymoronic way, but also prophetic
in that once Lavinia is deflowered
she becomes a trull in the eyes of
Demetrius and Chiron.
194 **panther** see on 2.1.21

184 fall –] *Q3;* fall *Q1*   184.1] *this edn*   184–5] Nay ... husband] *lineation new in this edn; 1 line
in Qq; divided after* mouth, *in* F, *but first sentence not joined with* 184   185 SD] *Oxf¹*   186.1–2]
Capell subst.; Exeunt F2; Exeunt Dem. Chi. Dragging Lav. / *Ravenscroft (who earlier has: Chir.
throws the Body into the Vault, Tam. the whilst holds Lav.)*   191 *Exit*] F   191.1 QUINTUS *and*
MARTIUS] *Capell*   192 AARON] F; *in Q1 implied by preceding entry SD*

QUINTUS

My sight is very dull, whate'er it bodes.   195

MARTIUS

And mine, I promise you; were it not for shame,

Well could I leave our sport to sleep awhile.

[Falls into the pit.]

QUINTUS

What, art thou fallen? What subtle hole is this,

Whose mouth is covered with rude-growing briers

Upon whose leaves are drops of new-shed blood   200

As fresh as morning dew distilled on flowers?

A very fatal place it seems to me.

Speak, brother, hast thou hurt thee with the fall?

MARTIUS   *[from below]*

O brother, with the dismall'st object hurt

That ever eye with sight made heart lament.   205

AARON   *[aside]*

Now will I fetch the king to find them here,

That he thereby may have a likely guess

How these were they that made away his brother.   *Exit.*

MARTIUS   *[from below]*

Why dost not comfort me and help me out

From this unhallowed and bloodstained hole?   210

195 **dull** lacking keenness of perception; also associated with a melancholy and foreboding mood (*OED a.* 2, 4)

197.1 *Falls into the pit* Waith (Oxf[1], followed by Oxf) includes in the SD at 186 '*and cover the opening with branches*', thus ensuring that Martius does not see the hole; if the stage was strewn with rushes, this is a possibility, but it presupposes a more 'realistic' staging than was required in the Elizabethan theatre. In the Warner production, the fall was managed by blacking out the main stage, taking the action onto the raised bridge that ran along the back of the stage, Aaron springing the trap and the middle section of the bridge dropping more than four feet.

198–201 **subtle hole ... flowers** on this imagery, see introduction, pp. 8–9

204 **object** spectacle provoking strong emotion (*OED sb.* 3b) – also used of dead bodies at *KL* 5.3.239

210 **unhallowed** F's correction of Q's 'vnhollow' ('"unhallowd" misread "unhollowe" before "hole"' – Cam[1]) **bloodstained** bloodstainèd. *OED*'s earliest citation is *1H4* 1.3.107 – it would be fitting if such a word were in fact coined here in *Titus*.

197.1] *Rowe subst.*   201 morning] *Q1;* mornings *Q3, F*   204 object hurt] *Q1;* obiect *Q3, F*   204 SD] *this edn (and for all subsequent speeches spoken from beneath the trap); under the stage / Collier MS*   206 SD] *Johnson*   208 SD] *Q1 (after 207)*   210 unhallowed] *F (*vnhallow'd*);* vnhollow *Qq*

QUINTUS

I am surprised with an uncouth fear;
A chilling sweat o'erruns my trembling joints;
My heart suspects more than mine eye can see.

MARTIUS   [*from below*]

To prove thou hast a true-divining heart,
Aaron and thou look down into this den,   215
And see a fearful sight of blood and death.

QUINTUS

Aaron is gone and my compassionate heart
Will not permit mine eyes once to behold
The thing whereat it trembles by surmise.
O tell me who it is, for ne'er till now   220
Was I a child to fear I know not what.

MARTIUS   [*from below*]

Lord Bassianus lies berayed in blood
All on a heap, like to a slaughtered lamb,
In this detested, dark, blood-drinking pit.

QUINTUS

If it be dark, how dost thou know 'tis he?   225

MARTIUS   [*from below*]

Upon his bloody finger he doth wear
A precious ring that lightens all this hole,
Which like a taper in some monument
Doth shine upon the dead man's earthy cheeks

---

211 **surprised** surprisèd. bewildered
    uncouth unfamiliar, strange
217 **compassionate** affected with sor-
    rowful emotion
219 **by surmise** even to imagine
222 ***berayed** defiled. Dover Wilson's
    emendation (Cam¹), on the assump-
    tion that Q1 misread 'bereied' as
    'bereud' (for a comparable minim
    misreading, see on 260). *OED*'s
    citations include a close parallel in

Holinshed's *Scottish Chronicle* (the
source of *Mac*): 'The king was slaine
... and the bed all beraied with
bloud'. For other possible emendations, see t.n.
227 **ring that lightens** 'There is sup-
    posed to be a gem called a *carbuncle*,
    which emits not reflected but native
    light' (Johnson).
229 **earthy** pale, lifeless as earth (more
    physical resonance than at 1.1.102)

---

220 who] *Q1;* how *Q3, F*   222 berayed in blood] *Cam¹;* bereaud in blood *Q1;* embrewed heere
Q2–3, F; heere reav'd of lyfe *early MS emendation in Folger copy of Q1;* bedaub'd *or* bedew'd in
blood *(Bolton)*   223 to a] *Q1;* to the *F*   227 this] *Q1;* the *Q3, F*   229 earthy] *Q1;* earthly *Q3, F*

And shows the ragged entrails of this pit.   230
So pale did shine the moon on Pyramus
When he by night lay bathed in maiden blood.
O brother, help me with thy fainting hand –
If fear hath made thee faint, as me it hath –
Out of this fell devouring receptacle,   235
As hateful as Cocytus' misty mouth.

QUINTUS   [*Reaches into pit.*]

Reach me thy hand that I may help thee out
Or, wanting strength to do thee so much good,
I may be plucked into the swallowing womb
Of this deep pit, poor Bassianus' grave.   240
I have no strength to pluck thee to the brink –

MARTIUS   [*from below*]

Nor I no strength to climb without thy help.

QUINTUS

Thy hand once more; I will not loose again
Till thou art here aloft or I below.
Thou canst not come to me – I come to thee.   245
                                        [*Falls into the pit.*]

230 **ragged entrails** rough interior. *entrails* strengthens the image of the pit as a body.
231 **Pyramus** In Ovid (*Met.*, 4.67–201, dramatized in *MND*) Pyramus and Thisbe were lovers who arranged to meet outside the city (where Semiramis was queen) because their parents resisted their union. While Thisbe waited, she was scared away by a lion and dropped her mantle, which it tore with its bloody teeth. Pyramus arrived and assumed Thisbe had been killed, so he killed himself; she returned and killed herself over his body.

232 **maiden blood** Thisbe's blood or Pyramus'? Pyramus and Bassianus are men (though Thisbe blazons the dead Pyramus as if he were a maiden at *MND* 5.1.324–41), so the image, with its hint of hymeneal blood, evokes the simultaneous offstage action in which Lavinia is being deflowered (as if for the second time in a few hours, with the difference that on the wedding-night it was consensual).
236 **Cocytus'** a river in hell, used here for hell generally
239 **womb** primary sense is 'stomach', but perhaps also a further image of the pit as a female body

230 this] *Q1*; the *F*   231 Pyramus] *Q2*; Priamus *Q1*   236 Cocytus'] *F2* (*Cocitus*); *Ocitus Qq*, *F*   237 SD] *this edn; Offering to help / Bevington*   245.1] *Pope subst.; Boths fall in F*

Enter the Emperor *and* AARON *the Moor* [*with Attendants*].

SATURNINUS
Along with me! I'll see what hole is here
And what he is that now is leapt into it.
[*Speaks into the pit.*]
Say, who art thou that lately didst descend
Into this gaping hollow of the earth?
MARTIUS   [*from below*]
The unhappy sons of old Andronicus,   250
Brought hither in a most unlucky hour
To find thy brother Bassianus dead.
SATURNINUS
My brother dead? I know thou dost but jest;
He and his lady both are at the lodge
Upon the north side of this pleasant chase.   255
'Tis not an hour since I left them there.
MARTIUS   [*from below*]
We know not where you left them all alive,
But, out alas, here have we found him dead.

Enter TAMORA, [TITUS] ANDRONICUS, *and* LUCIUS.

TAMORA
Where is my lord the king?
SATURNINUS
Here, Tamora, though gride with killing grief.   260

256 **hour** disyllabic
260 *****gride** Most eds have the very weak
'grieved with killing grief', following
Q2's emendation of Q1's 'griude'.
The next image ('search [i.e. probe]
my wound') suggests that the sense
should be 'piercing grief' – compare
4.4.31, where grief 'hath pierced him
deep and scarred his heart'. Line 4
of the February eclogue of Spenser's
Shepheardes Calender reads 'All as I
were through the body gryde' and is
glossed by EK, 'Gride, perced: an
olde word much used of Lidgate'.
OED (*v.* 1) also cites 'With many a
cruel wound [he] was through the
body gride' (Drayton's *Polyolbion*)
and 'Our own spirits gride with piercing wind' (Henry More). The poeti-
cism is an appropriate register of
Saturninus' insincerity and at the
same time cause for the compositor's
ignorance of the word; if the MS was
'gryde', it is a minim error.

245.2 *with Attendants*] *Ravenscroft subst., Theobald*   248 SD] *Bevington*   250 sons] *Q1;* sonne
Q2–3, F   256 them] *Q1;* him *Q3, F*   257 them] *Q1;* him *F*   258.1 TITUS] *Cam*   260 gride] *this*
edn; griude *Q1;* greeu'd/grieu'd *Q2–3, F;* griped *Cam¹ (J. C. Maxwell);* gored *(G. R. Proudfoot)*

183

TAMORA

Where is thy brother Bassianus?

SATURNINUS

Now to the bottom dost thou search my wound:
Poor Bassianus here lies murdered.

TAMORA

Then all too late I bring this fatal writ,
The complot of this timeless tragedy,   265
And wonder greatly that man's face can fold
In pleasing smiles such murderous tyranny.

                     She giveth Saturnine a letter.

SATURNINUS   [*reads*]

And if we miss to meet him handsomely,
Sweet huntsman – Bassianus 'tis we mean –
Do thou so much as dig the grave for him.   270
Thou know'st our meaning. Look for thy reward
Among the nettles at the elder tree
Which overshades the mouth of that same pit
Where we decreed to bury Bassianus.
Do this, and purchase us thy lasting friends.   275
O Tamora, was ever heard the like?
This is the pit and this the elder tree.
Look, sirs, if you can find the huntsman out
That should have murdered Bassianus here.

AARON   [*finding the money-bag*]

My gracious lord, here is the bag of gold.   280

---

263 **murdered** murderèd
264 **writ** document, paper (no specific legal sense)
265 **complot** design, conspiracy; Maxwell (Ard²) suggests a pun on the special theatrical sense of an outline of the action – this is supported by the proximity to *tragedy*
    timeless untimely
266–7 **face ... tyranny** a typically

Shakespearean image of the false face hiding cunning and murder; typical, too, in the irony of Tamora speaking it
268 **handsomely** conveniently
272 **elder tree** ill-omened and associated with betrayal: 'Judas was hanged on an elder' (*LLL* 5.2.606)
275 **purchase** win

268 SD] *Q1 (Saturninus reads the letter [centred])*   276] *Q1 repeats SP: King*   280 SD] *this edn;*
Shewing it / Johnson

SATURNINUS   [*to Titus*]
Two of thy whelps, fell curs of bloody kind,
Have here bereft my brother of his life.
Sirs, drag them from the pit unto the prison.
There let them bide until we have devised
Some never-heard-of torturing pain for them.   285
TAMORA
What, are they in this pit? O wondrous thing!
How easily murder is discovered.
                    [*Attendants pull Quintus, Martius and
                           Bassianus' body from the pit.*]
TITUS   [*kneeling*]
High emperor, upon my feeble knee
I beg this boon with tears not lightly shed:
That this fell fault of my accursed sons,   290
Accursed if the fault be proved in them –
SATURNINUS
If it be proved? You see it is apparent.
Who found this letter? Tamora, was it you?

---

281 **fell** fierce, cruel
   kind nature, disposition
285 **torturing** original pronunciation
   indicated by Q1's spelling, 'tortering'.
   The same phrase occurs in *Ironside*:
   'some new never-heard-of torturing
   pain' (1276).
287 **easily** pronounced 'eas'ly'
   discovered discoverèd
287.1–2 *Attendants ... pit* It would
   seem logical for Titus' sons to be
   pulled up before he pleads for their
   release, but this action could take
   place at any time between here and
   the end of the scene.
290, 291 **accursed** accursèd
293–4 **Who found ... take it up** Aaron
   tells Tamora to give the letter to
   Saturninus, as she does, yet now she
   says that Titus picked it up, which is
   neither plotted for nor seen. Does
   Tamora link it to Titus so as to be

sure that there is no suspicion that it
came from her or Aaron? Perhaps
Titus looks baffled for a moment
(since he *didn't* pick it up) but then
decides it's not worth quarrelling
(denying anything Tamora says will
not go down well with her new
husband) and accepts her false claim
so that he can move quickly on to try
to be his sons' bail. But at 5.1.106
Aaron mentions Titus finding the
letter: he is coming clean at this point
and has no need to sustain the fiction.
This suggests a genuine inconsistency, or unworked-through idea,
in the plotting – it is therefore noteworthy that, on the basis of supposed
'diffuseness and metrical monotony'
(Cam[1]), some eds consider 268–306 a
relic of 'an older and cruder version
of the story' (Ard[1]).

281 SD] *Ravenscroft, Rowe*   287.1–2] *Bevington subst.; Capell subst. at 303*   288 SD] *Bevington*   291 fault] *Ravenscroft, Rowe;* faults *Qq, F*

TAMORA

Andronicus himself did take it up.

TITUS

I did, my lord, yet let me be their bail,   295
For by my fathers' reverend tomb I vow
They shall be ready at your highness' will
To answer their suspicion with their lives.

SATURNINUS

Thou shalt not bail them. See thou follow me.
Some bring the murdered body, some the murderers. 300
Let them not speak a word: the guilt is plain;
For, by my soul, were there worse end than death
That end upon them should be executed.

TAMORA

Andronicus, I will entreat the king;
Fear not thy sons, they shall do well enough.   305

TITUS   [*rising*]

Come, Lucius, come; stay not to talk with them.
Exeunt [some taking the body, some guarding the prisoners].

2.3 [2.4]   *Enter the* Empress' Sons *with* LAVINIA, *her hands*
cut off and her tongue cut out, and ravished.

DEMETRIUS

So, now go tell, and if thy tongue can speak,
Who 'twas that cut thy tongue and ravished thee.

---

298 **their suspicion** the suspicion they
are under
300 **murderers** probably elided as
'murd'rers'
305 **Fear not** do not be afraid for
(preposition understood – Abbott,
§200)
306.1 *Exeunt* The staging seems to be
that Saturninus turns and leads off at
303, Tamora takes Titus aside before

following, and Attendants, probably
assisted by Aaron, obey Saturninus'
instruction regarding the body and
the prisoners.
2.3 The stage is empty for a moment,
but the action continues in the same
location. In the Warner production,
Chiron and Demetrius crawled on
first, parodying the movement of their
mutilated victim.

296 fathers'] *Delius;* fathers *Qq, F;* father's *Rowe*   306 SD] *Bevington*   306.1 *Exeunt*] *F; Capell*
has Emperor's party exiting at 305, then Titus and Lucius at 306; Oxf has Sat. exiting at 303   some
... prisoners] *Bevington subst.*   **2.3**] *this edn; 2.4 in edns since Dyce*   Location] The same part of
the Forest *Capell*

CHIRON

> Write down thy mind, bewray thy meaning so,
> And if thy stumps will let thee, play the scribe.

DEMETRIUS

> See how with signs and tokens she can scrawl.   5

CHIRON

> Go home, call for sweet water, wash thy hands.

DEMETRIUS

> She hath no tongue to call, nor hands to wash,
> And so let's leave her to her silent walks.

CHIRON

> And 'twere my cause, I should go hang myself.

DEMETRIUS

> If thou hadst hands to help thee knit the cord.   10
>
> *Exeunt [Chiron and Demetrius].*

Wind horns. Enter MARCUS *from hunting.* [LAVINIA *runs away.*]

MARCUS

> Who is this – my niece that flies away so fast?
> Cousin, a word. Where is your husband?
>
> [*Lavinia turns.*]
> If I do dream, would all my wealth would wake me;
> If I do wake, some planet strike me down
> That I may slumber an eternal sleep.   15

3 **bewray** divulge, reveal
5 **scrawl** Q1's 'scrowle' is a variant spelling of 'scrawl', 'to spread the limbs abroad in a sprawling manner' (*OED v.*[1]), with possible play on modern sense, 'to write carelessly or awkwardly' (*OED v.*[2], but no example before 1612), and perhaps also on 'scroll', 'to write down' (but *OED* has no example of this verb before 1606).
6 **sweet water** a sweet-smelling liquid preparation, similar to rose water
9 **and** if
   cause case

10.2 *from hunting* 'May indicate that his costume and those of others were appropriate for hunting' (Oxf[1]); see further, Dessen, *Conventions*, 32–4. *Lavinia runs away* initially Marcus sees her only from behind
11 **Who is this** could be elided to 'Who's this'
12 **Cousin** used for any collateral relative
12.1 *Lavinia turns* eliciting a long pause in the Warner production
14 **planet** adverse planet, star bringing ill fortune

5 scrawl] *Q1 (*scrowle*);* scowle *F*   10.1 *Chiron and Demetrius*] *Ravenscroft subst., Theobald*   10.2 *Wind horns*] *F   Lavinia runs away*] *this edn; Lavinia flees from him / Bevington*   11 MARCUS] *not in Q1, but implied by preceding entry SD*   12.1] *this edn; He sees her injuries / Bevington; He sees La. She turns away and hangs down her head / Ravenscroft*   15 an] *Q1; in Q2–3, F*

Speak, gentle niece, what stern ungentle hands
Hath lopped and hewed and made thy body bare
Of her two branches, those sweet ornaments
Whose circling shadows kings have sought to sleep in
And might not gain so great a happiness   20
As half thy love. Why dost not speak to me?
                                    [*Lavinia opens her mouth.*]
Alas, a crimson river of warm blood,
Like to a bubbling fountain stirred with wind,
Doth rise and fall between thy rosed lips,
Coming and going with thy honey breath.   25
But sure some Tereus hath deflowered thee
And, lest thou shouldst detect him, cut thy tongue.
Ah, now thou turn'st away thy face for shame,
And notwithstanding all this loss of blood,
As from a conduit with three issuing spouts,   30
Yet do thy cheeks look red as Titan's face,
Blushing to be encountered with a cloud.

17 **Hath** acceptable in Elizabethan usage
   with plural 'hands'
   lopped and hewed The forestry
   terms exactly echo those used of Alarbus' death.
21 **half** Theobald's emendation to 'have'
   is unnecessary: that merely having
   Lavinia half in love with you is the
   greatest happiness imaginable is an
   idea characteristic of Marcus' rhetorical excess in this speech.
21.1 *opens her mouth* spitting blood in
   the Warner production
24 **rosed** rosèd
26 **Tereus** For Tereus' rape of *Philomela*
   (38), the principal precedent for the
   plot, see introduction, pp. 90–2, and
   appendix, pp. 279–83.
27 ***him** 'them' in the early edns; a
   common compositorial error (in some
   Elizabethan secretary hands 'h' and
   'th' are easily confused, as are 'him'
   and 'hem'), perhaps precipitated here

by ignorance that Tereus is singular
30 **conduit** fountain, structure from
   which water is distributed
   ***three** 'their' in Qq,F: 'The MS
   probably had *thre*, misread as *ther*'
   (Ard²)
   issuing used by Shakespeare for both
   blood (e.g. *MV* 3.2.266) and tears
   (e.g. *H5* 4.6.34); 'issue' was a medical
   term for a discharge of blood from the
   body. In Golding's Ovid, Pyramus'
   'bloud did spin on hie / As when a
   Conduit pipe is crackt' (*Met.*, 4.147–
   8); for the Ovidianism of the whole
   of this speech, see Waith, 'Met.', and
   Bate, *Ovid*, 111–13.
31 **Titan's** the sun's
32 **Blushing … cloud** As Dover Wilson
   notes (Cam¹), the image is similarly
   developed in *R2* 3.3.62–7, where the
   king becomes 'the blushing dis-
   contented sun', his glory dimmed by
   'the envious clouds'. '*Encountered*

21 half] *Q1;* have *Theobald*   21.1] *this edn*   27 him] *Ravenscroft, Rowe;* them *Qq, F*   30 three]
Hanmer; their *Qq, F*

Shall I speak for thee? Shall I say 'tis so?
O that I knew thy heart, and knew the beast,
That I might rail at him to ease my mind!   35
Sorrow concealed, like an oven stopped,
Doth burn the heart to cinders where it is.
Fair Philomela, why she but lost her tongue,
And in a tedious sampler sewed her mind;
But, lovely niece, that mean is cut from thee.   40
A craftier Tereus, cousin, hast thou met,
And he hath cut those pretty fingers off,
That could have better sewed than Philomel.
O, had the monster seen those lily hands
Tremble like aspen leaves upon a lute   45
And make the silken strings delight to kiss them,
He would not then have touched them for his life.
Or had he heard the heavenly harmony
Which that sweet tongue hath made,
He would have dropped his knife and fell asleep,   50

means firstly only "meet", and then "be covered up"; but it is also the standard word for the accosting of a prostitute, and it is that source which is the root of Lavinia's blush, the shame which (however complete her innocence may seem) drove Lucrece to suicide' (Brooke, 16).

36–7 **Sorrow ... it is** A commonplace idea in the period (Dent, O89.1), but one that is crucial to the expression/expulsion of sorrow effected by rhetorical tragedy. Very similar thought and phrasing to *VA* 331–4.

36 **concealed** concealèd

38 **Philomela** Some eds emend to 'Philomel' for the sake of metre, but the name can be syncopated (as at *TNK* 5.5.124) and the final 'a' thrusts the line strongly onwards. The Latinless Q1 compositor frequently altered Shakespeare's correct classical

names to non-existent ones; it is therefore more likely that Shakespeare used the correct variant form 'Philomela' than that he wrote 'Philomel' and the compositor altered it by chance to a different but still correct form.

39 **tedious** laboriously executed
sampler piece of embroidery. The original sense was 'pattern, model, example to be imitated' (*OED sb.*[1]): the Philomel story is thus the 'sampler' for the rape of Lavinia.

45 **Tremble ... leaves** a poetical commonplace in the period, probably derived by Shakespeare from Golding's Ovid: 'Stoode trembling like an Aspen leafe' (*Met.*, 3.46)

47 **touched** transferred from the technical musical sense of 'playing' a stringed instrument; Lavinia has become the instrument, now untuned.

38 Philomela] *Q1;* Philomel *Cam*   why she] *Q1;* she *Q3, F*   41 cousin] *Q1; not in Q3, F, but F has* met withall

    As Cerberus at the Thracian poet's feet.
    Come, let us go and make thy father blind,
    For such a sight will blind a father's eye.
    One hour's storm will drown the fragrant meads:
    What will whole months of tears thy father's eyes?   55
    Do not draw back, for we will mourn with thee;
    O, could our mourning ease thy misery!

                                          Exeunt.

3.1 *Enter the [Tribunes as] Judges and [the] Senators, with*
    Titus' two sons [QUINTUS and MARTIUS] bound, passing on
    the stage to the place of execution, and TITUS going before
                      pleading.

TITUS
    Hear me, grave fathers; noble tribunes, stay!
    For pity of mine age, whose youth was spent
    In dangerous wars whilst you securely slept;
    For all my blood in Rome's great quarrel shed,
    For all the frosty nights that I have watched,   5
    And for these bitter tears which now you see
    Filling the aged wrinkles in my cheeks,
    Be pitiful to my condemned sons,

---

51 **Cerberus ... feet** Orpheus ('the
Thracian poet') played so sweetly
that Cerberus, the three-headed dog
guarding the entrance to the underworld, fell asleep at his feet. The same
allusion occurs in the context of rape
at *Luc* 552–3. On the fusion of Philomel and Orpheus in both play and
poem, as well as in *Edward III*, see
Bate, *Ovid*, 76–7, 111–13.
54 **hour's** disyllabic
    meads meadows
55 **What will ... thy** i.e. 'what effect
will ... have on thy'
3.1 The action returns to Rome.
0.1 **Tribunes as Judges* 'Judges' in Qq,

F. Eds add Tribunes, but the latter's
principal power was judicial, so they
are probably synonymous with Judges
here. Titus clearly addresses the Tribunes throughout the scene as if they
are the Judges.
0.2 **on** This being an otherwise unknown
phrasing for an SD, Wells (Oxf and
Oxf¹) emends to '*over*' on the assumption that the MS read 'ou"', but 'on'
has the advantage of indicating that
they cross the main stage, not the
above space.
7 **aged** agèd (also at 3.1.23, 3.1.59,
4.4.95, 5.2.130)
8 **condemned** condemnèd

3.1] *Actus Tertius. F* Location] *A street in Rome Theobald* 0.1 *the Tribunes ... Senators*] *this
edn; the Iudges and Senatours Qq, F; the Judges, Senators and Tribunes / edns since Capell* 0.2
QUINTUS *and* MARTIUS] *Capell*

Whose souls is not corrupted as 'tis thought.
For two-and-twenty sons I never wept,   10
Because they died in honour's lofty bed.
> *Andronicus lieth down, and the Judges pass by him.*
For these two, tribunes, in the dust I write
My heart's deep languor and my soul's sad tears.
Let my tears staunch the earth's dry appetite;
My sons' sweet blood will make it shame and blush.   15
> *Exeunt [all but Titus].*
O earth, I will befriend thee more with rain
That shall distil from these two ancient ruins
Than youthful April shall with all his showers.
In summer's drought I'll drop upon thee still;
In winter with warm tears I'll melt the snow   20
And keep eternal springtime on thy face,
So thou refuse to drink my dear sons' blood.

Enter LUCIUS *with his weapon drawn.*

O reverend tribunes, O gentle aged men,
Unbind my sons, reverse the doom of death,

---

10 **two-and-twenty** Mutius is now numbered among the sons who died honourably: perhaps Titus has forgiven him, perhaps Shakespeare has muddled his numbers, or perhaps the killing of Mutius was added after this scene was drafted.

12 ***these two** merely 'these' in Qq,F, but the metre seems to demand an extra word, which was first supplied by F2. Of the various conjectures (see t.n.) that of Jackson (supplied to Oxf) is neatest.

15.1 *Exeunt* F's SD, though printed one line below because this is a long line; Q1's *pass by him* at 11 implies they are on the way to an exit

17 **distil** trickle down

ruins Hanmer poetically emended to 'urns', but the sense of urns as waterpots (as opposed to containers of ashes) may not have emerged at this time (it is not in Cawdrey's 1604 dictionary, but is in the 1613 edition). Titus' comparison of his eyes to ruined buildings makes good sense.

19 **still** continually. 'Seldom used by Shakespeare in the modern sense' (Ard²).

22 **So** on condition that; i.e. 'drink my tears rather than my sons' blood'. Imagery of blood and tears drunk by the earth has a long history in tragedy, going back via Seneca and Euripides to Aeschylus' *Oresteia*.

24 **doom** sentence

---

9 is] *Q1;* are *F2*   12 these two] *Oxf;* these *Qq, F;* these, these *F2;* these, good *Malone;* these, O (*Jackson ShS*)   15.1 *Exeunt*] *F* all but Titus] *Capell subst.*   17 ruins] *Q1;* urns *Hanmer*   21 on thy] *Q2;* outhy *Q1* ('n' *set upside-down*)

191

And let me say, that never wept before,   25
My tears are now prevailing orators.

LUCIUS

O noble father, you lament in vain:
The tribunes hear you not, no man is by,
And you recount your sorrows to a stone.

TITUS

Ah Lucius, for thy brothers let me plead.   30
Grave tribunes, once more I entreat of you –

LUCIUS

My gracious lord, no tribune hears you speak.

TITUS

Why, 'tis no matter, man: if they did hear,
They would not mark me, or if they did mark,
They would not pity me; yet plead I must,   35
{And bootless unto them.}
Therefore I tell my sorrows to the stones,
Who, though they cannot answer my distress,
Yet in some sort they are better than the tribunes
For that they will not intercept my tale.   40
When I do weep, they humbly at my feet
Receive my tears and seem to weep with me,
And were they but attired in grave weeds
Rome could afford no tribunes like to these.
A stone is soft as wax, tribunes more hard than stones; 45
A stone is silent and offendeth not,

26 **prevailing orators** successful in
their suit
33–5 **if they … would not** a rhetorical
ladder strongly influenced by Kyd,
Sp. Trag., 1.3.23–7
34 **or if** 'if' in Q1; by supplying 'or', Q2
improves metre and logic
36 **And bootless unto them** i.e. it is
useless pleading to them. For the
status of this half-line, and the possibility that it should be cut, see introduction, pp. 100–1.
40 **intercept** interrupt
43 **attired** attirèd or 'atti-erd'
weeds perhaps punning on clothes
and weeds that grow between stones
45 **A … stones** a strong hexameter

28 you not] *Q1;* not *F*   34 or if] *Q2;* if *Q1;* oh if *F*   did mark] *Q1;* did heare *F*   35] *Q1; not
in Q3*   35–6 yet … them] *Q1; not in F*   36 And bootless] *Q1;* All bootlesse *Q3*   37 sorrows to]
Q1; sorrowes bootles to *Q3, F*   44 tribunes] *Q1;* Tribune *Q2–3, F*   45 soft as] *Q1;* as soft *F*

And tribunes with their tongues doom men to death.
But wherefore stand'st thou with thy weapon drawn?

LUCIUS
To rescue my two brothers from their death,
For which attempt the judges have pronounced   50
My everlasting doom of banishment.

TITUS [*rising*]
O happy man, they have befriended thee!
Why, foolish Lucius, dost thou not perceive
That Rome is but a wilderness of tigers?
Tigers must prey, and Rome affords no prey   55
But me and mine. How happy art thou then
From these devourers to be banished.
But who comes with our brother Marcus here?

Enter MARCUS *with* LAVINIA.

MARCUS
Titus, prepare thy aged eyes to weep,
Or if not so, thy noble heart to break: 60
I bring consuming sorrow to thine age.

TITUS
Will it consume me? Let me see it then.

MARCUS
This was thy daughter.

TITUS
Why, Marcus, so she is.

LUCIUS [*falling to his knees*]
Ay me, this object kills me.   65

48 **But wherefore** Titus presumably looks up at this point.
54 **Rome ... tigers** deconstructs the classic binary opposition between civilization (associated with the city, especially Rome) and *wilderness* (where the law of tigers reigns)
57 **banished** banishèd
58.1 *with Lavinia* in the Warner production, she remained behind Marcus' back until 62
63–5 **This was ... kills me** Some eds print 63–4 as a single line, but half-lines effectively convey the simplicity and dignity of the moment.
65 **Ay me** alas
object spectacle, something presented to the sight (as at 2.2.204)

52 SD] *Oxf¹*; *at 40 Hudson; at 47 Dyce*   58.1 *with*] *Q1; and F*   59 aged] *Q1;* noble *Q3, F*
65 SD] *Oxf¹ subst.*

TITUS

    Faint-hearted boy, arise and look upon her.

                                  [Lucius rises.]

    Speak, Lavinia, what accursed hand

    Hath made thee handless in thy father's sight?

    What fool hath added water to the sea?

    Or brought a faggot to bright-burning Troy?   70

    My grief was at the height before thou cam'st,

    And now like Nilus it disdaineth bounds.

    Give me a sword, I'll chop off my hands too,

    For they have fought for Rome, and all in vain;

    And they have nursed this woe in feeding life;   75

    In bootless prayer have they been held up,

    And they have served me to effectless use.

    Now all the service I require of them

    Is that the one will help to cut the other.

    'Tis well, Lavinia, that thou hast no hands,   80

    For hands to do Rome service is but vain.

LUCIUS

    Speak, gentle sister: who hath martyred thee?

MARCUS

    O, that delightful engine of her thoughts,

---

67 **Speak** Often at the beginning of a line a monosyllable containing a diphthong or long vowel is emphasized so as to dispense with an unaccented syllable (Abbott, §484).
accursed accursèd

69 **sea?** Oxf and Oxf[1] omit the question mark and run on the sentence, but the succession of three question marks in Qq,F is dramatically strong. The idea is proverbial (Tilley, W106).

70 **brought … Troy** proverbial idea of 'adding fuel to the fire', elaborated so as to develop the link between Rome and Troy

72 **Nilus** The river Nile was especially known for its annual flooding; a favourite Shakespearean image for overflowing passion.

73 **I'll chop … too** Dramatically ironic anticipation of future event, very like Lear's 'Old fond eyes, / Beweep this cause again, I'll pluck ye out' (*KL* 1.4.301–2), though there the anticipation is complicated by the double plot.

77 **effectless** fruitless (probably a Shakespearean coinage). 'The whole phrase is an oxymoron' (Ard[2]).

81 **For hands … vain** In the Warner production, Brian Cox threw off his breastplate, symbol of his service to Rome.

82 **martyred** mutilated. 'martred' in Q1, but 'martyr'd' in F (also at 108).

83 **engine** instrument; with implication of artfulness (as at *VA* 367)

66.1] *Oxf[1]*

That blabbed them with such pleasing eloquence,
Is torn from forth that pretty hollow cage   85
Where, like a sweet melodious bird, it sung
Sweet varied notes, enchanting every ear.

LUCIUS
O, say thou for her: who hath done this deed?

MARCUS
O, thus I found her, straying in the park,
Seeking to hide herself, as doth the deer   90
That hath received some unrecuring wound.

TITUS
It was my dear, and he that wounded her
Hath hurt me more than had he killed me dead.
For now I stand as one upon a rock,
Environed with a wilderness of sea,   95
Who marks the waxing tide grow wave by wave,
Expecting ever when some envious surge
Will in his brinish bowels swallow him.
This way to death my wretched sons are gone;
Here stands my other son, a banished man,   100
And here my brother, weeping at my woes.
But that which gives my soul the greatest spurn
Is dear Lavinia, dearer than my soul.
Had I but seen thy picture in this plight,
It would have madded me; what shall I do   105
Now I behold thy lively body so?
Thou hast no hands to wipe away thy tears,
Nor tongue to tell me who hath martyred thee;
Thy husband he is dead, and for his death
Thy brothers are condemned, and dead by this.   110

84 **blabbed** told what was better kept
   secret
89 **park** area enclosed for royal hunting
90 **deer** pun emphasized by Q1 spelling,
   'Deare'. The stricken deer with-
   drawing to die is proverbial (Tilley,
   D189).
91 **unrecuring** incurable (probably a
   Shakespearean coinage)
97 **Expecting ... when** waiting for the
   time when
   envious malignant
102 **spurn** hurt, blow
106 **lively** living
110 **by this** by this time

195

Look, Marcus, ah, son Lucius, look on her!
When I did name her brothers, then fresh tears
Stood on her cheeks, as doth the honey-dew
Upon a gathered lily almost withered.

MARCUS

Perchance she weeps because they killed her
  husband,   115
Perchance because she knows them innocent.

TITUS

If they did kill thy husband, then be joyful,
Because the law hath ta'en revenge on them.
No, no, they would not do so foul a deed:
Witness the sorrow that their sister makes.   120
Gentle Lavinia, let me kiss thy lips
Or make some sign how I may do thee ease.
Shall thy good uncle and thy brother Lucius
And thou and I sit round about some fountain,
Looking all downwards to behold our cheeks,   125
How they are stained like meadows yet not dry,
With miry slime left on them by a flood?
And in the fountain shall we gaze so long
Till the fresh taste be taken from that clearness
And made a brine pit with our bitter tears?   130
Or shall we cut away our hands like thine?
Or shall we bite our tongues and in dumb shows
Pass the remainder of our hateful days?
What shall we do? Let us that have our tongues
Plot some device of further misery   135
To make us wondered at in time to come.

---

114 **withered** Some eds (supported by the Q1 spelling) suggest 'witherèd', producing a hexameter; a pentameter with a redundant syllable is also possible.

118 **ta'en** pronounced according to Q1 spelling, 'tane'

120 **Witness … makes** One of many implied directions for Lavinia's 'dumb' actions; Ravenscroft incorporated relevant SDs for some of them (see t.n. at 111, 138, 144).

132 **bite our tongues** one of Hieronimo's last actions in *Sp. Trag.*

111] *Ravenscroft adds SD: Lav. makes signs of sorrow lifting up her eyes & then hanging down her head & moving her stumps* 116 them] *Q1;* him *Q3, F* 122 sign] *Q1;* signes *F* 126 like] *Q1;* in *Q2–3, F* 135 misery] *Q1;* miseries *F*

LUCIUS

Sweet father, cease your tears, for at your grief
See how my wretched sister sobs and weeps.

MARCUS

Patience, dear niece; good Titus, dry thine eyes.

[*Gives handkerchief.*]

TITUS

Ah Marcus, Marcus, brother, well I wot   140
Thy napkin cannot drink a tear of mine,
For thou, poor man, hast drowned it with thine own.

LUCIUS

Ah, my Lavinia, I will wipe thy cheeks.

TITUS

Mark, Marcus, mark! I understand her signs:
Had she a tongue to speak, now would she say   145
That to her brother which I said to thee.
His napkin with his true tears all bewet
Can do no service on her sorrowful cheeks.
O, what a sympathy of woe is this;
As far from help as limbo is from bliss.   150

Enter AARON *the Moor alone.*

AARON

Titus Andronicus, my lord the emperor
Sends thee this word: that if thou love thy sons,
Let Marcus, Lucius, or thyself, old Titus,
Or any one of you, chop off your hand
And send it to the king, he for the same   155

141 **napkin** handkerchief
144 **Mark, Marcus, mark** witty play on the common technique of beginning a line with a spondee formed by a repeated monosyllable
147 ***his true** 'her true' in Qq,F, an easy error in view of the surrounding pronouns and the MS similarity of 'his' and 'hir'; emended in F4

150 **limbo** abode of the unbaptised, on the borders of hell; compare 'in Tartar limbo, worse than hell' (*CE* 4.2.32)
155 **king,** Most eds punctuate more heavily here (Oxf has a full stop), but grammatically 'Let … king' is a conditional protasis whose apodosis is 'he will send'.

138] *Ravenscroft adds SD: Lav. turns up her eyes & then hangs down her head as weeping* 139.1] *Ravenscroft subst.* 144] *Ravenscroft adds SD: Lav. shakes her head & points at Mar. handkercher as refusing to have her eyes wip'd* 147 his true] *F4;* her true *Qq, F*

Will send thee hither both thy sons alive –
And that shall be the ransom for their fault.

TITUS

O gracious emperor, O gentle Aaron!
Did ever raven sing so like a lark
That gives sweet tidings of the sun's uprise?   160
With all my heart I'll send the emperor my hand.
Good Aaron, wilt thou help to chop it off?

LUCIUS

Stay, father, for that noble hand of thine
That hath thrown down so many enemies
Shall not be sent. My hand will serve the turn.   165
My youth can better spare my blood than you,
And therefore mine shall save my brothers' lives.

MARCUS

Which of your hands hath not defended Rome
And reared aloft the bloody battleaxe,
Writing destruction on the enemy's casque?   170
O, none of both but are of high desert.
My hand hath been but idle: let it serve
To ransom my two nephews from their death,
Then have I kept it to a worthy end.

AARON

Nay, come, agree whose hand shall go along,   175

---

159 **raven ... lark** reiterates antithesis
of 2.2.149
161 **With ... hand** a purposeful hexameter
170 ***casque** 'castle' in Q1, but the
redundant last syllable suggests a
compositor's error, easily made if the
MS spelling was 'caske'. The emendation is supported by a close parallel
in *R2*: 'let thy blows, doubly
redoubled, / Fall like amazing thunder on the casque / Of thy adverse
pernicious enemy' (1.3.80–2). But
'castle' is not impossible, since it

either literally or figuratively means
'helmet' in Holinshed (*Chronicles*
[1577], 2.185). A parallel in *Ironside*
also suggests that a soldier, not a
building, is being struck: 'In vain this
curtle-axe was reared aloft / Which
made a lane throughout thy foemen's
troops' (1665–6). Marcus' metaphor
of *writing* is one of many figures of
violent inscription upon the body –
compare the same character's 'foemen's *marks* upon his battered shield'
(4.1.127).
171 **both** either of you

---

170 Writing] *Q1* (Wrighting)   enemy's] *(Capell)*;   enemies *Qq, F*;   enemies' *Theobald*   casque]
Theobald;   castle *Qq, F*;   cask *Hanmer*;   crest *(Walker)*

For fear they die before their pardon come.

MARCUS

My hand shall go.

LUCIUS   By heaven it shall not go.

TITUS

Sirs, strive no more. Such withered herbs as these

Are meet for plucking up – and therefore mine.

LUCIUS

Sweet father, if I shall be thought thy son,   180

Let me redeem my brothers both from death.

MARCUS

And for our father's sake and mother's care,

Now let me show a brother's love to thee.

TITUS

Agree between you: I will spare my hand.

LUCIUS

Then I'll go fetch an axe.   185

MARCUS

But I will use the axe.   *Exeunt [Lucius and Marcus].*

TITUS

Come hither, Aaron. I'll deceive them both:

Lend me thy hand and I will give thee mine.

AARON   *[aside]*

If that be called deceit, I will be honest

And never whilst I live deceive men so.   190

But I'll deceive you in another sort,

And that you'll say ere half an hour pass.

He cuts off Titus' hand.

Enter LUCIUS *and* MARCUS *again.*

---

192 **that you'll say** i.e. 'you will say
    that I have deceived you': the villain
    takes pleasure in foreknowledge of his
    victims' reactions.
    hour disyllabic

192.1 *Titus' hand* We learn from 3.2.7
    that it is his left hand. The Warner
    production utilized cheese-wire and
    an old bucket, but Aaron's scimitar
    would presumably be available.

186.1 *Lucius and Marcus*] Theobald   189 SD] *Ravenscroft, Rowe*   192.1 *hand*] *Q1; left hand
Oxf¹   Collier MS adds SD: with an axe*

TITUS

Now stay your strife; what shall be is dispatched.
Good Aaron, give his majesty my hand.
Tell him it was a hand that warded him   195
From thousand dangers, bid him bury it:
More hath it merited; that let it have.
As for my sons, say I account of them
As jewels purchased at an easy price,
And yet dear too, because I bought mine own.   200

AARON

I go, Andronicus, and for thy hand
Look by and by to have thy sons with thee.
[*aside*] Their heads I mean. O, how this villainy
Doth fat me with the very thoughts of it.
Let fools do good and fair men call for grace,   205
Aaron will have his soul black like his face.   *Exit.*

TITUS

O, here I lift this one hand up to heaven
And bow this feeble ruin to the earth.   [*Kneels.*]
If any power pities wretched tears,
To that I call. [*Lavinia kneels.*]
                    What, wouldst thou kneel with me?   210
Do then, dear heart, for heaven shall hear our
     prayers,
Or with our sighs we'll breathe the welkin dim
And stain the sun with fog, as sometime clouds
When they do hug him in their melting bosoms.

MARCUS

O brother, speak with possibility,   215

---

193 **shall be** is destined (Abbott, §315)
195 **warded** defended, protected
202 **Look** expect
204 **fat** nourish, hence delight
205 **fair** pale-faced (white)
208 **ruin** his mutilated body: this vein of

imagery supports 'ruins' rather than
'urns' for his eyes at 3.1.17. In *Cym*
(4.2.354) a headless body is called a
'ruin'.
212 **welkin** poetic term for the skies
215 **with possibility** realistically

203 SD] *Rowe*   208 SD] *Ravenscroft subst.*   210 SD] *Collier MS*   wouldst] *Q1;* would *Q2–3;*
wilt *F*   215 possibility] *Q1;* possibilities *Q3, F*

And do not break into these deep extremes.

TITUS

Is not my sorrows deep, having no bottom?
Then be my passions bottomless with them.

MARCUS

But yet let reason govern thy lament.

TITUS

If there were reason for these miseries,   220
Then into limits could I bind my woes.
When heaven doth weep, doth not the earth
    o'erflow?
If the winds rage, doth not the sea wax mad,
Threatening the welkin with his big-swollen face?
And wilt thou have a reason for this coil?   225
I am the sea. Hark how her sighs doth blow.
She is the weeping welkin, I the earth.
Then must my sea be moved with her sighs,
Then must my earth with her continual tears
Become a deluge overflowed and drowned,   230
For why my bowels cannot hide her woes,

---

217 *sorrows Dyce's emendation of
'sorrow': 'them' in the following line
implies a plural, and the combination
of singular verb with plural noun
was common in Elizabethan usage,
especially in questions.
218 passions outbursts of feeling: a new
sense of the word that emerged
around 1580–90 (*OED sb.* 6d)
222 o'erflow become flooded: transferred from the water, in accordance
with the overflow of feeling. The
language of 222–30 is influenced by
that of *Sp. Trag.* – see appendix,
pp. 285–6.
224 Threatening ... face elisions:
'Threatning' (Q1), 'big-swoll'n' (Q1
'bigswolne')
225 coil turmoil
226 *blow 'flow' in Qq,F; F2 (and

Ravenscroft) emended to 'blow'
because Lavinia's sighs represent the
wind (an effect caught strongly by
both Warner and BBC). She is a
'weeping welkin' producing tears as
well as sighs, rain as well as wind,
so 'flow' is not impossible, but the
emendation is strongly supported by
the influence of *Sp. Trag.*, 'Blow,
sighs, and raise an everlasting storm'
(2.5.44).
228 moved movèd
231 For why because. Oxf prints as one
word.
    her Theobald emended to 'their' on
the assumption that the referent is
'bowels', but 'her' could mean 'their'
in Elizabethan usage, and the pronoun
nicely suggests the intermingling of
father's and daughter's woes.

---

217 sorrows] *(Dyce²)*; sorrow *Qq, F*   226 doth] *Q1;* doe *Q2–3, F*   blow] *F2;* flow *Qq, F*   231
her] *Q1;* their *Theobald*

But like a drunkard must I vomit them.
Then give me leave, for losers will have leave
To ease their stomachs with their bitter tongues.

Enter a Messenger *with two heads and a hand.*

[*Titus and Lavinia may rise here.*]

MESSENGER
Worthy Andronicus, ill art thou repaid   235
For that good hand thou sent'st the emperor.
Here are the heads of thy two noble sons,
And here's thy hand in scorn to thee sent back:
Thy grief their sports, thy resolution mocked,
That woe is me to think upon thy woes   240
More than remembrance of my father's death.
[*Sets down heads and hand, exit.*]

233 **losers ... leave** 'Give losers leave to
speak' was proverbial (Tilley, L458).
234 **stomachs** like 'heart' and 'bosom',
used to denote the inner seat of the
passions, but also sustains the imagery
of vomiting
234.2 *may rise here* The implied SDs
for Titus and Lavinia to kneel at 208
and 210 are clear. In the 'I am the
sea' sequence in which they meta-
phorically become forces of nature
they have been rooted to the earth,
Lavinia moaning like the wind, Titus
holding her in his arms (as in the
BBC production). But when do they
arise? Oxf and Oxf[1] keep them on
their knees for nearly seventy lines,
till 276 (they must be standing for
the business at 277ff.). It inhibits the
action to keep them down for so long,
and Lavinia must move if my SD at
250.1 is correct. They could rise in
response to the Messenger's entry:
even in his grief, Titus would not be
seen on his knees in front of a mere

messenger. But since this is conjectural I have included a tentative
SD here: each director or reader will
need to try out various options and
decide what is best for the rhythm of
the scene.
239 **grief their sports** In Q1 'griefe'
is singular and 'sports' plural; Q3
emended to 'griefes' (Titus has more
than one grief, the next line refers to
his 'woes'); Ravenscroft improved the
sound of the line by making 'sport'
singular. Actors may wish to try these
different possibilities, but emendation
is not necessary.
     resolution suggestive of Stoic endur-
ance (see introduction, p. 30)
240 **That woe is me** 'so that it is [more]
woeful to me'
241 **More ... death** Since the eighteenth
century, Shakespeare has been admired for the art of animating even
the smallest role through details such
as this.

234.2] *this edn; Oxf[1] has them rising at 276*   239 grief their sports] *Q1;* griefes their sports *Q3;*
griefs their sport *Ravenscroft*   241.1] *Bevington subst.*

MARCUS

Now let hot Etna cool in Sicily,
And be my heart an ever-burning hell!
These miseries are more than may be borne.
To weep with them that weep doth ease some deal,   245
But sorrow flouted at is double death.

LUCIUS

Ah, that this sight should make so deep a wound
And yet detested life not shrink thereat!
That ever death should let life bear his name,
Where life hath no more interest but to breathe!   250
[Lavinia kisses the heads.]

MARCUS

Alas, poor heart, that kiss is comfortless
As frozen water to a starved snake.

TITUS

When will this fearful slumber have an end?

MARCUS

Now farewell flattery, die Andronicus.
Thou dost not slumber. See thy two sons' heads,   255
Thy warlike hand, thy mangled daughter here,
Thy other banished son with this dear sight
Struck pale and bloodless, and thy brother, I,
Even like a stony image, cold and numb.
Ah, now no more will I control thy griefs: 260

---

242 **Etna** archetypal volcano
245 **weep ... weep** a biblical phrase (Romans, 12.15)
    some deal somewhat, a little
246 **flouted** mocked, jeered
248 **shrink** 'wither or shrivel through withdrawal of vital fluid' (*OED v.* 1)
249 **life ... name** life still be called life
250 **interest** figurative use of legal term for entitlement to possessions or enjoyment of them

250.1 ***kisses the heads** on this SD, see introduction, pp. 47–8. Lavinia must go to *both* heads: Marcus' singular *That* could refer to the two collectively or mean 'such a kind of kiss'.
252 **starved** starvèd. perished with cold
254 **flattery** self-delusion (*OED* 2, earliest example being *Son* 42.14). Two syllables: 'flattrie' (Q1).
257 **dear** grievous (*OED a.* 2)
260 **control** hold in check

250.1] *this edn; she walks to the heads and kisses them / G1620; To Lavinia, seeing her kiss the Heads of her Brothers / (Capell); Lucius Kisses one head / Ravenscroft; Lavinia kisses him [i.e. Lucius] / Johnson; Lavinia kisses Titus / Cam* 256 hand] *Q1;* hands *F* 257 son] *Q1;* sonnes *F* 260 thy] *Q1;* my *Q2–3, F*

Rend off thy silver hair, thy other hand
Gnawing with thy teeth, and be this dismal sight
The closing up of our most wretched eyes.
Now is a time to storm. Why art thou still?

TITUS

Ha, ha, ha!   265

MARCUS

Why dost thou laugh? It fits not with this hour.

TITUS

Why? I have not another tear to shed.
Besides, this sorrow is an enemy
And would usurp upon my watery eyes
And make them blind with tributary tears.   270
Then which way shall I find Revenge's cave?
For these two heads do seem to speak to me
And threat me I shall never come to bliss
Till all these mischiefs be returned again
Even in their throats that hath committed them.   275
Come, let me see what task I have to do.
You heavy people, circle me about,
That I may turn me to each one of you
And swear unto my soul to right your wrongs.

[*They make a vow.*]

The vow is made. Come, brother, take a head,   280

---

264 **Why ... still?** Ovid's Hecuba also
has a moment of silence at the height
of grief: 'The Trojane Ladyes shree-
ked out. But shee was dumb for
sorrow. / The anguish of her hart
forclosde as well her speech as eeke /
Her teares devowring them within'
(*Met.*, 13.645–7).

265 **Ha, ha, ha!** the play's pivotal inde-
corum: see introduction, pp. 11–12.
In the Warner production, Brian Cox
laughed maniacally for a full 10
seconds.

270 **tributary** see on 1.1.162

271 **Revenge's cave** Brian Cox paused
before this phrase, as if searching for
the idea of revenge.

273 **threat** portend, give ominous indication (*OED* threaten, 4, earliest
example: *WT* 3.3.4).
me 'to me that' understood

277 **heavy** sorrowful

279.1 ***They make a vow*** For the elaborate ritual at this point in the 1620
German version, see introduction, p.
46.

261 Rend] *Q1* (Rent)   267 Why?] *this edn* (G. R. Proudfoot); Why *Q1*   269 watery] *Q1*
(watrie)   275 hath] *Q1*; haue *Q2–3, F*   279.1] *this edn, after G1620*; They form a circle about
Titus, and he pledges them / Bevington

And in this hand the other will I bear.
And, Lavinia, thou shalt be employed:
Bear thou my hand, sweet wench, between thy teeth.
As for thee, boy, go get thee from my sight:
Thou art an exile and thou must not stay;   285
Hie to the Goths and raise an army there,
And if ye love me, as I think you do,
Let's kiss and part, for we have much to do.

                    [They kiss.] Exeunt. Lucius remains.

LUCIUS
Farewell, Andronicus, my noble father,
The woefull'st man that ever lived in Rome.   290
Farewell, proud Rome, till Lucius come again;
He loves his pledges dearer than his life.
Farewell, Lavinia, my noble sister,
O would thou wert as thou tofore hast been!
But now nor Lucius nor Lavinia lives   295
But in oblivion and hateful griefs.
If Lucius live, he will requite your wrongs
And make proud Saturnine and his empress
Beg at the gates like Tarquin and his queen.
Now will I to the Goths and raise a power,   300
To be revenged on Rome and Saturnine.   *Exit Lucius.*

282–3 *employed ... teeth In Q1 the
first of these two lines ends with an
incomprehensible 'imployde in these
Armes'. The likeliest explanation of
this (first advanced in Cam, 6.534) is
that a corrector could not believe that
the hand was really supposed to be
carried in the mouth and wrote
'Armes' above 'teeth', and the word
was incorporated into the adjacent
line; F tried to make sense of that
line by changing 'Armes' to 'things'.
Earlier in the line, the Q1 compositor
may have skipped over a repeated
pronoun: 'And thou, Lavinia, thou'.

Pace correctors and editors, the
emblem of the hand between the teeth
is perfectly appropriate: it accentuates
Lavinia's role as the *hand*maid of
Revenge.
292 **pledges** sureties, those left behind
as bail (i.e. his family)
294 **tofore** formerly (two words in Qq,F)
298 **empress** Q1's 'Emperesse' suggests
three syllables; 'and his' is probably
monosyllabic ('and's').
299 **Tarquin** For the importance of
Tarquin, Lucrece and Lucius Brutus,
see introduction, p. 92.

282 And] *Q1; not in F* employed] *Oxf;* imployde in these Armes *Q1;* employd in these things
F; employ'd in this *Hudson (Lettsom)* 283 between thy teeth] *Q1;* between thine arms *Oxf* 287
ye] *Q1;* you *Q2–3, F* 288.1 *They kiss] Bevington subst. Lucius remains] F (Manet Lucius)* 298
empress] *Q1* (Emperesse) 299 like] *Q1;* likes *F* 300 power] *Q1* (powre)

3.2   *A banquet. Enter* [TITUS] ANDRONICUS, MARCUS, LAVINIA
         and the Boy [YOUNG LUCIUS].

TITUS

So, so, now sit, and look you eat no more
Than will preserve just so much strength in us
As will revenge these bitter woes of ours.   [*They sit.*]
Marcus, unknit that sorrow-wreathen knot.
Thy niece and I, poor creatures, want our hands   5
And cannot passionate our tenfold grief
With folded arms. This poor right hand of mine
Is left to tyrannize upon my breast,
Who, when my heart, all mad with misery,
Beats in this hollow prison of my flesh,   10
Then thus I thump it down.
[*to Lavinia*]
Thou map of woe, that thus dost talk in signs,
When thy poor heart beats with outrageous beating,
Thou canst not strike it thus to make it still.

3.2 printed in a different typeface because it is an additional scene, first printed in F (see introduction, pp. 117–21)

0.1 *banquet* A table laid with dishes is brought on.

4 **sorrow-wreathen knot** Marcus' arms are folded in a gesture denoting grief.

6 **passionate** express with passion: a new verb in Elizabethan times (*OED v.* 2). The dialogue turns on the capacity of dramatic gesture to passionate grief.

8 **tyrannize** The formal gesture of the tyrant – a violent stabbing or thumping – can be performed with one hand, whereas the expression of grief needs two.

9–11 **Who ... down** The syntax is contorted here: the hand begins as the subject of the 'who' clause, beating

down the thumping heart, but 'I' later takes over. But the contortion is probably the result of Titus' derangement, not of the printer's incompetence: the confused syntax enacts the fragmentation of his self into the mutilated and racked parts of the body.

12 **map** used figuratively for a detailed representation in epitome: a map is a specially coded signifier which 'talk[s] in signs'. Compare Samuel Rowlands, *Guy of Warwick* (1607, p. 59), 'That in her face a map of sorrow wears'. Serpieri notes that maps were particularly associated with the Elizabethan charting of hitherto undiscovered New Worlds: Lavinia is thus an image of previously unimagined woe.

13 **outrageous** violent, excessive

3.2] *scene not in Qq, first printed in F; numbered 3.2 by Capell*   Location] An Apartment in Titus' House *Theobald*   0.1 *banquet*] *F1 (Bnaket)   Titus*] *Rowe*   0.2 YOUNG LUCIUS] *Rowe*   1 TITUS] *Rowe;* AN. *F (throughout scene, nowhere else)*   3 SD] *Oxf*   12 SD] *Johnson*   13 with outrageous] *F2;* without ragious *F*

Wound it with sighing, girl, kill it with groans,   15
Or get some little knife between thy teeth
And just against thy heart make thou a hole,
That all the tears that thy poor eyes let fall
May run into that sink and, soaking in,
Drown the lamenting fool in sea-salt tears.   20

MARCUS

Fie, brother, fie! Teach her not thus to lay
Such violent hands upon her tender life.

TITUS

How now, has sorrow made thee dote already?
Why, Marcus, no man should be mad but I.
What violent hands can she lay on her life?   25
Ah, wherefore dost thou urge the name of hands
To bid Aeneas tell the tale twice o'er
How Troy was burnt and he made miserable?
O handle not the theme, to talk of hands,
Lest we remember still that we have none.   30
Fie, fie, how franticly I square my talk,
As if we should forget we had no hands
If Marcus did not name the word of hands.
Come, let's fall to, and, gentle girl, eat this.

---

15 **Wound ... sighing** Each sigh was
thought to draw a drop of blood from
the heart.

16–17 **knife ... heart** sustains the image
of Lavinia as Philomel, who, once
metamorphosed into a nightingale,
pressed her breast against a thorn 'To
keep [her] sharp woes waking' (*Luc*
1136). 'Between thy teeth' recollects
the action of 3.1.283.

20 **fool** term of endearment, as in Lear
of Cordelia, 'And my poor fool is
hanged' (*KL* 5.3.306)

24 **no man ... but I** This line makes
clear the reason for the addition of
this scene: it is to dramatize Titus'
madness (compare the additions to
Sp. Trag.).

27 **Aeneas ... twice o'er** Allusion to

Aeneid, 2.2: when Dido asks Aeneas
to tell his story, he says that to repeat
it will renew his grief.

29 **handle ... hands** The sustained
verbal play is typical of the drama's
black wit, but Maxwell (Ard²) suggests a possible source for the motif
in Ovid's story of the transformed Io
(see note on 4.1.68 SD): 'when she
did devise, / To *Argus* for to lift hir
handes in meeke and humble wise, /
She sawe she had no handes at all'
(*Met.*, 1.787–9). To 'handle a theme'
was the technical term for dealing
with a subject in a formal rhetorical
discourse.

30 **remember still** keep continually in
mind

31 **square** shape to a pattern; regulate

Here is no drink! Hark, Marcus, what she says: 35
I can interpret all her martyred signs –
She says she drinks no other drink but tears,
Brewed with her sorrow, mashed upon her cheeks.
Speechless complainer, I will learn thy thought.
In thy dumb action will I be as perfect   40
As begging hermits in their holy prayers.
Thou shalt not sigh, nor hold thy stumps to heaven,
Nor wink, nor nod, nor kneel, nor make a sign,
But I of these will wrest an alphabet
And by still practice learn to know thy meaning.   45

BOY

Good grandsire, leave these bitter deep laments;
Make my aunt merry with some pleasing tale.

MARCUS

Alas, the tender boy in passion moved
Doth weep to see his grandsire's heaviness.

TITUS

Peace, tender sapling, thou art made of tears,   50
And tears will quickly melt thy life away.
                    Marcus strikes the dish with a knife.
What dost thou strike at, Marcus, with thy knife?

MARCUS

At that that I have killed, my lord – a fly.

---

35 **no drink** T. W. Craik proposes that
this should be 'to drink': Titus offers
Lavinia a drink and 37 is a response
to her refusal. This is attractive in
its potential for comic business of
pouring and passing a drink with one
hand. But F's question mark suggests
surprise on Titus' part – as if to
say, 'Haven't I got enough problems
without the servants forgetting to
provide drink?' Lavinia's gesture
would then be an attempt to calm
him, 'It's all right, Father, I don't
want a drink'.
36 **martyred** wounded, disfigured, as at
3.1.82: her mutilation impedes the

act of communicative *sign*ification and
requires special *interpret*ative work.
37 **drink but tears** a biblical figure
(compare Psalms, 80.5)
38 **mashed** part of the process of
brewing (still used in northern
England for making tea)
39 **complainer** suggestive of the 'complaint' tradition, a convention of
poetry written from the point of view
of the lamenting, deserted lover (see
Kerrigan)
40 **perfect** sustains the imagery of a language lesson (as in 'word-perfect')
45 **still** constant

35 no drink!] *F (*no drinke?*);* to drink *(T. W. Craik)*   38 mashed] *F (*mesh'd*)*   39 complainer]
Capell; complaynet *F;* complainant *Collier MS*   52 thy knife] *F2;* knife *F*   53 fly] *F2;* Flys *F*

TITUS

> Out on thee, murderer. Thou kill'st my heart.
> Mine eyes are cloyed with view of tyranny;   55
> A deed of death done on the innocent
> Becomes not Titus' brother. Get thee gone;
> I see thou art not for my company.

MARCUS

> Alas, my lord, I have but killed a fly.

TITUS

> 'But'?   60
> How if that fly had a father and a mother?
> How would he hang his slender gilded wings
> And buzz lamenting doings in the air.
> Poor harmless fly,
> That with his pretty buzzing melody   65
> Came here to make us merry, and thou hast killed
>   him.

MARCUS

> Pardon me, sir, it was a black ill-favoured fly,
> Like to the empress' Moor. Therefore I killed him.

TITUS

> Oh, Oh, Oh!
> Then pardon me for reprehending thee,   70
> For thou hast done a charitable deed.

---

54 ***thee** F3's emendation of F's 'the' –
'*The* for *thee* was a common 16th-
century spelling, and sometimes led
to confusion' (Ard²)

60–1 ***'But' ... a mother** One line in F
(where the lineation is very irregular),
which reads 'and mother'. See introduction, pp. 120–1, for discussion of
the emendation here.

63 **doings** actions, performances;
perhaps echoing the 'valiant doings'
of the Andronici (1.1.116) and thus

emphasizing the switch from valour
to lamentation. But the word is odd
here, and various emendations have
been proposed (see t.n.); the problem
with all these is that taken with
'lamenting' they are tautologous.

66–7 **Came ... fly** The metre is irregular and F printed in half-lines. Elision
of 'thou hast' and 'it was' might ease
the speaking of the lines, but in Titus'
case broken metre fits with his broken
mind.

---

54 thee] *F3;* the *F*   55 are cloyed] *F2;* cloi'd *F*   60–1] *1 line in F*   61 a father and a mother?]
Craig; a father and mother? *F;* father, brother? *Hudson (Ritson)*   63 doings] *F;* dolings *Theobald;*
dronings *Hudson;* dotings *(Walker);* dirges *Oxf*   66] *1 line in Capell; 2 lines in F, divided after*
merry,   67] *1 line in Pope; 2 lines in F, divided after* sir,

Give me thy knife; I will insult on him,
Flattering myself as if it were the Moor
Come hither purposely to poison me.
                              [*Takes knife and strikes.*]
There's for thyself, and that's for Tamora.   75
Ah, sirrah!
Yet I think we are not brought so low
But that between us we can kill a fly
That comes in likeness of a coal-black Moor.

MARCUS

Alas, poor man! Grief has so wrought on him   80
He takes false shadows for true substances.

TITUS

Come, take away. Lavinia, go with me;
I'll to thy closet and go read with thee
Sad stories chanced in the times of old.
Come, boy, and go with me; thy sight is young,   85
And thou shalt read when mine begin to dazzle.
                                            Exeunt.

4.1 *Enter Lucius' son* [YOUNG LUCIUS] *and* LAVINIA *running after him, and the Boy flies from her with his books under his arm.* [*He drops the books.*] *Enter* TITUS *and* MARCUS.

---

72 **insult on** triumph scornfully over
81 **shadows ... substances** one of
   Shakespeare's favourite antitheses
82 **take away** clear the table
83 **closet** private room
84 **sad ... old** Serpieri suggests an
   anticipation of Lear's image of himself
   and Cordelia in prison telling each
   other old tales (*KL* 5.3.12)
   chanced chancèd. occurring
86 **mine** my eyes (understood from 'thy
   sight')
4.1 Stagings with an interval, following
   in the tradition of F's act divisions,

usually begin the second half here.
0.1 YOUNG   LUCIUS   For   Young
   Lucius/Boy, see note to List of Roles.
0.3 *He drops the books* action indicated
   by 25. SD after 4 in Oxf and Oxf[1],
   but the sequence implied by 'down
   to throw my books and fly' suggests
   sooner rather than later. The obvious
   staging is for him to enter at one door
   with Lavinia in pursuit, disencumber
   himself of the books, flee across
   towards the other door and into the
   arms of Marcus and Titus, as they
   enter through it. The books would

---

73 myself] *F2;* my selfes *F*   74.1] *Bevington*   75 Tamora] *F (Tamira)*   75–6 *divided thus by
Capell; 1 line in F*   86 begin] *Q1;* begins *Rowe[3]*

4.1] *Rowe; Actus Quartus. F*   Location] Before Titus' House *Capell;* Rome. Titus' Garden
Cam   0.1 YOUNG LUCIUS] *F*   0.3 He ... books] *this edn; after 4 Oxf[1]*

BOY

Help, grandsire, help! My aunt Lavinia
Follows me everywhere, I know not why.
Good uncle Marcus, see how swift she comes.
Alas, sweet aunt, I know not what you mean.

MARCUS

Stand by me, Lucius; do not fear thine aunt.   5

TITUS

She loves thee, boy, too well to do thee harm.

BOY

Ay, when my father was in Rome she did.

MARCUS

What means my niece Lavinia by these signs?

TITUS

Fear her not, Lucius – somewhat doth she mean.

MARCUS

See, Lucius, see how much she makes of thee;   10
Somewhither would she have thee go with her.
Ah, boy, Cornelia never with more care
Read to her sons than she hath read to thee
Sweet poetry and Tully's *Orator*.
Canst thou not guess wherefore she plies thee thus?   15

---

then be lying centre stage, well placed
for the subsequent business. The use
of the doors at either edge of the stage
for the opening of this private scene
which begins the second half of the
play mirrors the use of them at the
opening of the public scene which
begins the first half.

10 *MARCUS Qq,F have Titus speaking
through to 15, but the Boy's reply is
addressed to Marcus, not to Titus
(*grandsire* is in the third person).
Capell gave 15 alone to Marcus, but
the reiterated vocative 'Lucius' in 9
and 10 is more logical in the first line

of Titus' and Marcus' speeches than
in both the first and second lines of a
single speech by Titus – many first
lines in speeches addressed to Young
Lucius in this scene include his
name.

12 **Cornelia** Roman mother, exemplary
for educating her sons, the Gracchi,
who became notable political
reformers

14 **Tully's** *Orator* one of Cicero's widely
studied treatises on rhetoric (*De
Oratore* or *Orator*)

15 **plies** importunes

1 BOY] *F;* PUER *Qq (throughout)*   5 thine] *Q1;* thy *F*   9 her not] *Q1;* not *F*   10 MARCUS]
Hudson; Qq, F continue to TITUS; *Capell assigns only 15 to* MARCUS   11 Somewhither] *Capell;*
Some whither *Q1*   12 Ah] *Q3;* A *Q1*

BOY

My lord, I know not, I, nor can I guess,
Unless some fit or frenzy do possess her.
For I have heard my grandsire say full oft
Extremity of griefs would make men mad,
And I have read that Hecuba of Troy   20
Ran mad for sorrow. That made me to fear,
Although, my lord, I know my noble aunt
Loves me as dear as e'er my mother did,
And would not but in fury fright my youth,
Which made me down to throw my books and fly,   25
Causeless perhaps. But pardon me, sweet aunt,
And, madam, if my uncle Marcus go,
I will most willingly attend your ladyship.

MARCUS

Lucius, I will.   [*Lavinia turns over the books.*]

TITUS

How now, Lavinia? Marcus, what means this?   30
Some book there is that she desires to see.
Which is it, girl, of these? Open them, boy.
[*to Lavinia*]
But thou art deeper read and better skilled:
Come and take choice of all my library,
And so beguile thy sorrow till the heavens   35
Reveal the damned contriver of this deed.

20 **Hecuba** In Ovid's *Metamorphoses* Hecuba (see note on 1.1.139–41) became frenzied with grief and eventually turned into a dog (13.679–85). Cooper's *Thesaurus* says she 'waxed madde'. For both Lavinia and Hecuba, 'Ran mad' suggests actual running as well as 'turning' mad. There is a strikingly close parallel passage in *Ironside*: 'like *Hecuba* the woeful Queen of Troy / who having

no avoidance for her grief / ran mad for sorrow 'cause she could not weep' (1478–80).
24 **fury** a fit of madness
27 **go** accompany us
33 **deeper … skilled** i.e. prepared for more advanced reading than Young Lucius' schoolroom texts, such as the *Metamorphoses*
36 **deed.** F adds, as a separate line, 'What booke?', anticipating 41 – Maxwell is

21 for] *Q1;* through *Q3, F*   29 SD] *Malone subst.*   33 SD] *Oxf*   36] *F adds separate line* What booke?

Why lifts she up her arms in sequence thus?

MARCUS
I think she means that there were more than one
Confederate in the fact. Ay, more there was –
Or else to heaven she heaves them for revenge.   40

TITUS
Lucius, what book is that she tosseth so?

BOY
Grandsire, 'tis Ovid's *Metamorphosis*;
My mother gave it me.

MARCUS   For love of her that's gone,
Perhaps she culled it from among the rest.

TITUS
Soft, so busily she turns the leaves!   *Helps her.*
What would she find? Lavinia, shall I read?   46
This is the tragic tale of Philomel,
And treats of Tereus' treason and his rape –
And rape, I fear, was root of thy annoy.

probably right to call it a 'compositor's vagary' (Ard²).

39 **Ay** Lavinia may nod or repeat her gesture to denote assent here.

41 **tosseth** turns the leaves of

42 **Ovid's *Metamorphosis*** the primary pattern of the play: see introduction, pp. 90–2. Singular and plural form of title used interchangeably in the Renaissance.

43 **gave it** perhaps elided to 'gave't'

45 ***Soft ... Helps her*** The line as printed in Q1 is a syllable short; 'Help her' is printed as the beginning of Titus' next line. Rowe emended to 'Soft, see how busily'; Riv adds 'Help her' to make up this line and reduce the next line, which as printed is a hexameter. But there is plenty of margin at the end of the first line, so it is hard to see why 'Help her' should have been carried over. It is quite fitting for a line beginning 'Soft' to be metrically headless. The second line is a strong pentameter without 'Help her' and it seems to be Titus not Marcus who goes to help her ('shall I read?'), so I agree with Dyce's conjecture that it is a stage direction not a spoken phrase (compare 'Stand up' at 1.1.489 and 'March away' at 5.1.165).

47–8 **Philomel ... Tereus'** the Ovidian precedent again

49 **annoy** mental anguish deriving from involuntary reception of external impressions (*OED sb.* 1)

38 were] *Q1;* was *Q3, F* 40 for] *Q1;* to *F* 42 *Metamorphosis*] *Qq, F; Metamorphoses Pope* 45 so] *Q1;* see how *Rowe Helps her*] as SD (*Dyce*); *Qq, F* text of 46 Help her, what would she finde? *Lauinia* shal I reade? 49 thy] *Q1;* thine *Q2–3, F*

MARCUS

　See, brother, see: note how she quotes the leaves.　　50

TITUS

　Lavinia, wert thou thus surprised, sweet girl,
　Ravished and wronged as Philomela was,
　Forced in the ruthless, vast and gloomy woods?
　[*Lavinia nods.*] See, see!
　Ay, such a place there is where we did hunt –　　55
　O, had we never, never hunted there! –
　Patterned by that the poet here describes,
　By nature made for murders and for rapes.

MARCUS

　O, why should nature build so foul a den,
　Unless the gods delight in tragedies?　　60

TITUS

　Give signs, sweet girl – for here are none but
　　friends –
　What Roman lord it was durst do the deed.
　Or slunk not Saturnine, as Tarquin erst,
　That left the camp to sin in Lucrece' bed?

MARCUS

　Sit down, sweet niece. Brother, sit down by me.　　65
　　　　　　　　　　　　　　　　　　[*They sit.*]

---

50 **quotes** observes, marks, perhaps with the more specific sense of citing a particular passage. Probably originally pronounced as spelt in Q1, 'coats'.

51–8 **wert thou ... for rapes** Marcus has already intuited this pattern at 2.3.26–43, but as if in a trance; it now has to be spelt out with painful explicitness.

51 **thou** Oxf italicizes to suggest the stress

53 **vast** waste, desolate

54 ***Lavinia nods** A gesture of assent is clearly indicated by 'See, see!': my SD is taken from the 1620 German acting version, where '*She sighs deeply and nods her head*'.

57 **patterned ... here** for the gloomy woodland setting, see *Met.*, 6.663–4 (appendix, p. 279)

60 **tragedies** The primary sense when Shakespeare uses the word is 'dire events', but there is often a play on the idea of tragedy as something plotted theatrically (as at 2.2.265), performed on a stage (e.g. 'Black stage for tragedies and murders fell' – *Luc* 766), or, as here, watched by a 'delighted' audience.

---

50 quotes] *Q1 (*coats)　54 SD] *this edn, after G1620*　54–5] *divided thus by Pope; 1 line in Qq,* F　65.1] *Bevington*

Apollo, Pallas, Jove or Mercury
Inspire me, that I may this treason find.
My lord, look here; look here, Lavinia.

He writes his name with his staff,
and guides it with feet and mouth.

This sandy plot is plain. Guide, if thou canst,
This after me. I here have writ my name   70
Without the help of any hand at all.
Cursed be that heart that forced us to this shift.
Write thou, good niece, and here display at last
What God will have discovered for revenge.
Heaven guide thy pen to print thy sorrows plain,   75
That we may know the traitors and the truth.

She takes the staff in her mouth,
and guides it with her stumps, and writes.

O do ye read, my lord, what she hath writ?

TITUS
Stuprum – Chiron – Demetrius.

MARCUS
What, what? The lustful sons of Tamora

66 **Apollo ... Mercury** Apollo was associated with the discovery of truth, Pallas Athene with law, Jove with the punishment of crime and the messenger-god Mercury with carrying forward the will of Jove.

68.1 *He writes his name* Maxwell (Ard²) proposes a source in Ovid: Io is raped by Jupiter and transformed into a cow; she tries to tell her father who she is, 'But for bicause she could not speake, she printed in the sande, / Two letters with hir foote, whereby was given to understande / The sorrowfull chaunging of hir shape' (*Met.*, 1.804–6). Io writes her own name; Shakespeare adapts the device into a substitute for Philomel's revelation of her rapist's identity in her 'tedious sampler'.

70 **after me** following my example

*I here have Q1's 'I have' produces an awkwardly truncated line, so I follow Oxf in adopting W. S. Walker's conjectural emendation – '*here* might easily have been omitted because of its resemblance to *have*' (*TxC*, 212).

72 **shift** dire expedient

74 **discovered for** revealed to require

78 *TITUS Q1–2 continue with Marcus speaking, but the repeated SP at 79 shows there is an error. Q3 tried to correct by assigning both 77 and 78 to Titus, but 'my lord' is how Marcus addresses his brother, not vice versa; Maxwell (Ard²) was surely right to give 78 alone to Titus. With his usual theatrical good sense, Ravenscroft saw that Titus must be the one who first reads out the terrible text.

Stuprum Latin: rape

68.1–2] *Q1; Collier places in 70 after me.* 70 I here have] *(Walker); I haue Q1; See, I have Keightley* 72 this shift] *Q1; that shift F* 78 TITUS] *Ravenscroft, Ard²; Q1–2 continue 77–8 to* MARCUS; *Q3,F assign 77–8 to* TITUS

Performers of this heinous bloody deed?   80

TITUS

Magni dominator poli,
Tam lentus audis scelera, tam lentus vides?

MARCUS

O calm thee, gentle lord, although I know
There is enough written upon this earth
To stir a mutiny in the mildest thoughts   85
And arm the minds of infants to exclaims.
My lord, kneel down with me; Lavinia, kneel;
And kneel, sweet boy, the Roman Hector's hope,

                                        [*They kneel.*]

And swear with me – as, with the woeful fere
And father of that chaste dishonoured dame,   90
Lord Junius Brutus swore for Lucrece' rape –
That we will prosecute by good advice
Mortal revenge upon these traitorous Goths,
And see their blood, or die with this reproach.

                                        [*They rise.*]

TITUS

'Tis sure enough, and you knew how.   95
But if you hunt these bear-whelps, then beware:
The dam will wake, and if she wind ye once

81–2 **Magni ... vides?** Senecan Latin:
'Ruler of the great heavens, are you
so slow to hear crimes, so slow to
see?' Demetrius announces the
intended rape of Lavinia with a quotation from *Hippolytus* at 1.1.635;
Titus reacts to the discovery of it with
a quotation from the same play. See
further, introduction, p. 30.
86 **exclaims** outcries, protests
88 **Roman Hector's** As Hector was the
greatest of the Trojan warriors, so
Lucius is claimed as a Roman equivalent and his son is implicitly made
into Astyanax, Hector's son (who was
thrown from the walls of Troy: this
raises the fleeting possibility that the

Boy will not survive; that he is on the
contrary a witness and a survivor was
a focal point of the BBC production).
89 **fere** spouse
91 **Junius ... rape** see introduction, pp.
18, 92
  ***swore** As F3 realized, the past tense
is needed here; I adopt the appropriate modernized form.
92 **prosecute ... advice** pursue by well-
considered means
95 **and** if
97 **The dam** The mother bear was traditionally ferocious when bereft of her
whelps.
  wind get wind of

---

81 *Magni*] *Q1*; *Magne Theobald*   88 hope] *Q2*; h op *Q1* (slipped to edge of page, with h
broken)   88.1] *Collier MS subst.*   91 swore] *F3* (sware); sweare *Qq, F*   94.1] *Bevington*   97 ye]
Q1; you *Q2–3, F*

She's with the lion deeply still in league,
And lulls him whilst she playeth on her back,
And when he sleeps will she do what she list.   100
You are a young huntsman, Marcus. Let alone,
And come, I will go get a leaf of brass
And with a gad of steel will write these words,
And lay it by. The angry northern wind
Will blow these sands like Sibyl's leaves abroad,   105
And where's our lesson then? Boy, what say you?

BOY

I say, my lord, that if I were a man
Their mother's bedchamber should not be safe
For these base bondmen to the yoke of Rome.

MARCUS

Ay, that's my boy! Thy father hath full oft   110
For his ungrateful country done the like.

BOY

And, uncle, so will I, and if I live.

TITUS

Come, go with me into mine armoury:
Lucius, I'll fit thee, and withal my boy
Shall carry from me to the empress' sons   115
Presents that I intend to send them both.
Come, come, thou'lt do my message, wilt thou not?

BOY

Ay, with my dagger in their bosoms, grandsire.

---

101 **young … alone** i.e. 'you're behaving like an inexperienced huntsman; leave off (*let alone*) the direct approach, let us store up (*lay by*) our revenge [until it can be carried out more subtly]'

102–3 **leaf … words** 'Injuries are written in brass' was proverbial (Tilley, I71). An inscription on brass should endure, unlike writing on sand (hence the blowing *leaves* at 105).

103 **gad** sharp spike, applied to a stylus

105 **Sibyl's leaves** The Cumaean Sibyl, renowned from Virgil and other classical sources, wrote her prophecies on leaves which were sometimes blown away before there was time to read them.

109 **bondmen** slaves; men in bondage, implicitly overturning Saturninus' freeing of Chiron and Demetrius in Act 1

114 **fit** furnish with arms

101 Let] *Q1;* let it *Q3, F*   106 our] *Q1;* you *Q2;* your *Q3, F*   109 base] *Q1;* bad *Q2–3, F*   117 my] *Q1;* thy *Q2–3, F*

217

TITUS

   No, boy, not so; I'll teach thee another course.

   Lavinia, come; Marcus, look to my house;   120

   Lucius and I'll go brave it at the court.

   Ay, marry, will we, sir, and we'll be waited on.

                              Exeunt [all but Marcus.]

MARCUS

   O heavens, can you hear a good man groan

   And not relent or not compassion him?

   Marcus, attend him in his ecstasy   125

   That hath more scars of sorrow in his heart

   Than foemen's marks upon his battered shield,

   But yet so just that he will not revenge.

   Revenge the heavens for old Andronicus!   *Exit.*

4.2   *Enter* AARON, CHIRON *and* DEMETRIUS *at one
door, and at the other door* YOUNG LUCIUS *and another, with
a bundle of weapons, and verses writ upon them.*

CHIRON

   Demetrius, here's the son of Lucius:

   He hath some message to deliver us.

AARON

   Ay, some mad message from his mad grandfather.

BOY

   My lords, with all the humbleness I may,

---

121 **brave it** swagger, put on a show (compare 'court it', 1.1.591)

122 **be waited on** 'i.e. not ignored as hitherto' (Cam[1])

124 **compassion** have compassion on: strong Shakespearean noun-to-verb conversion (*OED*'s earliest occurrence)

125 **ecstasy** fit of madness

126–7 **scars ... marks** yet another image of the inscription of wounds upon the body

129 **Revenge the heavens** i.e. 'let the heavens carry out the revenge, since he won't'

4.2 As in the first half of the play, so in the second, the second main sequence of action involves Aaron, Chiron and Demetrius.

0.2 *another* an attendant (hence Bevington's SD at 16.1)

122.1 *all but Marcus*] *Capell subst.*   123 good man] *Q1 (*goodman*)*

4.2] *Pope*   Location] The Palace *Theobald*   0.2 the other] *Q1; another Q2–3, F*

I greet your honours from Andronicus –   5
[*aside*] And pray the Roman gods confound you both.
DEMETRIUS
Gramercy, lovely Lucius. What's the news?
BOY   [*aside*]
That you are both deciphered, that's the news,
For villains marked with rape. [*to them*]
                       May it please you,
My grandsire, well advised, hath sent by me   10
The goodliest weapons of his armoury
To gratify your honourable youth,
The hope of Rome, for so he bid me say,
And so I do, and with his gifts present
Your lordships that, whenever you have need,   15
You may be armed and appointed well.
                [*Attendant presents the weapons.*]
And so I leave you both [*aside*] like bloody villains.
                    Exit [*with Attendant*].
DEMETRIUS
What's here? A scroll, and written round about?
Let's see:
[*reads*] *Integer vitae, scelerisque purus,*   20
Non eget Mauri iaculis, nec arcu.

---

7 **Gramercy** thank you (as at 1.1.499)
8 **deciphered** discovered, but perhaps also with sense of 'interpreted'
10 **well advised** in his right mind (contradicts line 3)
15 ***that** The word is lacking in the early edns, but both sense and metre require it; written in abbreviated form, it could easily have been overlooked by a compositor.
16 **armed** armèd
17 *aside* 'Q1 indicates the aside by a capital for *Like*, preceded by a rather long space and a colon after *both*' (Ard[2]). In the Warner production, the line was thrown back as the Boy ran off.
20–1 *Integer . . . arcu* Latin: 'the man of upright life and free from crime does not need the javelins or bows of the Moor' (Horace, *Odes*, 1.22.1–2). 'Quite literally, a barbed allusion' (James, 132). 'Mauris' in modern edns of Horace, but 'Mauri' in the grammar cited in 23.

6 SD] *Capell (also at 8, 17)*   8] *Q1; not in F (which thus attribs. 9–17 to Deme.)*   9 SD] *this edn; Aloud / Ard[2]* villains] *Q1;* villainie's *F*   13 bid] *Q1;* bad *Q3, F*   15 that] *Pope*   16.1] *Bevington*   17.1 *with Attendant*] *Capell subst.*   20 SD] *Capell*   20–1] *divided thus by Theobald; 1 line in Qq; 2 lines (prose) in F*   21 arcu] *Q1;* arcus *Q2–3, F*

CHIRON

O, 'tis a verse in Horace, I know it well:
I read it in the grammar long ago.

AARON

Ay, just – a verse in Horace, right, you have it.
[*aside*] Now what a thing it is to be an ass.   25
Here's no sound jest! The old man hath found their
        guilt,
And sends them weapons wrapped about with lines
That wound beyond their feeling to the quick.
But were our witty empress well afoot
She would applaud Andronicus' conceit.   30
But let her rest in her unrest awhile.
[*to them*]
And now, young lords, was't not a happy star
Led us to Rome, strangers and, more than so,
Captives, to be advanced to this height?
It did me good before the palace gate   35
To brave the tribune in his brother's hearing.

DEMETRIUS

But me more good to see so great a lord
Basely insinuate and send us gifts.

---

23 **in the grammar** Lily's Latin grammar (*Brevissima Institutio*), the standard text-book in schools from 1540 onwards, in which the quotation occurs twice.
24 **just** just so, precisely
25 *aside* T. W. Craik conjectures that only 'an ass' is spoken aside, as if Aaron begins to say 'Now what a thing it is to be a scholar', then turns the sentiment around (a technique often used in *The Jew of Malta*). But since this is a long aside continuing to 31 it would be awkward to begin it with a line that is initially addressed to the others.
26 **no sound jest** ironic: it could not be sounder. For ironic use of negative, compare 'Here's no foppery' in

Jonson, *Every Man in his Humour*, 4.2.17.
28 **wound ... quick** i.e. the message does touch the matter to the quick, but the boys are so stupid that they don't sense it
29 **witty** quick-witted
   afoot up and about. Together with 'rest in her unrest' (31) and 'her pains' (47), first intimations of Tamora's pregnancy
31 **rest ... unrest** see on 2.2.8–9, though here there is the added sense of the *pains* (47) of labour
34 **advanced** advancèd
38 **insinuate** Demetrius misinterprets the message as a strategy for gaining entrance at court.

24 Ay, just –] I just, *Q1*   25 SD] *Johnson*   27 them] *Q1*; the *Q3, F*   32 SD] *Collier MS*

AARON

    Had he not reason, Lord Demetrius?

    Did you not use his daughter very friendly? 40

DEMETRIUS

    I would we had a thousand Roman dames

    At such a bay, by turn to serve our lust.

CHIRON

    A charitable wish, and full of love.

AARON

    Here lacks but your mother for to say amen.

CHIRON

    And that would she, for twenty thousand more. 45

DEMETRIUS

    Come, let us go and pray to all the gods

    For our beloved mother in her pains.

AARON

    Pray to the devils; the gods have given us over.

Trumpets sound.

DEMETRIUS

    Why do the emperor's trumpets flourish thus?

CHIRON

    Belike for joy the emperor hath a son. 50

DEMETRIUS

    Soft, who comes here?

Enter Nurse *with a blackamoor child.*

NURSE

    Good morrow, lords.

    O tell me, did you see Aaron the Moor?

---

40 **friendly** kindly (ironic); for grammatical form, see on 1.1.223
42 **At such a bay** cornered thus (the
hunting metaphor again)
47 **beloved** belovèd

50 **Belike** probably
52 **Good morrow** 'God morrow' in Q1,
'Good' in Q3: alternative contractions
of 'God give you good morrow'

48.1] *Q1; Flourish F* 51.1] *Q1; Collier MS adds SD / hiding its face* 52 Good] *Q3;* God
Q1 52–3] *divided thus in F; 1 line in Q q*

221

AARON

Well, more or less, or ne'er a whit at all:
Here Aaron is, and what with Aaron now?   55

NURSE

O gentle Aaron, we are all undone.
Now help, or woe betide thee evermore!

AARON

Why, what a caterwauling dost thou keep!
What dost thou wrap and fumble in thy arms?

NURSE

O, that which I would hide from heaven's eye,   60
Our empress' shame and stately Rome's disgrace:
She is delivered, lords, she is delivered.

AARON

To whom?

NURSE

I mean she is brought abed.

AARON

Well, God give her good rest. What hath he sent
her?   65

NURSE

A devil.

AARON

Why then, she is the devil's dam: a joyful issue.

NURSE

A joyless, dismal, black and sorrowful issue.
Here is the babe, as loathsome as a toad
Amongst the fair-faced breeders of our clime.   70
The empress sends it thee, thy stamp, thy seal,

---

54 **more** A pun to please the ground-
     lings?
55 **what** what's your business
67 **devil's dam** 'The Devil and his dam
     [mother]' was proverbial (Tilley,
     D225).
67, 68 **issue** plays on (1) outcome (2)
     offspring

69 **toad** proverbially loathsome (Tilley,
     T361)
70 **fair-faced** *OED*'s interpretation of
     Q1's 'fairefast' (supported by 'bare-
     faste', the spelling of 'barefaced' in
     Ham Q2, 4.5.165 – Oxf[1])
71 **stamp, seal** means of inscription
     denoting possession

---

59 thy] *Q1;* thine *Q2–3, F*   70 fair-faced] *Cam[1]* (following *OED*); fairefast *Q1;* fairest *Q3, F*

And bids thee christen it with thy dagger's point.

AARON

Zounds, ye whore, is black so base a hue?

[*to the baby*]

Sweet blowze, you are a beauteous blossom, sure.

DEMETRIUS

Villain, what hast thou done?   75

AARON

That which thou canst not undo.

CHIRON

Thou hast undone our mother.

AARON

Villain, I have done thy mother.

DEMETRIUS

And therein, hellish dog, thou hast undone her.

Woe to her chance and damned her loathed choice,   80

Accursed the offspring of so foul a fiend.

CHIRON

It shall not live.

AARON

It shall not die.

NURSE

Aaron, it must: the mother wills it so.

AARON

What, must it, nurse? Then let no man but I   85

Do execution on my flesh and blood.

---

73 **Zounds** The play's only oath (from
  'God's wounds'), censored out of the
  Folio text because of the 1606 Act
  against profanity in stage plays.
74 **blowze** 'a ruddy fat-faced wench'
  (Johnson): wittily inverted to apply to
  a black male baby (also used ironically
  by Webster, *White Devil*, 5.6.3). The
  editor of 1948 thought the joke concerned the doll representing the baby
  ('to raise a laugh at a hideous sort of

golliwog' – Cam[1]); the more racially
sensitive editor of 1984 suggested that
in applying the phrase ironically
'Aaron continues his reaction against
the nurse's contempt for blackness'
(Oxf[1]).

78 **done** pun on bawdy sense of 'copulate
  with'
80 **loathed** loathèd (*damned* is one
  syllable)

---

73 Zounds, ye] *Q1;* Out you *F*   74 SD] *Oxf[1]*   78] *Q1; not in F*   79 undone her] *Q1;* undone
Q3, F

DEMETRIUS

I'll broach the tadpole on my rapier's point.
Nurse, give it me; my sword shall soon dispatch it.

AARON

Sooner this sword shall plough thy bowels up.
        [*Draws his sword and takes the child.*]
Stay, murderous villains, will you kill your brother?   90
Now, by the burning tapers of the sky
That shone so brightly when this boy was got,
He dies upon my scimitar's sharp point
That touches this, my first-born son and heir.
I tell you, younglings, not Enceladus   95
With all his threatening band of Typhon's brood,
Nor great Alcides, nor the god of war,
Shall seize this prey out of his father's hands.
What, what, ye sanguine, shallow-hearted boys,
Ye white-limed walls, ye alehouse painted signs!   100
Coal-black is better than another hue
In that it scorns to bear another hue;
For all the water in the ocean
Can never turn the swan's black legs to white,
Although she lave them hourly in the flood.   105

---

87 **broach** stick, as on a spit
93 **scimitar's** In the Victorian production, Ira Aldridge held a splendid weapon (Fig. 6).
95 **Enceladus** one of the Giants who fought against the Olympian gods
96 **threatening** 'threatning' (Q1)
   Typhon's brood Typhon was another giant (and father of monsters) who fought against the gods; originally in Greek mythology, both Enceladus and Typhon were sons of Ge, the earth-mother, but poets often conflated different giants/monsters and confused their relations.
97 **Alcides** Hercules, of legendary strength

the god of war Mars, completing the catalogue of strong men
99 **sanguine** red-faced (in contrast to black)
100 **white-limed** daubed with lime, but punning on 'white-limbed'
   alehouse painted signs crudely painted. The whole passage inverts the traditional idea that white is the 'natural' colour, making it on the contrary a crude artificial covering, where black is authentic and incapable of bearing false face.
102 **scorns ... hue** proverbial: 'black will take no other hue' (Tilley, B436)
103 **ocean** three syllables (also at 4.3.6)
104–5 **swan's ... flood** neat adaptation

89.1] *Capell subst.; Aron takes the child from the Woman / Ravenscroft*   97 Alcides] *Q2; Alciades Q1*   100 white-limed] *Q1 (whitelimde); white limbde Q2–3; white-limb'd F; white-lim'd F3*

Tell the empress from me I am of age
To keep mine own, excuse it how she can.

DEMETRIUS

Wilt thou betray thy noble mistress thus?

AARON

My mistress is my mistress, this myself,
The vigour and the picture of my youth.   110
This before all the world do I prefer,
This maugre all the world will I keep safe,
Or some of you shall smoke for it in Rome.

DEMETRIUS

By this our mother is for ever shamed.

CHIRON

Rome will despise her for this foul escape.   115

NURSE

The emperor in his rage will doom her death.

CHIRON

I blush to think upon this ignomy.

AARON

Why, there's the privilege your beauty bears.
Fie, treacherous hue, that will betray with blushing
The close enacts and counsels of thy heart.   120

---

of the proverbial 'To wash [*lave*] an Ethiop/blackamoor/Moor white' (Tilley, E186)

106–7 **I am ... mine own** i.e. 'I am not so young that a guardian will be required for the child' – but perhaps still a reminder that Tamora's lovers are younger than herself.

110 **vigour** a transferred epithet: the child is the result of Aaron's sexual energy. Compare Marston, *Antonio's Revenge*, 3.1.44, where a father refers to his son as 'Thou vigour of my youth, juice of my love'. Oxf notes that 'vigour' could be an old spelling of 'figure' and emends accordingly (see Wells, *Re-Editing*, 55–6), but this

reduces the phrase to a tautology rather than a 'characteristic Shakespearean hendiadys' (Cam[1]).

112 **maugre** in spite of (French *malgré*)

113 **smoke** suffer (originally from burning at the stake)

115 **escape** sexual transgression; in *WT*, the contracted form 'scape' is used for the 'behind-door-work' which has led to the birth of an apparently illegitimate child (3.3.72)

117 **ignomy** common contracted form of 'ignominy'

120 **close enacts** secret actions, purposes; typically Shakespearean verb-to-noun conversion

---

110 vigour] *Q1*; figure *Oxf*   117 ignomy] *Q1*; ignominie *F*   120 thy] *Q1*; the *Q3, F*

Here's a young lad framed of another leer:
Look how the black slave smiles upon the father,
As who should say, 'Old lad, I am thine own.'
He is your brother, lords, sensibly fed
Of that self blood that first gave life to you,   125
And from that womb where you imprisoned were
He is enfranchised and come to light.
Nay, he is your brother by the surer side,
Although my seal be stamped in his face.

NURSE
Aaron, what shall I say unto the empress?   130

DEMETRIUS
Advise thee, Aaron, what is to be done
And we will all subscribe to thy advice.
Save thou the child, so we may all be safe.

AARON
Then sit we down and let us all consult.
My son and I will have the wind of you.   135
Keep there. [*They sit.*]
                    Now talk at pleasure of your safety.

121 **leer** The primary sense is 'complexion', but *OED* (*sb.*[2]) cites Shakespeare (*MW* 1.3.45) for the first usage of the new sense of 'A side glance; a look or roll of the eye expressive of slyness, malignity': if the baby is like either of its parents, it may have a smiling countenance, as Aaron claims, but its true nature will be expressed in the glance and the aside.

124 **sensibly** 'perceptibly' (*OED adv.* 1) seems perfectly acceptable in context, but eds more frequently gloss as 'made capable of sensation' (Oxf[1]).

125 **self** abbreviated form of 'self-same'

126 *****that** 'your' in Q1, which sounds very odd in context. I follow other eds in accepting Q3's emendation; Waith (Oxf[1]) suggests that if 'that' were written 'y", it could easily have been read as 'y".

127 **enfranchised** enfranchisèd. Baildon (Ard[1]) notes the same line of imagery in *WT*: 'This child was prisoner to the womb, and is / By law and process of great Nature thence / Freed and enfranchised' (2.2.57–9).

128 **surer side** 'Mamma's baby, Pappa's maybe', as the saying has it: Tilley (M1205) quotes a speech of Henry V in Hall's *Chronicle* (1548), 'if the old and trite proverb be true that the woman's side is the surer side'.

129 **stamped** stampèd

133 **so** provided that (compare 1.1.602)

135 **have the wind of** watch as a hunter does from the security of a downwind position

136 *They sit* The SD, first introduced by Ravenscroft, is demanded by the dialogue.

126 that] *Q3, F;* your *Q1*   136 SD] *Rowe subst. (at end of line); All sit down upon the ground, and the Moor at a distance with his Sword between / Ravenscroft*

DEMETRIUS   [*to the Nurse*]
How many women saw this child of his?
AARON
Why, so, brave lords, when we join in league
I am a lamb – but if you brave the Moor,
The chafed boar, the mountain lioness,   140
The ocean, swells not so as Aaron storms.
[*to the Nurse*]
But say again, how many saw the child?
NURSE
Cornelia the midwife, and myself,
And no one else but the delivered empress.
AARON
The empress, the midwife and yourself.   145
Two may keep counsel when the third's away.
Go to the empress, tell her this I said: *He kills her.*
'Wheak, wheak!' – so cries a pig prepared to the
    spit.
                                          [*All stand up.*]
DEMETRIUS
What mean'st thou, Aaron? Wherefore didst thou
    this?

138 **Why ... league** The line is one
syllable short. See t.n. for proposed
emendations, but monosyllables containing vowel followed by 'r' were
often prolonged (ló-rds), and Ravenscroft, who often regularized, saw
no need to alter the line.
138–9 **brave ... brave** The adjectival
usage refers to the cocky bravado
the boys have shown throughout, the
verbal one warns them not to defy
Aaron (who is truly fearless, as they
are not).
140 **chafed** chaféd; angry, irritated
143 **Cornelia** In seeking a Roman name
for the midwife, Shakespeare's mind

went back to 4.1.12.
145 **empress** three syllables: 'Emperess'
(Capell)
146 **Two ... away** proverbial (Dent,
T642.1), like many of the idioms in
this scene
148 **prepared** preparèd
148.1 *All stand up* Modern eds such as
Wells (Oxf) and Bevington include a
direction to sit, but not one to stand;
the exact moment of standing and its
relation to the killing of the Nurse
would have to be worked out in
rehearsal, but Ravenscroft (see t.n.)
stages the moment effectively.

137 SD] *Oxf¹ (also at 142)*   138 we join] *Q1;* we all ioyne *F2;* we are join'd *(Ard²)*; we do join
Oxf   147 SD] *Q1;* Collier MS adds SD: she cries out   148.1] *Ravenscroft (Aron Stabs the Woman,
she dyes, all stands up)*

AARON

O Lord, sir, 'tis a deed of policy: 150
Shall she live to betray this guilt of ours?
A long-tongued, babbling gossip? No, lords, no.
And now be it known to you, my full intent.
Not far one Muly lives, my countryman:
His wife but yesternight was brought to bed;   155
His child is like to her, fair as you are.
Go pack with him and give the mother gold,
And tell them both the circumstance of all,
And how by this their child shall be advanced
And be received for the emperor's heir,   160
And substituted in the place of mine,
To calm this tempest whirling in the court;
And let the emperor dandle him for his own.
Hark ye, lords, you see I have given her physic,
And you must needs bestow her funeral;   165
The fields are near and you are gallant grooms.

---

150 **policy** expedience, shading into cunning (*OED sb.*[1] 4)
152 **long-tongued** chattering
154 *****Muly lives** Qq, F have '*Muliteus my Countriman / His wife but ...*' Though grammatically possible, this is awkward, especially since 'him' in the next sentence reads better if the man is the subject of the previous sentence. Steevens conjectured: 'This line being too long by a foot, *Muliteus*, no Moorish name (or indeed any name at all), and the verb *lives* wanting to the sense in the old copy, I suspect the designation of Aaron's friend to be a corruption, and that our author wrote: "Not far, one *Muley* lives, my countryman." "Muley lives" was easily changed by a blundering transcriber, or printer, into *Muliteus*.' Peele's *Battle of Alcazar* was also known, after its villainous Moor, as *Muly Mahomet*.

156 **like to her** i.e. in contrast to Aaron's son, this is a white child of a mixed union
157 **pack** make an arrangement, conspire
160 **received** receivèd
164 **physic** medicine (ironic)
165 **bestow** give (*OED* 6c), perhaps also playing on two other senses, to stow away and to provide with a resting-place (*OED* 2, 3)
166 **grooms** Most eds gloss 'fellows', but more specific senses are relevant: in the Elizabethan court, Groom was the designation of various officers who would undertake arrangements for special events (such as funerals); in pastoral poetry, the word was frequently applied, often contemptuously, to herdsmen (for whom Chiron and Demetrius might be mistaken while about their burying business in the fields).

---

154 Muly lives] *(Steevens)*; Muliteus *Q q, F;* Muliteus lives *Rowe*   164 you] *Q1;* ye *Q3, F*   physic] *Q1; Johnson adds SD / Pointing to the Nurse*

This done, see that you take no longer days,
But send the midwife presently to me.
The midwife and the nurse well made away,
Then let the ladies tattle what they please.   170

CHIRON
Aaron, I see thou wilt not trust the air
With secrets.

DEMETRIUS
                        For this care of Tamora,
Herself and hers are highly bound to thee.
        Exeunt [Chiron and Demetrius, with the Nurse's body].

AARON
Now to the Goths, as swift as swallow flies,
There to dispose this treasure in mine arms   175
And secretly to greet the empress' friends.
Come on, you thick-lipped slave, I'll bear you hence,
For it is you that puts us to our shifts.
I'll make you feed on berries and on roots,
And fat on curds and whey, and suck the goat,   180
And cabin in a cave, and bring you up
To be a warrior and command a camp.   *Exit.*

---

167 **days** time
168 **presently** immediately
171 **Aaron ... air** Theobald's lineation
    (see t.n.) highlights the pun by
    placing Aaron and air at the beginning
    and end of the line. 'Trust the air'
    was proverbial (Dent, A94.2).
178 **puts ... shifts** literally, 'causes us
    to have recourse to stratagems', but
    more generally 'creates trouble for us'
    (proverbial – Tilley, S337).
180 *****fat** Qq,F repeat the previous line's
    'feed'. Wells gives good reasons for
    adopting Cartwright's conjecture:

'The repetition of both word and
construction seems implausible; a
baby seems more likely to "fat" than
to "feast" [Hanmer's conj.] *on curds
and whey*' (*TxC*, 212). Aaron uses the
verb at 3.1.204.
curds and whey coagulated milk,
roughly the Elizabethan equivalent of
yoghurt; the diet of Tacitus' idealized
Germans
suck drink the milk of
181 **cabin** lodge (very new usage, by
noun-to-verb conversion)

171–2] *divided thus by Theobald;* aire with secrets. / For this *Qq, F* 173.1 *Chiron ... body] Capell
subst.*   180 fat] *(Cartwright);* feed *Qq, F;* feast *Hanmer*

4.3 *Enter* TITUS, OLD MARCUS, YOUNG LUCIUS, *and other Gentlemen* [*Marcus' son* PUBLIUS; *kinsmen of the Andronici,* CAIUS *and* SEMPRONIUS] *with bows; and Titus bears the arrows with letters on the ends of them.*

TITUS

Come, Marcus, come; kinsmen, this is the way.
Sir Boy, let me see your archery.
Look ye draw home enough, and 'tis there straight.
Terras Astraea reliquit: be you remembered, Marcus,
She's gone, she's fled. Sirs, take you to your tools.   5
You, cousins, shall go sound the ocean
And cast your nets:
Happily you may catch her in the sea;
Yet there's as little justice as at land.
No, Publius and Sempronius, you must do it,   10
'Tis you must dig with mattock and with spade,
And pierce the inmost centre of the earth.
Then, when you come to Pluto's region,

2 **Sir Boy** could be two vocatives, 'Sir, boy,' but 'Sir Boy' is an appropriately chivalric form of address for the context. F capitalizes 'Boy' here, but has it lower-case for vocatives elsewhere.
3 **home** term in archery for drawing bow to full extent
4 *Terras ... reliquit* 'Astraea [goddess of Justice] has left the earth' (Ovid, *Met.*, 1.150). Twice quoted in English in *Sp. Trag.*, 3.13.108, 140. The departure of Astraea heralds the Age of Iron, a time of violence and social/familial discord. Queen Elizabeth was frequently mythologized as Astraea.
5–15 **She's gone ... for justice** Titus' language wildly literalizes the metaphoric search above and below for the absent Astraea/Justice.

6 **ocean** trisyllabic
7–8 **And ... sea** One very long line in Q1; F abbreviates *happily* ('perhaps') to 'haply' to shorten it slightly. Capell's relineation of 4–7 (see t.n.) is attractive in that it gives the Latin tag a line to itself, as is common in the play, and it avoids the introduction of a short line, but it is metrically awkward in places. Since the lines cannot be regularized, it seems best, as Waith says (Oxf¹), to interfere with the Q1 lineation as little as possible.
11 **mattock** agricultural tool, similar to pick, used for loosening hard ground. In *Sp. Trag.* (3.12.65–78) Hieronimo cries 'Justice, O justice!' and digs with his dagger in the ground.
13 **Pluto's region** the classical underworld

4.3] *Capell* Location] A Street near the Palace *Theobald* 0.2 *Marcus' son* PUBLIUS] *Bevington subst. kinsmen of the Andronici*] *this edn* 0.3 CAIUS *and* SEMPRONIUS] *Cam* 0.4 *ends*] *Q1; end F* 2 let] *Q1; now let F2* 7–8] *divided thus by* Ard²; *1 line in* Qq, *F; Capell lines: reliquit,*/fled/shall/nets/ 8 Happily] *Q1;* haply *F* catch] *Q1;* finde *Q3, F*

I pray you deliver him this petition.
Tell him it is for justice and for aid,   15
And that it comes from old Andronicus,
Shaken with sorrows in ungrateful Rome.
Ah, Rome! Well, well, I made thee miserable
What time I threw the people's suffrages
On him that thus doth tyrannize o'er me.   20
Go, get you gone, and pray be careful all,
And leave you not a man-of-war unsearched:
This wicked emperor may have shipped her hence,
And, kinsmen, then we may go pipe for justice.

MARCUS
O Publius, is not this a heavy case,   25
To see thy noble uncle thus distract?

PUBLIUS
Therefore, my lords, it highly us concerns
By day and night t'attend him carefully
And feed his humour kindly as we may,
Till time beget some careful remedy.   30

MARCUS
Kinsmen, his sorrows are past remedy,
But [let us live in hope that Lucius will]

19, 20 **suffrages, tyrannize** key terms from the political lexicon
24 **pipe for** look in vain for (like 'whistle for')
25 **heavy case** sad state of affairs
26 **distract** distracted. Oxf modernizes to 'distraught', but since Shakespeare used both forms ('distract' more frequently) it is better not to alter it, thus retaining the colouring together of *OED v.* 5, 6: 'To throw into a state of mind in which one knows not how to act'; 'To derange the mind, drive mad'.
28, 30 **carefully, careful** the adverbial use suggests both 'attentively' and 'with solicitude' (picking up line 21), the adjectival use, 'solicitude-bringing', or possibly 'costing trouble'; dramatic irony suggests the opposite

sense of the word, 'bringing griefs, cares'. The usage in 30 is odd and might be an error caused by the presence of the word in 28 – 'we should substitute *cureful*, if this were a Shakespearian word' (Schmidt, 172).
29 **feed his humour** 'humour him', indulge his strange mood
32 *__But__ ... A line (or more) is missing in Q1: sig.G4ᵛ ends with the catchword 'But', but H1ʳ begins 'Join with the Goths'. The speech begins with Titus supposed beyond hope and ends with the Goths and vengeance: Lucius is surely the link in this train of thought, so he forms the basis of my conjecture as to the lost line, but since it is pure conjecture I place it in square brackets.

26 thus] *Q1;* this *Q*   32 But] *Q1 catchword; remainder of line / this edn*

Join with the Goths and with revengeful war
Take wreak on Rome for this ingratitude,
And vengeance on the traitor Saturnine.   35
TITUS
Publius, how now? How now, my masters?
What, have you met with her?
PUBLIUS
No, my good lord, but Pluto sends you word
If you will have Revenge from hell, you shall.
Marry, for Justice, she is so employed,   40
He thinks with Jove in heaven or somewhere else,
So that perforce you must needs stay a time.
TITUS
He doth me wrong to feed me with delays.
I'll dive into the burning lake below
And pull her out of Acheron by the heels.   45
Marcus, we are but shrubs, no cedars we,
No big-boned men framed of the Cyclops' size,
But metal, Marcus, steel to the very back,
Yet wrung with wrongs more than our backs can
    bear.
And sith there's no justice in earth nor hell,   50
We will solicit heaven and move the gods
To send down Justice for to wreak our wrongs.

---

34 **wreak** vengeance (as in 35, word varied for rhetorical effect)
37 **her** i.e. Astraea/Justice
40 **so** Hanmer emended to 'now', improving both sense and grammar, but improvement is not strictly necessary.
44 **burning lake** *Acheron* (45) and the fiery Phlegethon were among the rivers of the classical underworld, but Elizabethan poets often referred to them as lakes.
46 **shrubs, no cedars** proverbially contrasted (Tilley, C208; compare *Luc* 664)
47 **Cyclops'** giants (Polyphemus, known

to Shakespeare from Ovid, *Met.*, 13, was one of them)
48 **steel ... back** proverbial (Tilley, S842)
49 **wrung** racked, wrenched, pressed down upon; a highly physical image, tied to *wrongs* by near homonymy
50–1 **And ... the gods** an inventive reversal of one of the most famous lines in Virgil, 'flectere si nequeo superos, Acheronta movebo' (*Aen.*, 7.312): 'Since heavens I may not moove, yet pits of Hell I will uprake' (Phaer's trans. 7.325)
50 **sith** since

40 so] *Q1*; now *Hanmer*   49 backs] *Q1*; backe *F*

Come, to this gear. You are a good archer, Marcus:
                              He gives them the arrows.
'*Ad Jovem*', that's for you; here, '*ad Apollinem*';
'*Ad Martem*', that's for myself;   55
Here, boy, 'to Pallas'; here, 'to Mercury';
'To Saturn', Caius – not to Saturnine:
You were as good to shoot against the wind.
To it, boy; Marcus, loose when I bid.
Of my word, I have written to effect: 60
There's not a god left unsolicited.

MARCUS
Kinsmen, shoot all your shafts into the court;
We will afflict the emperor in his pride.

TITUS
Now, masters, draw. [*They shoot.*]
                              O, well said, Lucius,
Good boy: in Virgo's lap! Give it Pallas.   65

MARCUS
My lord, I aimed a mile beyond the moon:

---

53 **gear** business
54–5 *Ad Jovem ... Martem* Latin: 'to
  Jove', 'to Apollo', 'to Mars'. See on
  4.1.66; Mars was the god of war.
  'Apollinem' is Rowe's correction of
  Q1's 'Apollonem', justifiable on the
  grounds that the erroneous Latin is
  more likely to be the compositor's
  than Shakespeare's.
57 ***Saturn** The Q1 printer, influenced
  by the end of the line and not per-
  ceiving the verbal play, set as *Saturnine.*
58 **You ... wind** 'you might as well
  shoot against the wind as appeal to
  Saturninus' (a proverbial idiom –
  Dent, W435.2)
59 **loose** let fly
64 *They shoot* presumably towards the
  gallery at the back of the stage. The
  Elizabethan stage canopy seems to
  have been decorated with zodiacal

signs. In the Warner production there
was a definite sense of danger among
those sitting at the side of the stage,
played off against the comedy of
Titus' attempt to draw a bow with
one hand.
  well said well done, well shot: the
  Andronici are now speaking with
  actions, not words
65 **Virgo's** the constellation associated
  with Astraea
  Pallas Athene, also associated with
  virginity
66 ***aimed** 'aime' in Qq,F, but the sense
  demands a past tense and the mistaking of a 'd' for an 'e' was an easy
  error (the printer could have misread
  the MS or taken his type from the
  case adjacent to the one he intended).
  'To cast beyond the moon' was proverbial (Tilley, M1114).

---

54 *Apollinem*] *Rowe; Apollonem Q1*   57 Saturn', Caius] *Capell subst.; Saturnine, to Caius Qq,
F*   64 SD] *Rowe*   66 aimed] *Hudson;* aime *Qq, F*

Your letter is with Jupiter by this.
TITUS
Ha, ha! Publius, Publius, what hast thou done?
See, see, thou hast shot off one of Taurus' horns.
MARCUS
This was the sport, my lord: when Publius shot,   70
The Bull, being galled, gave Aries such a knock
That down fell both the Ram's horns in the court,
And who should find them but the empress' villain!
She laughed and told the Moor he should not
    choose
But give them to his master for a present.   75
TITUS
Why, there it goes; God give his lordship joy.

Enter the Clown *with a basket and two pigeons in it.*

News, news, from heaven! Marcus, the post is come.
Sirrah, what tidings? Have you any letters?
Shall I have justice? What says Jupiter?
CLOWN   Ho, the gibbet-maker? He says that he hath taken   80

69 **See ... horns** in a literal staging, something would need to drop from aloft to provoke this line. In the Warner production it was a dead pigeon, but perhaps it was originally a piece of masonry or statuary (perhaps resembling a horn), imagined to be from the palace. *Taurus*, the *Bull*, and *Aries* (71), the *Ram*, are adjacent horned zodiacal signs.

71 **galled** grazed

73 **villain** servant, but playing on Aaron's wickedness

75 **give ... master** This image of Aaron giving Saturninus the cuckold's horns implies that the affair with Tamora is now public knowledge (if it were not already at 2.2.86–7).

76 **there it goes** 'the hunter's cry of encouragement' (Cam[1]) – as the revenge gathers pace, the hunters of Act 2 become the hunted.

76.1 **Clown** 'The word meant both a rustic and the actor who played low-comic parts' (Oxf[1]).

77 **News ...** Assigned to Titus in Q2; Q1 gave the line to the Clown, probably on the erroneous supposition that the entry direction carried an implied SP, as happens elsewhere in the play, and that 'News, news' would be spoken by the bringer not the receiver of it.

80 **gibbet-maker** This misunderstanding was borrowed by Heywood in his play *The Golden Age* (1611). A Clown enters with letters for the king, then asks 'is there not one in your Court, cal'd (let me see) have you here never a gibbet-maker?' Jupiter himself

67 Jupiter] *Q2; Iubiter Q1*   76 his] *Q1; your Q3, F*   77] *1 line in Rowe[3]; divided after* heauen, *in Qq, F; Q1 has SP* CLOWNE; *Q2 repeats SP* TITUS   78] *Q1 has SP* TITUS   79 Jupiter] *Q2; Iubiter Q1*   80 Ho] *Q1; Who? Rowe*

them down again, for the man must not be hanged
till the next week.
TITUS
But what says Jupiter, I ask thee?
CLOWN   Alas, sir, I know not Jubiter, I never drank
with him in all my life.   85
TITUS
Why, villain, art not thou the carrier?
CLOWN
Ay, of my pigeons, sir – nothing else.
TITUS
Why, didst thou not come from heaven?
CLOWN   From heaven? Alas, sir, I never came there.
God forbid I should be so bold to press to heaven in my   90
young days. Why, I am going with my pigeons to the
tribunal plebs to take up a matter of brawl betwixt
my uncle and one of the emperal's men.

replies, 'Sirra, here's one cal'd *Jup-*
iter', eliciting the Clown's 'By *Jupiter*,
that's he that I would speak with'
(sig.F3ʳ).
80–1 **taken them down** i.e. taken down
the gallows because the execution has
been postponed. For a possible contemporary allusion, see introduction,
p. 77.
83 **But what says ...** In his dialogue
with the Clown between here and the
end of the scene Titus shifts between
prose and sometimes irregular verse.
This may be considered a symptom of
his mental instability or may suggest a
movement between the formality of
patrician command and the infor-
mality of collusive intimacy (he also
shifts between 'you' and 'thou').
84 **Jubiter** Q1 has this spelling at 67, 79
and 83 as well as here; Q2 corrected
all four occurrences to 'Jupiter'. I
follow Dover Wilson (Cam¹) in assuming that this is the one occasion on

which the error belongs to the character rather than to the compositor: it
is one of the Clown's several mis-
pronunciations, the 'b' sound necessary for the play on *gibbet-maker*.
86 **carrier** message-bearer (*OED*'s first
usage in this sense)
88 **from heaven** This fantasy was dramatized in the Brook production, in
which the Clown descended in a
basket as a parodic *deus ex machina*.
90 **press** aspire; thrust into the 'presence'
of the great. He only aspires to the
'tribunal plebs', not as high as the
emperor, let alone heaven.
92 **tribunal plebs** malapropism for
'tribuni plebis' – the Tribunes in their
capacity as magistrates protecting the
plebeians in law
     take up make an amicable settlement
of a legal dispute (the pigeons to serve
as a peace offering)
93 **emperal's** another malapropism,
repeated at 4.4.40

83 Jupiter] *Q2; Iubiter Q1*   84 Jupiter] *Q1; Iupiter Q2–3, F*   84–5] *prose Capell; verse, divided*
after Iubiter, Q1   88 Why, didst] *Q2; Why didst Q1*   89 From ... there] *prose Pope; verse Q q,*
F   91 Why ...] *prose F; begins new line, as if new paragraph, in Q q*   93 emperal's] *Q1; Emperialls*
Q2–3, F

{MARCUS   [*to Titus*] Why, sir, that is as fit as can be
     to serve for your oration, and let him deliver the   95
     pigeons to the emperor from you.
TITUS   Tell me, can you deliver an oration to the
     emperor with a grace?
CLOWN   Nay, truly, sir, I could never say grace in all
     my life.}   100
TITUS
     Sirrah, come hither; make no more ado,
     But give your pigeons to the emperor.
     By me thou shalt have justice at his hands.
     Hold, hold – meanwhile here's money for thy
          charges.   104
     Give me pen and ink.   [*Writes.*]
     Sirrah, can you with a grace deliver up a supplication?
CLOWN
     Ay, sir.
TITUS   [*Gives letter.*] Then here is a supplication for
     you, and when you come to him, at the first approach
     you must kneel, then kiss his foot, then deliver up   110
     your pigeons, and then look for your reward. I'll be
     at hand, sir; see you do it bravely.
CLOWN
     I warrant you, sir, let me alone.
TITUS
     Sirrah, hast thou a knife? Come, let me see it.

94–100 MARCUS … life. These lines are
     in wavy brackets because they may
     well be a 'false start' – see intro-
     duction, pp. 101–3.
104 Hold The Clown has probably
     started to leave, assuming that the
     instruction is simply to deliver his
     pigeons to the emperor instead of to
     the Tribunes; Titus has to stop him
     while he writes the supplication.
     here's money Bevington and Oxf

add the SD 'giving money'. Titus
     may do so, but in the spirit of a mad
     scene he may merely mime doing so,
     as the mad Lear does with 'press-
     money' at *KL* 4.6.87.
     charges expenses
111 your reward dramatically ironic, in
     view of what it proves to be
112 bravely in good style
113 let me alone leave it to me (as at
     1.1.454)

94 SD] *Oxf¹*   105 SD] *Oxf¹*   106 up] *Q1; not in Q2–3, F*   108 SD] *Bevington subst.*

Here, Marcus, fold it in the oration;   115
[*to the Clown*]
For thou must hold it like an humble suppliant,
And when thou hast given it to the emperor,
Knock at my door and tell me what he says.

CLOWN

God be with you, sir. I will.   *Exit.*

TITUS

Come, Marcus, let us go; Publius, follow me.   *Exeunt.*

4.4   *Enter* Emperor *and* Empress *and her two sons,* [*and*
  Attendants.] *The Emperor brings the arrows in his hand that*
                    Titus shot at him.

SATURNINUS

Why, lords, what wrongs are these! Was ever seen
An emperor in Rome thus overborne,
Troubled, confronted thus, and for the extent
Of equal justice used in such contempt?
My lords, you know, as know the mightful gods,   5
However these disturbers of our peace

---

116 ***thou must hold** Previous eds have
failed to make sense of this clause
because they have assumed that 'thou'
means Marcus. But Titus calls him
'you' throughout the scene (e.g. at 4,
53, 54), whereas he calls the Clown
'thou' several times. T. W. Craik's
proposed emendation of the early
texts' 'hast made' to 'must hold', an
error easily made by the eye reversing
the first letter of the two words, makes
beautiful sense (an alternative emendation, with the same effect, would
be 'must make').
4.4 Capell was the first to introduce a
new scene number here; Waith (Oxf¹)

assumes there is a throne for Saturninus.
2 **overborne** oppressed, had authority
exercised upon, as when Marlowe's
Edward II claims that he has been
'overborne' by his proud barons
(3.2.9)
3 **extent** exercise (*OED*'s earliest usage
in this sense)
4 **equal** 'egall' in Q1, from French *égal*
5 ***know, as know** just 'know' in Qq,F,
producing a short line and a non-
sensical sentence; almost certainly a
printer's error due to eyeskip – Cam's
emendation is universally adopted.

---

116 SD] *this edn*   thou must hold] *this edn (T. W. Craik);* thou hast made *Qq, F;* then hast made
Riv; thou must make *(Bate)*   117 it to the] *Q1;* it the *Q3, F*

4.4] *Capell*   Location] The Palace *Theobald*   0.1–2 *and Attendants*] *Malone subst.*   4 equal] *Q1*
*(*egall*)*   5 know, as know] *Cam;* know *Qq, F*

Buzz in the people's ears, there nought hath passed
But even with law against the wilful sons
Of old Andronicus. And what and if
His sorrows have so overwhelmed his wits?   10
Shall we be thus afflicted in his wreaks,
His fits, his frenzy and his bitterness?
And now he writes to heaven for his redress.
See, here's 'to Jove', and this 'to Mercury',
This 'to Apollo', this 'to the god of war':   15
Sweet scrolls to fly about the streets of Rome!
What's this but libelling against the senate
And blazoning our injustice everywhere?
A goodly humour, is it not, my lords?
As who would say, in Rome no justice were.   20
But if I live, his feigned ecstasies
Shall be no shelter to these outrages,
But he and his shall know that justice lives
In Saturninus' health, whom, if she sleep,
He'll so awake as she in fury shall   25
Cut off the proud'st conspirator that lives.

TAMORA

My gracious lord, my lovely Saturnine,
Lord of my life, commander of my thoughts,
Calm thee and bear the faults of Titus' age,
Th'effects of sorrow for his valiant sons   30

---

7 **passed** plays on (1) happened (2) exercised legal sentence
8 **even** in exact agreement
9 **what and if** what if, supposing that
11 **wreaks** acts of vengeance (compare 4.3.34)
17 **libelling** Titus' messages are viewed as legal documents instituting an accusation.
18 **blazoning** proclaiming, displaying
19 **humour** whim, caprice
21 **feigned** feignèd. Baildon (Ard¹) notes

that Saturninus is the only one to suspect that Titus' madness is not genuine.
24–5 *__she ... she 'he' in both lines in the early edns. Since Justice is personified as a woman in the previous scene, I follow Rowe's emendation. Waith (Oxf¹) retains 'he', arguing that it is Saturninus rather than Justice who is sleeping, but he would hardly admit this himself.

18 injustice] *F;* vniustice *Q1*   24–5 she ... she] *Rowe;* he ... he *Q1*   30 Th'effects] *Q1* (The'ffects)

Whose loss hath pierced him deep and scarred his
  heart;
And rather comfort his distressed plight
Than prosecute the meanest or the best
For these contempts.
                            [*aside*] Why, thus it shall become
High-witted Tamora to gloze withal.   35
But, Titus, I have touched thee to the quick;
Thy life-blood out, if Aaron now be wise,
Then is all safe, the anchor in the port.

                    Enter Clown.

How now, good fellow, wouldst thou speak with us?
CLOWN
  Yea, forsooth, and your mistress-ship be emperial.   40
TAMORA
  Empress I am, but yonder sits the emperor.
CLOWN   'Tis he. God and Saint Stephen give you good e'en.
  I have brought you a letter and a couple of pigeons here.
                            [*Saturninus*] *reads the letter.*
SATURNINUS
  Go, take him away and hang him presently!
CLOWN
  How much money must I have?   45
TAMORA
  Come, sirrah, you must be hanged.
CLOWN   Hanged, by'Lady? Then I have brought up a

32 **distressed** distressèd
35 **gloze** use fair, false words
   *withal Most eds follow the early
   texts' 'with all', but I think that the
   sense is adverbial: it is not Tamora
   glozing with everybody, but glozing
   'with this', i.e. with what she is
   saying. 'Withal' is always spelt
   'withall' in Q1.
40 **and** if

42 **good e'en** Q1 has the old form
   'godden'.
43.1 *reads the letter* Presumably his
   reaction is provoked by the knife
   folded therein, which he might take
   out or which might fall to the ground.
47 **brought up** plays on (1) nurture,
   raise (2) give utterance to a report or
   legal claim (*OED bring*, 27d)

34 SD] *F (at end of 35)*   35 withal] *Pope;* with all *Qq, F*   38 anchor] *Q1;* Anchor's *Q3, F*   42
good e'en] *Q1 (*godden*);* good den *Q3, F*   43.1 *Saturninus*] *Johnson subst.;* He *Qq, F*   47 by'Lady]
*Q1 (*be Lady*);* ber Lady *F*

239

neck to a fair end.   *Exit [under guard].*

SATURNINUS

Despiteful and intolerable wrongs!
Shall I endure this monstrous villainy?   50
I know from whence this same device proceeds.
May this be borne as if his traitorous sons,
That died by law for murder of our brother,
Have by my means been butchered wrongfully?
Go, drag the villain hither by the hair: 55
Nor age nor honour shall shape privilege.
For this proud mock I'll be thy slaughterman,
Sly frantic wretch that holp'st to make me great
In hope thyself should govern Rome and me.

         Enter EMILLIUS, *a Messenger.*

What news with thee, Emillius?   60

EMILLIUS

Arm, arm, my lords! Rome never had more cause:

48 **neck** plays on (1) his own neck, by which he will be hanged (2) the laying of a charge in law (*OED sb.*[1] 3c)
end plays on (1) death, at the rope's end (2) completion of legal case, outcome of action (ironic with *fair*)

52 **borne as if** Most eds follow F's 'borne? As if', but Q1 has no mid-line punctuation and 52–4 makes a good (and dramatically ironic) sentence.

55 **the villain** i.e. Titus

56 **shape privilege** create immunity from prosecution (technical legal term)

57 **slaughterman** executioner. Word also used for man whose job it was to kill cattle for food: a low, undignified role for an emperor; also dramatically ironic in view of the abattoir quality of 5.2.

58 **holp'st** archaic form of 'helped'

59.1 EMILLIUS, *a Messenger* Q1 has 'Nutius' (erroneous reading of 'Nuntius', Latin for 'messenger', which would have been 'Nūtius' in MS); for the spelling of the proper name, see note on List of Roles.

61 ***Arm, arm** Only one 'arm' in Q1, but the line is a syllable short and the repetition could easily have been missed by a printer's eye; I therefore adopt Ravenscroft's emendation, especially since every parallel usage in early Shakespeare has the repetition (e.g. *KJ* 3.1.107, *1H4* 5.2.75, *1H6* 2.1.38, *R3* 5.3.288, the last of these being a close parallel: 'Arm, arm, my lord, the foe vaunts in the field').
lords Capell assumed that Emillius was addressing Saturninus alone and emended to 'lord', but he could be addressing both emperor and empress.

48 *under guard*] *Capell subst.*   52 borne as if] *Q1*; borne? As if *F*   59.1 EMILLIUS, *a Messenger*] *this edn*; *Nutius Emillius Q1*; *Nuntius Emillius Q2–3, F*; *Aemilius Theobald*   61 Arm, arm] *Ravenscroft, Warburton*; Arme *Q1*

The Goths have gathered head, and with a power
Of high-resolved men bent to the spoil
They hither march amain under conduct
Of Lucius, son to old Andronicus,   65
Who threats in course of this revenge to do
As much as ever Coriolanus did.

SATURNINUS

Is warlike Lucius general of the Goths?
These tidings nip me and I hang the head
As flowers with frost or grass beat down with
   storms.   70
Ay, now begins our sorrows to approach.
'Tis he the common people love so much;
Myself hath often heard them say,
When I have walked like a private man,
That Lucius' banishment was wrongfully,   75
And they have wished that Lucius were their
   emperor.

TAMORA

Why should you fear? Is not your city strong?

SATURNINUS

Ay, but the citizens favour Lucius

63 **high-resolved** high-resolvèd (not
hyphenated in Q1)
bent to the spoil determined on
their attack, straining for an encounter
64 **amain** in full force or at full speed
conduct leadership
66 **this** should perhaps be 'his' (a
common printer's error), but 'this
revenge' makes sufficient sense to
stand
67 **ever** may be elided to 'e'er'
Coriolanus joined with his former
enemy to march against the Rome
that had exiled him; Shakespeare read
his life in Plutarch and, of course,
returned to it later in his career.
72 **the common people love** a theme
from the Tarquin and Lucius Junius

Brutus precedent, where Lucius is
the people's leader against the tyrant.
Also suggestively proleptic of Claudius' fear of young leaders – Laertes,
Hamlet – whom the common people
love.
73 **Myself ... say** a short line
74 **walked ... man** walkèd. The motif
of the ruler going among his people
in disguise and discovering what they
think of him is common in both classical history and Renaissance drama
(most notably *H5* and *MM*).
75 **wrongfully** It was common Elizabethan usage to have an adverb where
an adjective might be expected; the
effect is an elliptical form of 'wrongfully done' (compare 'mildly' at
1.1.480).

66 this] *Qq, F;* his *Rowe*   77 your] *Q1;* our *F*

And will revolt from me to succour him.

TAMORA

King, be thy thoughts imperious like thy name.   80
Is the sun dimmed, that gnats do fly in it?
The eagle suffers little birds to sing,
And is not careful what they mean thereby,
Knowing that with the shadow of his wings
He can at pleasure stint their melody: 85
Even so mayst thou the giddy men of Rome.
Then cheer thy spirit, for know thou, emperor,
I will enchant the old Andronicus
With words more sweet and yet more dangerous
Than baits to fish or honey-stalks to sheep,   90
When as the one is wounded with the bait,
The other rotted with delicious feed.

SATURNINUS

But he will not entreat his son for us.

TAMORA

If Tamora entreat him, then he will,
For I can smooth and fill his aged ears   95
With golden promises that, were his heart
Almost impregnable, his old ears deaf,
Yet should both ear and heart obey my tongue.
[*to Emillius*] Go thou before to be our ambassador:

80 **thy name** i.e. Saturninus, with its
suggestion of Saturn, supposedly king
of Rome in the golden age
81 **sun ... gnats** the sun for the king
and gnats for the commoners recur at
3H6 2.6.8–9: 'The common people
swarm like summer flies, / And
whither fly the gnats but to the sun'
82 **eagle ... little birds** imagery from
the 'great chain of being', in which
hierarchies in society are made to
correspond with those in the natural
world. *suffers*: allows.
83 **is not careful** does not care
85 **stint** stop
86 **giddy** (1) fickle in allegiance (2)

intoxicated with the thought of revolt
90 **honey-stalks** 'clover flowers, which
contain a sweet juice. It is common
for cattle to over-charge themselves
with clover, and die' (Johnson)
95 **smooth** flatter
98 **obey my tongue** These lines on the
power of the tongue suggest a contrast
with the powerlessness of the tongue-
less Lavinia – but a reversal will be
effected when Tamora acts out her
plan.
99 **to be** metre suggests that 'be' is contracted, as it often was before a vowel
(Cercignani, 291)

87 know thou, emperor] *Kittredge;* know thou Emperour *Q1;* know, thou Emperour *F4*   92 feed]
Q3; seede *Q1–2;* foode *F*   97 ears] *F;* yeares *Qq*   99 SD] *Rowe*   to be] *Q1;* to *F*

Say that the emperor requests a parley   100
Of warlike Lucius, and appoint the meeting
Even at his father's house, the old Andronicus.

SATURNINUS
Emillius, do this message honourably,
And if he stand in hostage for his safety,
Bid him demand what pledge will please him best.   105

EMILLIUS
Your bidding shall I do effectually.   *Exit.*

TAMORA
Now will I to that old Andronicus,
And temper him with all the art I have
To pluck proud Lucius from the warlike Goths.
And now, sweet emperor, be blithe again   110
And bury all thy fear in my devices.

SATURNINUS
Then go incessantly and plead to him.

Exeunt [by different doors].

5.1   *Flourish. Enter* LUCIUS *with an army of* Goths *with
Drums and Soldiers.*

100 **parley** peace conference under conditions of truce
104 **stand in** insist upon. Most eds adopt
F4's emendation to 'stand on', but
Waith (Oxf[1]) points out that,
although this is *OED*'s only usage for
this meaning (72e), there are many
examples of the closely related 'per-
severe, persist in' (72b). The correctors of edns from Q2 to F3 had no
difficulty with Q1's reading, which
suggests that it was an acceptable
usage.
106 **effectually** to the purpose,
explicitly

108 **temper** work on (as of clay, suggesting moulding by rhetorical
persuasion)
112 ***incessantly** immediately. Capell's
emendation of Q1's 'sucessantly', an
otherwise unrecorded word. The
compositor may have mistaken 'i' for
long 's'; 'u' for 'n' is a common error.
5.1 The action moves outside the city for
the first time since the second act.
0.2 *Soldiers* in effect repeats *army*,
leading Capell to emend to *Colours*
(as in F's opening SD for 1.1); the
phrasing has the improvised feel of a
foul paper SD

102] *Q1; not in Q3, F*   104 in] *Q1;* on *F4*   112 incessantly] *Capell;* sucessantly *Q1;* successantly
Q2–3, F   to] *Q1;* for *F*   112.1 *by different doors*] *this edn; severally* Oxf

5.1] *Rowe; Actus Quintus. F*   Location] A Camp, at a small Distance from Rome *Theobald;* Plains
near Rome *Capell*   0.1 *Flourish*] *F*   0.2 *Drums*] *Q1;* Drum *Q3, F*

243

LUCIUS

Approved warriors and my faithful friends,
I have received letters from great Rome.
Which signifies what hate they bear their emperor,
And how desirous of our sight they are.
Therefore, great lords, be as your titles witness, 5
Imperious, and impatient of your wrongs,
And wherein Rome hath done you any scath
Let him make treble satisfaction.

1 GOTH

Brave slip sprung from the great Andronicus,
Whose name was once our terror, now our comfort, 10
Whose high exploits and honourable deeds
Ingrateful Rome requites with foul contempt,
Be bold in us. We'll follow where thou lead'st,
Like stinging bees in hottest summer's day
Led by their master to the flowered fields, 15
And be avenged on cursed Tamora.

ALL GOTHS

And as he saith, so say we all with him.

LUCIUS

I humbly thank him, and I thank you all.
But who comes here, led by a lusty Goth?

Enter a Goth, *leading of* AARON *with his child in his arms.*

1 **Approved** approvèd. well-tried
2 **received** receivèd
3 **signifies** *letters* was often used for a single communication; grammatically, this is another plural noun coupled with singular verb form
7 **scath** harm
8 **satisfaction** five syllables
9 **slip** offspring (used figuratively for a child, originally for a cutting taken from a plant for grafting)
13 **bold** confident

15 **master** in Shakespeare's time, queen bees were assumed to be masculine
flowered original pronunciation probably indicated by Q1's spelling, 'flowred'
16 **cursed** cursèd
17 *ALL GOTHS This SP, clearly required by the sense, is missing in the early edns, and was first supplied by F2.
19 **lusty** vigorous

9 1 GOTH] *Capell subst. (also at 121, 162);* GOTH *Qq, F* 13 Be bold] *Q1;* Behold *F* 17 ALL GOTHS] *F2 (*OMN.*); Qq, F continue to* GOTH

2 GOTH

 Renowned Lucius, from our troops I strayed   20
 To gaze upon a ruinous monastery,
 And as I earnestly did fix mine eye
 Upon the wasted building, suddenly
 I heard a child cry underneath a wall.
 I made unto the noise, when soon I heard   25
 The crying babe controlled with this discourse:
 'Peace, tawny slave, half me and half thy dame!
 Did not thy hue bewray whose brat thou art,
 Had nature lent thee but thy mother's look,
 Villain, thou mightst have been an emperor.   30
 But where the bull and cow are both milk-white,
 They never do beget a coal-black calf.
 Peace, villain, peace,' – even thus he rates the babe –
 'For I must bear thee to a trusty Goth
 Who, when he knows thou art the empress' babe, 35
 Will hold thee dearly for thy mother's sake.'
 With this my weapon drawn, I rushed upon him,
 Surprised him suddenly, and brought him hither
 To use as you think needful of the man.

LUCIUS

 O worthy Goth, this is the incarnate devil   40
 That robbed Andronicus of his good hand;
 This is the pearl that pleased your empress' eye,
 And here's the base fruit of her burning lust.

---

20 **Renowned** renownèd
21 **ruinous monastery** for the Reformation context, see introduction, pp.
 19–21
22 **earnestly** with sincere feeling
23 **wasted** ruined (lain waste by Henry
 VIII?)
26 **controlled** calmed
27 **tawny** black (not 'yellowish brown',
 as now)
 dame mother (edns after Q1 have

the alternative form 'dam')
28 **bewray** reveal
 brat sometimes a term of affection,
 not abuse
33 **rates** scolds
37 **this my weapon** He presumably
 entered at 19.1 with sword drawn.
39 **use** deal with
42 **pearl ... eye** proverbial: 'a black man
 is a jewel/pearl in a fair woman's eye'
 (Tilley, M79)

20 2 GOTH] *Capell subst;* GOTH *Qq, F* Renowned] *Q1* (Renowmed*)* 27 dame] *Q1;* dam *Q2–3,*
F 43 here's] *Q2;* her's *Q1* her] *Q1;* his *Q3, F*

[*to Aaron*]
Say, wall-eyed slave, whither wouldst thou convey
This growing image of thy fiend-like face?   45
Why dost not speak? What, deaf? Not a word?
A halter, soldiers! Hang him on this tree,
And by his side his fruit of bastardy.

AARON
Touch not the boy, he is of royal blood.

LUCIUS
Too like the sire for ever being good.   50
First hang the child, that he may see it sprawl:
A sight to vex the father's soul withal.
Get me a ladder.

> [*A Goth brings a ladder, which Aaron is*
> *made to climb; another Goth takes the child.*]

AARON   Lucius, save the child,
And bear it from me to the empress.
If thou do this, I'll show thee wondrous things   55
That highly may advantage thee to hear.
If thou wilt not, befall what may befall,
I'll speak no more but 'Vengeance rot you all!'

---

44 **wall-eyed** having glaring eyes, indicative of anger ('wall-eyed wrath': *KJ* 4.3.49)
45 **fiend-like** because devils were portrayed as black. *OED*'s earliest citation of the word is *Mac* 5.9.35.
46 **Not a word?** The line is a syllable short, which may be acceptable since it is broken up into a string of questions; it could, however, be regularized by emending to 'what, not a word?' (Oxf, after Keightley).
50 **sire** father
51 **sprawl** in convulsive death motion
53 *****Get me a ladder** Assigned by Q1 to Aaron, but this must be Lucius' command – the compositor misinterpreted the mid-line change of speaker. Signet follows Q1, implying that Aaron is offering to die on condition that his son is saved; the Santa Cruz production followed this reading, but the point seemed dramatically forced. At Elizabethan executions, a ladder was climbed to ascend the scaffold; here it was perhaps leant against one of the onstage pillars.
54 **empress** pronounced 'emperess' (Pope)

44 SD] *Oxf*   53 Get me a ladder] *assigned to* LUCIUS *Theobald; to* AARON *Qq, F*   53.1–2 *A Goth ... climb*] *Capell subst.*   53.2 *another ... child*] *this edn*   58 'Vengeance ... all'] *quot. marks first in Cam*

LUCIUS

Say on, and if it please me which thou speak'st,
Thy child shall live and I will see it nourished.   60

AARON

And if it please thee? Why, assure thee, Lucius,
'Twill vex thy soul to hear what I shall speak:
For I must talk of murders, rapes and massacres,
Acts of black night, abominable deeds,
Complots of mischief, treasons, villainies,   65
Ruthful to hear yet piteously performed;
And this shall all be buried in my death
Unless thou swear to me my child shall live.

LUCIUS

Tell on thy mind; I say thy child shall live.

AARON

Swear that he shall and then I will begin.   70

LUCIUS

Who should I swear by? Thou believest no god.
That granted, how canst thou believe an oath?

AARON

What if I do not? – as indeed I do not –
Yet for I know thou art religious
And hast a thing within thee called conscience,   75
With twenty popish tricks and ceremonies
Which I have seen thee careful to observe,

---

59 **and if** This does not seem to be a case of 'and if' meaning 'if' (though Aaron makes it that at 61) – here the sense suggests a genuine connective.

60 **nourished** nursed, brought up; probably pronounced 'nursht'

65 ***treasons** Singular in Qq,F, but the catalogue of plurals suggests that this is one of the Q1 compositor's several errors of grammatical number. Compare 'fit for treasons, stratagems and spoils' (*MV* 5.1.85).

66 **Ruthful ... performed** 'lamentable

to hear about, yet done in order to excite pity' (a good definition of the complots of tragedy, to use the phrase of 2.2.265); refers to the full list going back to 'murders' (Oxf omits comma after 'villainies', implicitly narrowing the referent of this line).

69, 70 **shall** has the force of a decree

71 **Thou ... god** Atheism is a characteristic of the stage Machiavel.

75 **called** callèd

76 **popish** sustains the Reformation context introduced by 21

65 treasons] *this edn (Ard²)*; treason *Qq, F*   67 in] *Q1*; by *Q3, F*

Therefore I urge thy oath; for that I know
An idiot holds his bauble for a god,
And keeps the oath which by that god he swears,   80
To that I'll urge him, therefore thou shalt vow
By that same god, what god soe'er it be
That thou adorest and hast in reverence,
To save my boy, to nurse and bring him up,
Or else I will discover nought to thee.   85

LUCIUS
Even by my god I swear to thee I will.

AARON
First know thou I begot him on the empress.

LUCIUS
O most insatiate and luxurious woman!

AARON
Tut, Lucius, this was but a deed of charity
To that which thou shalt hear of me anon.   90
'Twas her two sons that murdered Bassianus;
They cut thy sister's tongue and ravished her
And cut her hands and trimmed her as thou sawest.

LUCIUS
O detestable villain, call'st thou that trimming?

AARON
Why, she was washed and cut and trimmed, and
'twas   95
Trim sport for them which had the doing of it.

---

79 **bauble** court fool's stick with carved head. 'To dote more than a fool on his bauble' was proverbial (Tilley, F509).
83 **adorest** possibly elided to 'ador'st'
84 ***nurse** 'nourish' in Qq, F, but this may be regarded as a variant spelling, and the monosyllable suits the metre, as it does when the same word occurs in *2H6* 3.1.348.

85 **discover** reveal
88 **luxurious** lecherous, unchaste
90 **To** common contraction of 'compared to'
93 **trimmed** plays on slang for sexual intercourse (Partridge, 205)
94 **detestable** stressed on first syllable: 'dee-test-able'
95 **washed ... trimmed** like dead meat

84 nurse] *Oxf;* nourish *Qq, F*   88 and] *Q1; not in Q3, F*   93 hands] Q1; hands off *F*   95–6] *divided thus by Capell; Qq, F divide after* trimd   96 which] *Q1;* that *Q2–3, F*

LUCIUS

   O barbarous, beastly villains, like thyself!

AARON

   Indeed, I was their tutor to instruct them.
   That codding spirit had they from their mother,
   As sure a card as ever won the set.   100
   That bloody mind I think they learned of me,
   As true a dog as ever fought at head.
   Well, let my deeds be witness of my worth:
   I trained thy brethren to that guileful hole
   Where the dead corpse of Bassianus lay;   105
   I wrote the letter that thy father found,
   And hid the gold within that letter mentioned,
   Confederate with the queen and her two sons;
   And what not done that thou hast cause to rue
   Wherein I had no stroke of mischief in it?   110
   I played the cheater for thy father's hand,
   And when I had it, drew myself apart
   And almost broke my heart with extreme laughter;
   I pried me through the crevice of a wall

---

97 **barbarous** Q1's spelling is 'barberous', suggesting a possible pun on 'barber', though the same spelling occurs with no possible pun at 5.3.4.

99 **codding** lecherous (from 'cod': testicle). *OED*'s sole occurrence.

100 **sure ... set** i.e. their mother's lecherousness guaranteed theirs, as certain cards are guaranteed to win a game (the simile is proverbial: Tilley, C74)

102 **at head** Bulldogs were admired for attacking the bull head on, an ironic claim in view of Aaron's deviousness. The parallel construction of this simile and that in 100 emphasizes that Chiron and Demetrius are the products of Tamora's nature and Aaron's nurture.

104 **trained** lured (*OED* v.4), from

'train', a trap or snare for catching wild animals – the hunting imagery persistently associated with events in the forest

106 **thy father found** see on 2.2.294–5

111 **cheater** play on 'one who cheats' and 'escheator', officer appointed to look after estates forfeited to the crown (Titus' hand thus becomes an 'escheat')

112–13 **drew ... laughter** These lines led Waith (Oxf¹) to add the SD *'Laughs as he moves to one side'* at 3.1.204, but this seems too literal-minded, as would a direction, implied by the next line, to have Aaron peeping round the back wall ('I pried me') and laughing at Titus' grief.

113 *extreme* stressed on first syllable

107 that] *Q1; the Q2–3, F*

When for his hand he had his two sons' heads,   115
Beheld his tears and laughed so heartily
That both mine eyes were rainy like to his;
And when I told the empress of this sport,
She sounded almost at my pleasing tale
And for my tidings gave me twenty kisses.   120

1 GOTH
What, canst thou say all this and never blush?

AARON
Ay, like a black dog, as the saying is.

LUCIUS
Art thou not sorry for these heinous deeds?

AARON
Ay, that I had not done a thousand more.
Even now I curse the day – and yet I think   125
Few come within the compass of my curse –
Wherein I did not some notorious ill,
As kill a man or else devise his death,
Ravish a maid or plot the way to do it,
Accuse some innocent and forswear myself,   130
Set deadly enmity between two friends,
Make poor men's cattle break their necks,
Set fire on barns and haystacks in the night
And bid the owners quench them with their tears.
Oft have I digged up dead men from their graves   135
And set them upright at their dear friends' door,
Even when their sorrows almost was forgot,

---

119 **sounded** variant spelling of 'swooned'

122 **as the saying** 'To blush like a black dog' was proverbial for having a brazen face (Tilley, D507).

124–44 **Ay ... more** a catalogue of crimes imitating those of Barabas and Ithamore in *The Jew of Malta* (see appendix, pp. 286–7). The setting upright of a dead man's body (136) is

an action that they actually perform in 4.1.

132 **Make ... necks** a short line. Hudson suggested that Aaron set pitfalls, so conjecturally emended to 'cattle fall and break'; Gary Taylor conjectures 'cillie [i.e. "seely/silly", innocent] and an eyeskip error' (*TxC*, 212).

136 **friends'** usually means relatives, kinsfolk

---

119 sounded] *Q1*; swooned *F3*   121–4] *Q1 centres SPs*   126 the] *Q1*; few *F*   133 haystacks] *Q1* (haystalks)   134 their] *Q1*; the *F*

And on their skins, as on the bark of trees,
Have with my knife carved in Roman letters,
'Let not your sorrow die though I am dead.'   140
Tut, I have done a thousand dreadful things
As willingly as one would kill a fly,
And nothing grieves me heartily indeed
But that I cannot do ten thousand more.

LUCIUS
Bring down the devil, for he must not die   145
So sweet a death as hanging presently.
                                  [*Aaron is made to climb down.*]

AARON
If there be devils, would I were a devil,
To live and burn in everlasting fire,
So I might have your company in hell
But to torment you with my bitter tongue.   150

LUCIUS
Sirs, stop his mouth and let him speak no more.
                                              [*Aaron is gagged.*]

Enter EMILLIUS.

A GOTH
My lord, there is a messenger from Rome
Desires to be admitted to your presence.

LUCIUS
Let him come near.

---

139 **carved** carvèd. Yet another figure of
   writing on the body.
141 ***Tut,** 'But' in Q1, glossed in Ard²
   as 'but why should I go on itemizing'.
   Q2's emendation is, however, very
   attractive (especially since Aaron uses
   the same idiom at 89). 'But' may
   have arisen from the compositor's eye
   skipping forward to 144.
142 **kill a fly** The line that perhaps
   sowed the seed of the added fly scene?

146 **presently** instantly
148 **burn ... fire** as he does onstage in
   the rewritten endings in the Vos and
   Ravenscroft versions
152 A GOTH Could be the '1st' Goth
   who acts like a leader, but might be
   another. It is unnecessary to have a
   Goth entering here, as Capell and
   Malone do: he can simply come
   forward from the group, which Emillius will have approached.

141 Tut,] *Q2–3, F;* But *Q1* 146.1] *Bevington subst.* 151.1] *Bevington; Capell adds SD /* Enter a
Goth; *Enter a Goth with Aemilius / Malone* 152 A GOTH] *Oxf¹;* GOTH *Qq, F;* 3RD GOTH *Capell*

Welcome, Emillius: what's the news from Rome?   155

EMILLIUS
Lord Lucius and you princes of the Goths,
The Roman emperor greets you all by me,
And for he understands you are in arms,
He craves a parley at your father's house,
Willing you to demand your hostages   160
And they shall be immediately delivered.

1 GOTH
What says our general?

LUCIUS
Emillius, let the emperor give his pledges
Unto my father and my uncle Marcus,   164
And we will come.   *Flourish. [They] march away.*

5.2   *Enter* TAMORA *and her two* Sons *disguised.*

TAMORA
Thus, in this strange and sad habiliment,
I will encounter with Andronicus
And say I am Revenge, sent from below
To join with him and right his heinous wrongs.
Knock at his study, where they say he keeps   5
To ruminate strange plots of dire revenge;
Tell him Revenge is come to join with him

158 **for** since
160 **Willing ... hostages** i.e. such hos-
    tages as you may require
162 1 GOTH As at 152, simply 'GOTH' in
    Qq,F, but here almost certainly the
    1st Goth whose dialogue with Lucius
    began the scene, which thus closes
    symmetrically.
165 ***They march away** Q1 scrupulously
    ends every other scene with *Exit* or
    Exeunt. Here there is no SD, but
    Lucius' line ends 'March away'
    (without closing punctuation). Stee-

vens is surely right that this is an SD
which has crept into the text. I restore
it and add F's trumpet flourish.
1 **sad** dark-coloured (*OED a.* 8): she is
    almost certainly covered in a black
    robe
5 **keeps** stays (*OED v.* 33), but other
    senses – 'takes note, watches, lies in
    wait' (*OED* 4–6) – may be ironically
    present at Tamora's expense
7 **Tell him** 'I will tell him'; syntax
    carries on from 'I will encounter'.

165] *this edn (Steevens);* And we will come, march away *Q1; Flourish (at end of previous line)* And
we will come: march away. *Exeunt. F*

5.2] *Rowe*   Location] Rome. Court of Titus' House. *Capell*

And work confusion on his enemies.

They knock, and TITUS [*aloft with papers*] *opens his study door.*

TITUS   [*aloft*]
Who doth molest my contemplation?
Is it your trick to make me ope the door,   10
That so my sad decrees may fly away
And all my study be to no effect?
You are deceived, for what I mean to do
See here in bloody lines I have set down,
And what is written shall be executed.   15

TAMORA
Titus, I am come to talk with thee.

TITUS   [*aloft*]
No, not a word. How can I grace my talk,
Wanting a hand to give it action?

8.1 TITUS ... **door** 14 indicates that
Titus is holding papers (compare
4.3.105 for the comic business of
holding both pen and paper with one
hand); 67 suggests that he is in the
aloft space, Tamora's speech at 70–80
covering the time it takes for him to
come down. An alternative staging,
supported by the direction to open the
door, would have him in the discovery
space.

9 **Who ... contemplation?** One of
Olivier's most memorable lines in the
Brook production; also memorable in
Shakespeare's own time, to judge
from a parody in Thomas Dekker's
play, *The Welsh Embassador*: '*Enter
Clowne in his study writinge: one
knockes within. Clo:* whoe does molest
our Contemplations, what are you[?]'
(Malone Soc. Reprint, 1920, lines
1962–3).

11 **sad decrees** grave resolutions, and
more specifically his papers; the image
as a whole perhaps echoes 4.1.105

12 **study** relates to the idea of learning
how to revenge through studying
exemplary texts – on the play's fre-
quent schoolroom language, see Bate,
Ovid, 106–9

14 **bloody lines** writing describing
bloody deeds, but also as if written in
his own blood ('crimson lines' at 22)

16 **Titus** Metrically, a pause after a vocative sometimes stands in for a missing
syllable (Abbott, §507).

18 ****give it action** F's excellent emendation of Qq's 'giue that accord'. The
image (familiar from Cicero and
Quintilian) is of the orator's hand-
gestures corresponding to his words,
as in the opening speech of 3.2.
'*Action*, corresponding in classical
rhetoric to *pronuntiatio*, was the fifth
and last phase of the recitation and
staging of discourse, after *inventio*,
dispositio, *elocutio* and *memoria*. The
term denoted both intonation and gesture' (Serpieri). The similarity of 'yt'
and the MS form of 'that' may have

8.1 *aloft with papers*] *this edn; above / Capell*   9 *aloft*] *this edn (and for subsequent speeches from
upper stage)*   14 set down] *Q1; Collier MS adds SD: Showe Paper*   18 give it action] *F;* giue that
accord *Q1*

Thou hast the odds of me, therefore no more.

TAMORA

If thou didst know me, thou wouldst talk with me.   20

TITUS   [*aloft*]

I am not mad, I know thee well enough:
Witness this wretched stump, witness these crimson
    lines,
Witness these trenches made by grief and care,
Witness the tiring day and heavy night,
Witness all sorrow, that I know thee well   25
For our proud empress, mighty Tamora.
Is not thy coming for my other hand?

TAMORA

Know, thou sad man, I am not Tamora:
She is thy enemy and I thy friend.
I am Revenge, sent from th'infernal kingdom   30
To ease the gnawing vulture of thy mind
By working wreakful vengeance on thy foes.
Come down and welcome me to this world's light,
Confer with me of murder and of death.
There's not a hollow cave or lurking place,   35

---

led Q1 into error. Maxwell (Ard²)
cites in support of the emendation: 'I
cannot give due action to my words'
(*2H6* 5.1.8) and a striking allusion in
Middleton's *Father Hubbard's Tale*,
'my lamentable action of one arm,
like old Titus Andronicus' (*Works*, ed.
Bullen, 8.94).
19 **odds of** advantage over (i.e. two
hands to one)
22 **Witness ... lines** a hexameter,
causing some eds to omit the second
'witness', but the play has a number
of longer lines and the relentless rhetorical repetition of the verb is powerful. Compare 'Witness this arm ...
Witness these scars' in *Ironside* (1710–
12); also *Selimus*, 1476–86, repro-

duced in my appendix.
24 **tiring ... night** not merely poetic
figures, but also suggestive of Titus'
perpetual mental anguish and the
wearying work of getting through the
day with only one hand
31 **gnawing vulture** suggestive of Prometheus (see on 1.1.516). A physical
image for mental anguish.
32 **wreakful** vengeful (rhetorical
reinforcement of the noun, though
strictly tautologous)
35 **lurking place** Oxf hyphenates,
'lurking-place', clarifying the sense
but upsetting the rhythmic balance
with 'hollow cave'. The language of
35–7 echoes that associated with the
place of rape and murder in 2.2.

22 witness these] *Q1;* these *Theobald*   31 thy] *Q1;* the *F*   32 thy] *Q1;* my *F*

No vast obscurity or misty vale
Where bloody murder or detested rape
Can couch for fear, but I will find them out,
And in their ears tell them my dreadful name,
Revenge, which makes the foul offender quake.   40
TITUS [*aloft*]
Art thou Revenge? And art thou sent to me
To be a torment to mine enemies?
TAMORA
I am, therefore come down and welcome me.
TITUS [*aloft*]
Do me some service ere I come to thee.
Lo by thy side where Rape and Murder stands;   45
Now give some surance that thou art Revenge:
Stab them or tear them on thy chariot wheels,
And then I'll come and be thy waggoner,
And whirl along with thee about the globe,
Provide thee two proper palfreys, black as jet,   50
To hale thy vengeful waggon swift away
And find out murderers in their guilty caves;

45 **stands** As often, the verb is inflected '-s' with a plural subject, contrary to modern use.

46 **surance** guarantee, pledge (from 'assurance')

47 **thy chariot wheels** Waith (Oxf[1]) assumes that this implies a literal staging in which Tamora has actually entered in her chariot. But Revenge traditionally rode in a chariot, so it can be assumed rather than shown, and the sustained references from 47 to 55 seem to work to supply in the imagination what is not physically present on stage. If there were a chariot, Chiron and Demetrius could draw it on, but since they do not exit with Tamora there would be no way of getting it off.

49 ***globe** Q1's 'globes' is almost certainly an error, perhaps caused by the proximity of many other plurals.

50 **Provide thee two** Rowe emended to 'Provide two' to improve the metre, but Q1 is defensible on the ground that every other line from 44 to 51 has a second-person pronoun, so it is rhetorically damaging to omit one here.

proper handsome (*palfreys* was usually used for delicate horses ridden by women)

black as jet proverbial (Tilley, J49)

51 **hale** archaic form of 'haul'

52 ***murderers** pronounced as two syllables, 'murd'rers'. Q1 has 'murder'; the MS was probably 'murdrers'.

38 them out] *Q2*; the mout *Q1*   40 offender] *Q1*; offenders *Q3, F*   49 globe] *Dyce (Capell)*; Globes *Qq, F*   50 thee two] *Q1*; two *Rowe*   black] *Q1*; as blacke *Q3, F*   52 murderers] *Capell*; murder *Qq, F*   caves] *F2*; cares *Qq, F*

And when thy car is loaden with their heads,
I will dismount and by thy waggon wheel
Trot like a servile footman all day long,   55
Even from Hyperion's rising in the east
Until his very downfall in the sea.
And day by day I'll do this heavy task,
So thou destroy Rapine and Murder there.

TAMORA
These are my ministers, and come with me.   60

TITUS   [*aloft*]
Are these thy ministers? What are they called?

TAMORA
Rape and Murder, therefore called so
'Cause they take vengeance of such kind of men.

TITUS   [*aloft*]
Good Lord, how like the empress' sons they are,

---

56 ***Hyperion's** Not merely a conventional reference to Hyperion as the sun-god, but, sustaining the passage's line of imagery, an allusion to the Ovidian myth of Hyperion's son, Phaëthon, attempting to drive the chariot of the sun, being unable to control the horses and crashing into the sea (*Met.*, 1.944–2.420) – hence *downfall*. The unclassical Q1 compositor printed the name as '*Epeons*'; F's Compositor E fared little better, changing it to '*Eptons*'.

57 **very** possibly an error for 'weary' (Cam[1] conj.) – 'plausible particularly considering the high incidence of error in this passage' (*TxC*, 213)

59 **Rapine** interchangeable with rape

61 ***these** Dyce's emendation of Qq,F's 'them'; F2's 'they' is also possible. 'Them' could conceivably be correct, in that accusative was occasionally used in place of nominative in Elizabethan English, but this passage has

an unusually high number of compositorial errors.
What … called? Tamora/Revenge does not name her attendants at the beginning of the scene: Titus does so at 45ff. 'He has recognized, not impersonations designed by Tamora, but the men themselves, and, under cover of his supposed madness, christens them after his knowledge of what they have done' (Ard[2], 132). Tamora first tries to deny the identification, saying they are merely her *ministers*, but when forced to name them plays along, *closing with* Titus – she thinks she is humouring him in his lunacy, but in fact he has now taken control of the scene.

62 **Rape** F2 emended to 'Rapine' to regularize the metre, but Maxwell defends this as 'an effectively solemn headless line' (Ard[2]).
called callèd

---

54 thy] *Q1*; the *Q2–3, F*   56 Hyperion's] *F2*; *Epeons Qq*; *Eptons F*   57 very] *Q1*; weary (*Cam[1]*)   61 these] *Dyce*; them *Qq, F*; they *F2*   62 Rape] *Q1*; Rapine *F2*

And you the empress! But we worldly men   65
Have miserable, mad, mistaking eyes.
O sweet Revenge, now do I come to thee,
And if one arm's embracement will content thee,
I will embrace thee in it by and by.   *[Exit aloft.]*

TAMORA

This closing with him fits his lunacy.   70
Whate'er I forge to feed his brainsick humours
Do you uphold and maintain in your speeches,
For now he firmly takes me for Revenge,
And, being credulous in this mad thought,
I'll make him send for Lucius his son,   75
And whilst I at a banquet hold him sure,
I'll find some cunning practice out of hand
To scatter and disperse the giddy Goths,
Or at the least make them his enemies.
See, here he comes, and I must ply my theme.   80

[Enter TITUS, *below.]*

TITUS

Long have I been forlorn, and all for thee.
Welcome, dread Fury, to my woeful house;
Rapine and Murder, you are welcome too.
How like the empress and her sons you are!
Well are you fitted, had you but a Moor;   85

65 **worldly** of this world, as opposed to the underworld where Revenge is supposed to have come from
70 **closing** agreeing (*OED*'s first citation for this meaning is *MM* 5.1.342)
71 **forge** invent, with suggestion of cunning
    brainsick humours links his whimsical caprices to his disturbed temperament
72 **maintain** stress on first syllable
77 **practice** plot, scheme

out of hand immediately, extempore
78 **To scatter … Goths** similar to Barabas' plan against the Turks in Marlowe's *Jew of Malta*. Possible wordplay on 'giddy goats'.
80 **ply my theme** work at my exercise: schoolroom language again
82 **Welcome …** presumably, as indicated by 68, attempting a comic one-handed embrace
85 **fitted** shaped, fitted out

65 worldly] *Q2*; wordlie *Q1*   69 SD] *Rowe subst.*   71 humours] *Q1*; fits *Q2–3*, F   76 banquet]
Q1 (banket)   80 ply] *Q1*; play F   80.1] *Rowe subst.*

Could not all hell afford you such a devil?
For well I wot the empress never wags
But in her company there is a Moor,
And would you represent our queen aright
It were convenient you had such a devil.   90
But welcome as you are. What shall we do?

TAMORA
What wouldst thou have us do, Andronicus?

DEMETRIUS
Show me a murderer, I'll deal with him.

CHIRON
Show me a villain that hath done a rape,
And I am sent to be revenged on him.   95

TAMORA
Show me a thousand that hath done thee wrong,
And I will be revenged on them all.

TITUS   [*to Demetrius*]
Look round about the wicked streets of Rome,
And when thou find'st a man that's like thyself,
Good Murder, stab him: he's a murderer.   100
[*to Chiron*]
Go thou with him, and when it is thy hap
To find another that is like to thee,
Good Rapine, stab him: he is a ravisher.
[*to Tamora*]
Go thou with them, and in the emperor's court,
There is a queen attended by a Moor –   105
Well shalt thou know her by thine own proportion,
For up and down she doth resemble thee –

---

87 **wags** makes the slightest movement,
   goes anywhere
93 **deal with** engage with, set to work
   upon, i.e. kill
97 **revenged** revengèd
98–107 **Look ... resemble thee** In the
   modern-dress Cambridge production
   (1991), Titus took Polaroid photos to

serve as 'mugshots' and handed them
over on 'him', 'him' and 'thee'. Titus'
routine here is very similar to Timon's
at *Tim* 5.1.100–11.
103 **he is** probably elided to 'he's', as in
   100
107 **up and down** in every respect (an
   opportunity for the actor to look her

96 hath] *Q1;* haue *Q2–3, F*   97 I will] *Q1;* Ile *F*   98 SD] *Oxf¹*   101 SD] *Oxf¹*   104 SD]
Bevington   106 shalt] *Q1;* maist *Q2–3, F*   thine] *Q1;* thy *Q3, F*

I pray thee, do on them some violent death:
They have been violent to me and mine.

TAMORA

Well hast thou lessoned us; this shall we do.   110
But would it please thee, good Andronicus,
To send for Lucius, thy thrice-valiant son,
Who leads towards Rome a band of warlike Goths,
And bid him come and banquet at thy house?
When he is here, even at thy solemn feast,   115
I will bring in the empress and her sons,
The emperor himself and all thy foes,
And at thy mercy shall they stoop and kneel,
And on them shalt thou ease thy angry heart.
What says Andronicus to this device?   120

TITUS

Marcus, my brother! 'Tis sad Titus calls.

Enter MARCUS.

Go, gentle Marcus, to thy nephew Lucius;
Thou shalt enquire him out among the Goths.
Bid him repair to me and bring with him
Some of the chiefest princes of the Goths.   125
Bid him encamp his soldiers where they are.
Tell him the emperor and the empress too
Feast at my house, and he shall feast with them.
This do thou for my love, and so let him,
As he regards his aged father's life.   130

MARCUS

This will I do, and soon return again.   [*Exit.*]

up and down)
112 **thrice-valiant** The tone may be
ingratiating but with an ironic under-
tow.
115–20 **When ... device** strong dramatic irony: this happens, but as
Titus' device instead of Tamora's

121.1 *Enter* MARCUS This SD is placed
a line earlier in Qq,F.
126 **Bid ... are** Lucius does not in fact
leave his army behind (Marcus may
realize that this instruction is for the
deception of Tamora).

121 TITUS] *Q1; Oxf¹ adds SD / calling*   121.1] *placed here by Theobald; after 120 in Qq, F*   128
Feast] *Q1; Feasts F*   131 SD] *F2*

TAMORA
> Now will I hence about thy business,
> And take my ministers along with me.

TITUS
> Nay, nay, let Rape and Murder stay with me –
> Or else I'll call my brother back again   135
> And cleave to no revenge but Lucius.

TAMORA   [*aside to her sons*]
> What say you, boys, will you abide with him
> Whiles I go tell my lord the emperor
> How I have governed our determined jest?
> Yield to his humour, smooth and speak him fair,   140
> And tarry with him till I turn again.

TITUS   [*aside*]
> I knew them all, though they supposed me mad,
> And will o'erreach them in their own devices –
> A pair of cursed hellhounds and their dam.

DEMETRIUS
> Madam, depart at pleasure, leave us here.   145

TAMORA
> Farewell, Andronicus: Revenge now goes
> To lay a complot to betray thy foes.

TITUS
> I know thou dost – and sweet Revenge, farewell.
>   [*Exit Tamora.*]

CHIRON
> Tell us, old man, how shall we be employed?

TITUS
> Tut, I have work enough for you to do.   150

---

136 **revenge ... Lucius** Revenge is thus still personified, but now as Lucius.
139 **governed ... jest** managed, administered the exploit we have planned
140 **smooth ... fair** flatter and humour him
141 **turn** return
144 **cursed** cursèd

137 SD] *Hanmer*   abide] *Q1;* bide *Q2–3, F*   140 Yield] *Q1* (Yeeld, l *broken, resembling apostrophe);* Yeede *Q2*   142 SD] *Rowe*   knew] *Q1;* know *Q2–3, F*   supposed] *Q1* (supposd); suppose *Q2–3, F*   144 dam] *Q1* (Dame)   148.1] *Capell; Rowe places after 147*   150 Tut] *Q1;* But *Q3*

Publius, come hither; Caius and Valentine.

[*Enter* PUBLIUS, CAIUS *and* VALENTINE.]

PUBLIUS
What is your will?
TITUS
Know you these two?
PUBLIUS
The empress' sons I take them: Chiron, Demetrius.
TITUS
Fie, Publius, fie, thou art too much deceived.   155
The one is Murder and Rape is the other's name,
And therefore bind them, gentle Publius;
Caius and Valentine, lay hands on them.
Oft have you heard me wish for such an hour,
And now I find it; therefore bind them sure,   160
And stop their mouths if they begin to cry.   [*Exit.*]
CHIRON
Villains, forbear! We are the empress' sons.
PUBLIUS
And therefore do we what we are commanded.
                              [*They bind and gag them.*]
Stop close their mouths; let them not speak a word.
Is he sure bound? Look that you bind them fast.   165

Enter TITUS ANDRONICUS *with a knife,*
and LAVINIA *with a basin.*

TITUS
Come, come, Lavinia: look, thy foes are bound.
Sirs, stop their mouths; let them not speak to me,

---

154 **The ... Demetrius** An unmetrical
line, probably broken up with gestures
towards the brothers.
163 **therefore** precisely for that reason

163.1 *They bind ... them* Publius is
ordering the action; he may or may
not physically assist.

151.1] *Rowe subst.*   156 and] *Q1; not in Q2–3, F*   161] *Q1; not in F*   161 SD] *Rowe*   163.1]
Oxf; Publius, &c. lay hold on Chiron and Demetrius / Malone (after 161)   165 fast.] *Q1; fast.*
Exeunt. F

But let them hear what fearful words I utter.
O villains, Chiron and Demetrius,
Here stands the spring whom you have stained with
    mud,   170
This goodly summer with your winter mixed.
You killed her husband, and for that vile fault
Two of her brothers were condemned to death,
My hand cut off and made a merry jest,
Both her sweet hands, her tongue, and that more
    dear   175
Than hands or tongue, her spotless chastity,
Inhuman traitors, you constrained and forced.
What would you say if I should let you speak?
Villains, for shame you could not beg for grace.
Hark, wretches, how I mean to martyr you: 180
This one hand yet is left to cut your throats,
Whiles that Lavinia 'tween her stumps doth hold
The basin that receives your guilty blood.
You know your mother means to feast with me,
And calls herself Revenge and thinks me mad.   185
Hark, villains, I will grind your bones to dust,
And with your blood and it I'll make a paste,
And of the paste a coffin I will rear,
And make two pasties of your shameful heads,
And bid that strumpet, your unhallowed dam,   190
Like to the earth swallow her own increase.
This is the feast that I have bid her to,

---

187 **paste** mixture of flour and water (for which ground bones and blood here substitute): pastry
188 **coffin** pie-crust, with obvious pun
189 **pasties** meat-pies
191 **earth ... increase** Simile from the traditional idea of mother-earth taking back her children in death (compare the 'swallowing womb' of 2.2.239); *increase* is common in Shakespeare for 'offspring'.

192–5 **feast ... revenged** At the climax of the Philomel story, 'King *Tereus* sitting in the throne of his forefathers, fed / And swallowed downe the selfe same flesh that of his bowels bred' (*Met.*, 6.824–5). Dinner was served by the raped Philomel's sister, *Progne* (otherwise spelt Procne). Also alluded to during the bloody banquet in *Tamburlaine*: 'And may this banquet prove as ominous / As Procne's to

182 Whiles] *Q1;* Whilst *Q2–3, F*   191 own] *Q1; not in F*

And this the banquet she shall surfeit on:
For worse than Philomel you used my daughter,
And worse than Progne I will be revenged.   195
And now, prepare your throats. Lavinia, come,
Receive the blood, and when that they are dead
Let me go grind their bones to powder small,
And with this hateful liquor temper it,
And in that paste let their vile heads be baked.   200
Come, come, be everyone officious
To make this banquet, which I wish may prove
More stern and bloody than the Centaurs' feast.
                                           He cuts their throats.
So, now bring them in, for I'll play the cook,
And see them ready against their mother comes.   205
                                           Exeunt [with the bodies.]

5.3 *Enter* LUCIUS, MARCUS *and the* Goths [*with* AARON
        prisoner and one carrying his child].

LUCIUS
Uncle Marcus, since 'tis my father's mind
That I repair to Rome, I am content.

---

th'adulterous Thracian king / That
fed upon the substance of his child'
(pt 1, 4.4.23–5).
197 **Receive the blood** a dark parody
of the language of the holy eucharist?
199 **temper** moisten
201 **officious** diligent in duties. Four
syllables.
203 **Centaurs' feast** another bloody
mythological allusion, to the battle
with the human/horses which took
place at the wedding-feast of the Lap-
ithae (Ovid's *Met.*, 12.239–592)

204 **now ... play** metrically awkward;
could be amended to 'So bring them
in, for now I'll play the cook', on the
assumption that the printer got the
word-order wrong; alternatively, *So*
can be treated as a separate line and
I'll expanded to *I will*.
205 **against** in anticipation of. Could be
elided to *'gainst* for the sake of the
metre.
5.3 The scene is imagined to begin
outside Titus' house and then move
inside it.

---

193 banquet *Q1* (banket*)*   202 may] *Q1;* might *F*   205 against] *Q1;* gainst *F*   205.1 *with the*
bodies] *Capell subst.*

5.3] *Capell; Pope continues the scene*   Location] The Same [as 5.2] *Capell*   0.1–2 *with* AARON
prisoner] *Rowe*   0.2 *and ... child*] *Kittredge subst.*

1 GOTH

And ours with thine, befall what fortune will.

LUCIUS

Good uncle, take you in this barbarous Moor,
This ravenous tiger, this accursed devil;   5
Let him receive no sustenance, fetter him
Till he be brought unto the empress' face
For testimony of her foul proceedings.
And see the ambush of our friends be strong:
I fear the emperor means no good to us.   10

AARON

Some devil whisper curses in my ear,
And prompt me that my tongue may utter forth
The venomous malice of my swelling heart.

LUCIUS

Away, inhuman dog, unhallowed slave!
Sirs, help our uncle to convey him in.   15
            [*Exit Aaron under guard.*] *Sound trumpets.*
The trumpets show the emperor is at hand.

Enter Emperor *and* Empress, *with Tribunes and Others*
            [*including* EMILLIUS].

3 **ours** i.e. our minds accord with yours
5 **accursed** accursèd
6 **sustenance** 'sustnance' (Q1)
9 **ambush** refers to those disposed in
an ambush
13 **venomous ... heart** Envy was often
associated with the swelling heart (as
at *1H6* 3.1.26 and *Arden of Faversham*,
1.325).
15.1 *under guard* Who takes Aaron
away? Lucius has asked Marcus to do
so, but he is back by 19. Most eds
since Rowe have '*Exeunt Goths with
Aaron*'; Oxf has Goths re-entering in
the tumult at 65. But this implies that

no Goths remain on stage during the
banquet, which flies in the face of
Titus' welcome to them at 27. The
likeliest staging is that one or two
Goths serve as guards and take Aaron
off, Marcus showing them the way in
but not actually leaving the stage.
Some Goths will remain, including
the one (who may be female, perhaps
played by the actor who was previously the Nurse) holding Aaron's
baby.
16.1 *Others* These would probably be
those who have previously played
Senators and the imperial guard.

3 1 GOTH] *Capell subst.*; GOTH *Qq, F*   7 empress'] *Q1* (*Empresse*); Emperours *Q3*; Emperous
F   11 my] *Q1, F*; mine *Q2–3*   15.1 *Exit ... guard*] *this edn*; Exeunt Goths, *with Aaron / Rowe
(after 14)   Sound trumpets*] *Q1 (after 16*); Flourish *F (placed here)*   16.2 *including* EMILLIUS]
Dyce subst. (*Aemilius*)

SATURNINUS

What, hath the firmament more suns than one?

LUCIUS

What boots it thee to call thyself a sun?

MARCUS

Rome's emperor, and nephew, break the parle;

These quarrels must be quietly debated.   20

The feast is ready which the careful Titus

Hath ordained to an honourable end,

For peace, for love, for league and good to Rome,

Please you therefore, draw nigh and take your
places.

SATURNINUS

Marcus, we will.   25

Trumpets sounding, a table brought in. [They sit.] Enter TITUS
like a cook, placing the dishes, and LAVINIA *with a veil over her
face [and* YOUNG LUCIUS].

Emillius and an unnamed Roman
Lord are numbered among them (this
could be one and the same actor:
see on 72). Strikingly, the SD has
Tribunes and not Senators. Lucius is
eventually acclaimed by the Tribunes
and the 'common voice', with the
Goths in support: the collective voice
of the patrician class is conspicuous
by its absence.

17 **more** F's 'modernization' of Qq's
'mo' (a long line of type in Q1, so
the shortened form may have been a
compositor's expedient). 'Two suns
cannot shine in one sphere' was proverbial (Tilley, S992).

18 **boots it** use is it

19 **break the parle** open the nego-

tiations: i.e. stop slanging each other
and 'quietly debate' the issue. *Parle*
probably monosyllabic.

21 **careful** afflicted with care. Possible
subliminal pun in that the audience
(not Marcus) know that Titus is
taking care of the arrangements.

24 **therefore** stress on second syllable

25.1 *Trumpets* F has hautboys (ancestors
of modern oboe, French *haut bois*),
perhaps since this is not an imperial
entrance, as are those heralded by
trumpets.
table probably brought in by Publius,
Caius and Valentine/Sempronius. In
the Warner production it was brought
in to the whistling of 'Heigh-ho,
heigh-ho, it's off to work we go'.

17 more] *F;* mo *Q1*   25.1 *Trumpets sounding] Q1; Hoboyes F   a table brought in] F   They sit]
Capell subst.*   25.2 *dishes] Q1; meat on the Table Q2–3, F   25.3 and* YOUNG LUCIUS] *this edn;*
Young Lucius, and others / Malone

TITUS

> Welcome, my gracious lord; welcome, dread queen;
> Welcome, ye warlike Goths; welcome, Lucius;
> And welcome, all. Although the cheer be poor,
> 'Twill fill your stomachs. Please you, eat of it.

SATURNINUS

> Why art thou thus attired, Andronicus?   30

TITUS

> Because I would be sure to have all well
> To entertain your highness and your empress.

TAMORA

> We are beholden to you, good Andronicus.

TITUS

> And if your highness knew my heart you were.
> My lord the emperor, resolve me this: 35
> Was it well done of rash Virginius
> To slay his daughter with his own right hand,
> Because she was enforced, stained and deflowered?

SATURNINUS

> It was, Andronicus.

TITUS   Your reason, mighty lord?

SATURNINUS

> Because the girl should not survive her shame,   40
> And by her presence still renew his sorrows.

TITUS

> A reason mighty, strong, and effectual;

---

26 *gracious A Q2 addition which was probably the result of the damage to the copy of Q1 from which it was set (this is the bottom line of sig.K2ʳ, and the preceding SD is also altered), but which nevertheless greatly improves the balance, rhythm and irony of the line.

28 cheer hospitality, food

33 beholden see on 1.1.401

34 And if if

36 Virginius another patterning narrative: in Livy, the centurion Virginius slew his daughter Virginia to prevent her being raped by Appius Claudius; in some versions of the story he killed her *because* she had been raped (see Nørgaard)

37 right hand Titus' surviving one

40 Because in order that

42 and omitted by Hanmer to improve the metre, but the rhetorical structure is symmetrical with the following line

26 my gracious lord] *Q2;* my Lord *Q1*   33 beholden] *Q1* (beholding*)*   42 and] *Q1;* om. *Hanmer*

A pattern, precedent, and lively warrant
For me, most wretched, to perform the like.

                              [*Unveils Lavinia.*]

Die, die, Lavinia, and thy shame with thee,   45
And with thy shame thy father's sorrow die.

                              He kills her.

SATURNINUS
What hast thou done, unnatural and unkind?

TITUS
Killed her for whom my tears have made me blind.
I am as woeful as Virginius was,
And have a thousand times more cause than he   50
To do this outrage, and it now is done.

SATURNINUS
What, was she ravished? Tell who did the deed.

TITUS
Will't please you eat? Will't please your highness
    feed?

TAMORA
Why hast thou slain thine only daughter thus?

TITUS
Not I, 'twas Chiron and Demetrius: 55
They ravished her and cut away her tongue,
And they, 'twas they, that did her all this wrong.

---

43 **pattern, precedent** key ideas in the
structuring of the play: see introduction, pp. 90–2
lively striking (*OED*'s first usage for
this sense, *a.* 4c); perhaps plays on the
more usual Elizabethan sense, 'living'
(compare 3.1.106), ironically in that
it is a death-warrant
warrant Several senses are relevant:
authoritative witness, conclusive
proof, one whose command justifies
an action, sanction, token of autho-
rization, document or writ licensing
execution.

44.1 *Unveils Lavinia the logical place
for this SD, though Ravenscroft waits
till after Titus kills her. Eds since
Rowe print Q1's entrance '*with a veil*'
but have no SD for its removal.

46.1 *He kills her* In the Warner production, he crisply snapped her neck;
at Santa Cruz, she stepped towards
him as he held out the knife, actively
embracing both her father and death.

52–65 **What … deed** The verse moves
into couplets, emphasizing the effect
of revenge as echoic reciprocation.

---

43 precedent] *Q1* (president) 44.1] *this edn; Titus pulls off Lavinias Veil / Ravenscroft (placed
three lines later)* 46.1] *Q3* 47 hast thou] *Q1*; hast *F* 51] *Q1*; not in *F* now is] *Q1*; is now
Q3 54 thus] *Q1*; not in *Q3, F*

SATURNINUS

  Go, fetch them hither to us presently.

TITUS

  Why, there they are, both baked in this pie,

  Whereof their mother daintily hath fed,   60

  Eating the flesh that she herself hath bred.

  'Tis true, 'tis true, witness my knife's sharp point.

                         He stabs the Empress.

SATURNINUS

  Die, frantic wretch, for this accursed deed.

                              [He kills Titus.]

LUCIUS

  Can the son's eye behold his father bleed?

  There's meed for meed, death for a deadly deed.   65

               [He kills Saturninus. Uproar.

     The Goths protect the Andronici, who go aloft.]

---

59 **there they are** Titus points to the pie. Oxf's SD for the heads to be shown (see t.n.) supposes that they have been baked whole rather than ground with the bones, but that would make a stew rather than a pie. In the Warner production, Brian Cox virtually threw away the line, then laughed, Estelle Kohler's Tamora laughed too, and then as he continued she realized it was not a joke.

baked bakèd

60 **daintily** with delicate attention to the palate. Both word and context suggest the bloody banquet in *Tamburlaine*: 'Are you so daintily brought up, you cannot eat your own flesh?' (pt 1, 4.4.36–7).

63 **accursed** accursèd

65 **meed for meed** proverbial: 'measure for measure'. 'Death for death' was also proverbial (Dent, D139.1).

65.1–2 **Uproar ... aloft* Most eds have

'*A great tumult*' here; my '*Uproar*' is suggested by 67. When Lucius stabs the emperor, the followers of Saturninus would attempt to detain him; the Goths come to his defence, as agreed at the beginning of the scene (*ambush* at 9 may suggest that more Goths join those already on stage, though this would depend on the number of actors available). It is apparent from lines 129–35 that the Andronici have taken refuge aloft; the Goths probably guard their passage as they exit, then take up stations in front of the doors to prevent an assault from the Romans – though, as the ensuing dialogue shows, the latter are confused to the point of temporary paralysis in the state. Marcus has returned aloft, where he began the play and from where the choice of emperor will be made again, this time in favour of the Andronici.

---

59 this] *Q1*; that *Q2–3, F*; *Oxf* adds SD at this line: *revealing the heads*   63.1] *Ravenscroft, Rowe subst.*   65.1 *He kills Saturninus*] *Ravenscroft, Rowe subst.*   *Uproar*] *this edn*; *A great tumult* / *Capell*   65.2] *this edn*; *Lucius, Marcus, and others go up into the balcony* / *Cam*

MARCUS [*aloft*]
    You sad-faced men, people and sons of Rome,
    By uproars severed, as a flight of fowl
    Scattered by winds and high tempestuous gusts,
    O let me teach you how to knit again
    This scattered corn into one mutual sheaf,   70
    These broken limbs again into one body.
A ROMAN LORD
    Let Rome herself be bane unto herself,
    And she whom mighty kingdoms curtsy to,
    Like a forlorn and desperate castaway,
    Do shameful execution on herself!   75
    But if my frosty signs and chaps of age,
    Grave witnesses of true experience,
    Cannot induce you to attend my words,

70 **mutual sheaf** reciprocally sup-
porting structure, like a haystack
72 ROMAN LORD This SP is clearly
printed in Q1; I see no case for erasing
it and giving the whole speech to
Marcus, as most eds since Capell have
done. The speech is Rome's reply to
Marcus' offer to teach the state how
to knit itself together. Riv (following
a suggestion of Sisson) makes the
Roman Lord synonymous with Emillius, who has a similar function at
136–9; this is economical from the
point of view of casting, but not
necessary – any senior-looking Roman
can deliver the speech (76 indicates
he has white hair and wrinkles: 'frosty
signs and chaps of age').
72–5 **Let Rome ... herself** Far from
mending itself, the body of the state
might as well execute itself (be its
own *bane*): with the imperial couple
and the old Andronicus dead, and the
Goths in the very heart of once-all-
conquering Rome, this is an understandable reaction. But if the tone is
misread it sounds curious coming
from a Roman, which is probably why
F changed the SP 'ROMANE LORD'
to 'GOTH'. In fact, the Goths are
definitely present but uncannily silent
in this final sequence.
76–8 **But if ... my words** If Rome
won't do as advised and commit collective suicide, then Marcus may as
well speak and explain how the dis-
aster has come about. Sisson, Riv
and Wells (Oxf) have an alternative
reading: they make 72–8 into a single
sentence (with a comma at the end of
75), meaning 'If you cannot be
induced to listen to me, let Rome
execute itself'; the problem with this
(quite apart from the full stop at the
end of 75 in all the early texts) is that,
far from demanding further attention,
the Lord goes straight on to ask
someone else to speak.

66 *aloft*] *this edn (and for subsequent speeches from upper stage)*   67 as] *Q1; like Q3,* F   72 A
ROMAN LORD] *Q1 (*ROMANE LORD*);* GOTH F; *Capell continues to* MARCUS *with* Lest *for* Let
and comma after body *at end of previous line;* AEMIL. *Riv (Sisson)*   73 curtsy] *Q1 (*cursie*)

Speak, Rome's dear friend, as erst our ancestor
When with his solemn tongue he did discourse   80
To lovesick Dido's sad-attending ear
The story of that baleful burning night
When subtle Greeks surprised King Priam's Troy.
Tell us what Sinon hath bewitched our ears,
Or who hath brought the fatal engine in   85
That gives our Troy, our Rome, the civil wound.
MARCUS [*aloft*]
My heart is not compact of flint nor steel,

79 **Speak, Rome's dear friend** Rome's
reply to Marcus' request to speak. As
a tribune who stands in special party
for the people of Rome (1.1.20–1),
Marcus is indeed a 'dear friend' to
the state, yet every modern ed. follows
Rowe in having these lines addressed
'[*To Lucius*]'. Even though Lucius has
popular support, it is hard to imagine
a Lord addressing him as a dear friend
to Rome when he has just led an
enemy army into the city and per-
sonally killed the emperor – only
when events are explained will he
be acclaimed. Throughout the play,
Lucius is associated with action,
Marcus with explanation.

79–86 **our ancestor ... our Troy** The
ancestor is Aeneas. The Lord is under
the impression that Rome has fallen
to the Goths in exactly the same way
that Troy (Rome's *atavus*) fell to the
Greeks: he assumes that the bloody
banquet was a trick of the same order
as the Trojan horse. *Sinon* tricked the
Trojans into accepting the horse; the
Lord wants Marcus to tell the
assembled company the identity of
the equivalent figure here. But we
already know that the Sinon is not
an outsider, but rather the emperor
Saturninus himself: the situation is
analogous not to that of Troy, but to
that of Rome in *Lucrece*, where

Tarquin (to whom Saturninus has
twice been compared) explicitly
becomes Sinon (*Luc* 1520–61).

86 **our Troy, our Rome** on the translation of empire, see introduction, pp.
17–21
civil wound the body of the state
self-wounded by civil war

87 **MARCUS In Q1, lines 87–94 are a
continuation of the Roman Lord's
speech, but that speech comes to a
natural end with the 'Tell us' sentence. The language of the next eight
lines is very similar to that associated
with the Andronici in the third act
(the heart under stress, bitter grief,
tears and oratory, broken utterance).
Capell's instinct that these lines are
Marcus' led him to erase the SP
'ROMANE LORD' and give Marcus
the whole speech, but a missing SP
here is much easier to account for
than an incorrectly added one at 72.
Compositorial eyeskip across an
abbreviated SP (M., Ma. or Mar.) to
'My hart' is easily imaginable.
compact composed, made up

87–94 **My heart ... him speak** Having
requested to speak, and now been
given permission to do so, Marcus
realizes that in recounting the events
his eloquence will be overcome with
emotion; he therefore asks Lucius to
speak instead.

87 MARCUS] *this edn; Q1 continues to* ROMANE LORD

Nor can I utter all our bitter grief,
But floods of tears will drown my oratory
And break my utterance even in the time   90
When it should move ye to attend me most,
And force you to commiseration.
Here's Rome's young captain: let him tell the tale,
While I stand by and weep to hear him speak.

LUCIUS   [*aloft*]
    Then, gracious auditory, be it known to you   95
That Chiron and the damned Demetrius
Were they that murdered our emperor's brother,
And they it were that ravished our sister;
For their fell faults our brothers were beheaded,
Our father's tears despised and basely cozened   100
Of that true hand that fought Rome's quarrel out
And sent her enemies unto the grave;
Lastly myself, unkindly banished,
The gates shut on me, and turned weeping out

89 **But ... will drown** without ...
    drowning
91 **ye** The plural pronoun here suggests
    that this is Marcus addressing all the
    Romans, not the Lord addressing
    Marcus.
92 **commiseration** In his *Apology for
    Poetry*, Sir Philip Sidney wrote that
    tragedy arouses 'admiration' and
    'commiseration', terms derived from
    Aristotle's 'terror' and 'pity'.
93 **Rome's young captain** This phrase
    supports my assignment of these
    lines: the Roman Lord would not call
    Lucius this, since from the point of
    view of Rome he is a traitor and an
    invader; Marcus takes the opportunity
    to indicate Lucius' loyalty to Rome.
94 **While ... by** While I stand beside
    him: further evidence that this is

Marcus speaking, from aloft, shoulder
to shoulder with his nephew.
95 **Then ... you** metre suggests elisions:
    'auditry', 'be't' (Cercignani, 277, 289)
96 **damned** monosyllabic
97 **murdered**   murderèd   (hence
    'emp'ror's')
98 **they it were** transposed word order
    adds emphasis (Abbott, §425)
    ravished ravishèd
100 **cozened** cheated
101 **fought ... out** fought to the finish;
    quarrel hostilities, war
103 **unkindly** unnaturally
    banished banishèd
103–16 **Lastly myself ... praise** For
    the very strong similarities to Cori-
    olanus throughout this speech, see
    introduction, pp. 13–15.

90 my] *Q1;* my very *Q3, F*   utterance] *Q1 (*vttrance*)*   91 ye] *Q1;* you *Q2–3, F*   92] *Q1;* Lending
your kind commiseration *Q2–3, F (F adds* hand *after* kind*)*   93 Here's Rome's young] *Q1;* Heere
is a *Q2–3, F*   94 While I stand by] *Q1;* Your harts will throb *Q2–3, F*   95 Then] *Q1;* This
F   gracious] *Q1;* noble *Q2–3, F*   96 Chiron and the damned] *Q1;* cursed Chiron and *Q2–3, F*

To beg relief among Rome's enemies,   105
Who drowned their enmity in my true tears
And oped their arms to embrace me as a friend.
I am the turned-forth, be it known to you,
That have preserved her welfare in my blood,
And from her bosom took the enemy's point,   110
Sheathing the steel in my adventurous body.
Alas, you know I am no vaunter, I;
My scars can witness, dumb although they are,
That my report is just and full of truth.
But soft, methinks I do digress too much,   115
Citing my worthless praise. O pardon me,
For when no friends are by, men praise themselves.
MARCUS   [*aloft*]
Now is my turn to speak. [*Points to Aaron's baby.*]
                        Behold the child:
Of this was Tamora delivered,
The issue of an irreligious Moor,   120
Chief architect and plotter of these woes.
The villain is alive in Titus' house,
And as he is to witness this is true,

---

107 **to embrace** possibly elided to 't'em-
    brace'
108 **turned-forth** turnèd forth
    be it elided to 'be't'
111 **adventurous** willing to incur risk.
    Pronounced 'adventrous', to judge
    from Q1 spelling.
113 **scars can witness** another image of
    the wounded body articulating more
    clearly than speech
117 **when ... themselves** proverbial
    (Tilley, N117)
118 **my turn to speak** Marcus is now
    able to speak, Lucius having recounted
    the woes of the Andronici which he
    would have found unspeakable.
    Behold the child Presumably the
    baby has been in the arms of a Goth
    throughout the scene; Marcus now
    points down to it (or conceivably

some of the Goths, including the one
with the baby, have accompanied the
Andronici to the upper stage). I
assume that Lucius has kept his word
to Aaron and the baby is still alive,
but in the BBC production Marcus
at this point held up a box containing
its dead body.
119 **delivered** deliverèd
121 **architect** *OED*'s earliest citation in
    sense of one who plans, schemes; the
    original sense of 'master-builder' was
    first used in the 1560s (*plotter* is also
    very new at this time: *OED*'s first
    citation is Nashe, 1589; it has the
    same figurative origin, 'plot'/'plat'
    meaning the ground-plan of a
    building).
123 **true** F has a full stop here, but Q1's
    comma makes reasonable sense.

---

108 I am the] *Q1*; and I am the *Q3*; And I am *F*   118 SD] *Oxf¹*   the] *Q1*; this *Q3*, *F*

Now judge what cause had Titus to revenge
These wrongs unspeakable, past patience,   125
Or more than any living man could bear.
Now have you heard the truth: what say you,
    Romans?
Have we done aught amiss, show us wherein,
And from the place where you behold us pleading,
The poor remainder of Andronici   130
Will hand in hand all headlong hurl ourselves
And on the ragged stones beat forth our souls
And make a mutual closure of our house.
Speak, Romans, speak, and if you say, we shall,
Lo, hand in hand, Lucius and I will fall.   135

EMILLIUS
Come, come, thou reverend man of Rome,
And bring our emperor gently in thy hand,
Lucius, our emperor, for well I know
The common voice do cry it shall be so.

---

125 **patience** three syllables
128 **Have we** conditional: 'if we have'
130 **remainder of Andronici** This suggests that the Boy, Young Lucius, is aloft with his father and great-uncle: three generations of Andronici stand hand in hand aloft, threatening to end the house by throwing themselves off the building that represents Titus' house. An allusion to Rome's Tarpeian rock, from which those found guilty of treason were hurled.
132 **ragged** rough
133 **closure** *OED*'s first citation for the sense of 'bringing to a conclusion'. Given the reference to *house*, may be transferred from a technical term in architecture: 'the scutcheon or closure of a Tymber vault, where the ends of

the branches thereof doe meet' (*OED* 7c, though not linked to the sense given for the usage here). 'Mutual closure' is presented by Marcus as the alternative to the rebuilding into a 'mutual sheaf' which he proposed at 70.
136 **Come, come** a short line, which could be made up with 'Come, Marcus, come' (as 4.3.1), assuming eyeskip across the vocative
137 **our emperor** Lucius is acclaimed not only because of his popularity but because of Marcus' threat: if Lucius, the general of the invading army, were to jump to his death, Rome would be left to the mercy of the Goths. As emperor, he will be able to make an accommodation with them.

---

124 cause] *F4;* course *Qq, F*   127 have you] *Q1;* you haue *Q2–3, F*   129 pleading] *Q1;* now *Q2–3, F*   131 hurl ourselves] *Q1;* cast vs downe *Q2–3, F*   132 souls] *Q1;* braines *Q2–3, F*   136 Come, come] *Q1* (Come come*);* Come, Marcus, come *(Ard²)*

MARCUS   [*aloft*]
   Lucius, all hail, Rome's royal emperor!   140
   [*to others*] Go, go into old Titus' sorrowful house
   And hither hale that misbelieving Moor
   To be adjudged some direful slaughtering death
   As punishment for his most wicked life.
                  [*Exeunt some into the house.*
      A long flourish till the Andronici come down.]
ALL ROMANS
   Lucius, all hail, Rome's gracious governor!   145

140 MARCUS Though clearly ascribed to
Marcus in the early texts, most eds
assume a missing SP and give this
line to 'ALL THE ROMANS'. But the
moment echoes 1.1.234–7, and there
it is Marcus, speaking for 'Patricians
and plebeians', who proclaims 'Long
live our emperor Saturnine!' Compare
R3 3.7.240–1, where first Buckingham
acclaims Richard, then 'ALL' respond.

141 **Go, go** Having proclaimed Lucius
emperor, Marcus now gives the order
for Aaron to be fetched. But by
whom? Eds follow Capell and have
'*To Attendants*', but Goths have taken
Aaron into the house, so it would be
logical for them to bring him out.
Q1's 'Goe goe' could conceivably be
a misreading of 'Goths, go' or 'Go,
Goths'. Alternatively, if fellow-
Andronici such as Publius and Caius
are with Marcus, he may turn and
address the line to them. Since it is
an open question, I do not name a
specific addressee here and I use the
vague '*some*' for SD at 144, and '*under
guard*' for the re-entry at 174.

143 **slaughtering** 'slaughtring' (Q1)

144.2 *A long flourish ... A trumpet
flourish would cover the Andronici's
descent and proclaim Lucius as

emperor, echoing '*a long flourish till
they come down*' at the corresponding
moment at 1.1.237.

145 *ALL ROMANS In the early texts, this
is the last line of Marcus' speech, but
since Lucius replies to the collectivity
of 'gentle Romans', it may be assumed
that this line is spoken by them as he
comes on to the main stage and that
the SP 'ALL' has dropped out (one
missing SP is much more likely than
the two assumed by eds who also give
140 to 'ALL'). Ravenscroft gave this
line to 'OMNES'. Dessen (p. 102)
makes the case for leaving both accla-
mations with Marcus ('perhaps acting
as cheerleader'). Directors might wish
to try this as an alternative staging.
Whether or not the Goths join in the
cry is another interesting decision that
would have to be made in production:
if they do, it would be as if Romans
and Goths have been united; if not,
they remain as a silent – and potentially sinister – guard for Lucius. Like
Fortinbras in *Ham*, Octavius in *AC*
and Malcolm in *Mac*, Lucius is a
bringer of order to the fragmented
state, but it is left open whether he
will usher in an age of peace or resort
to strong-arm tactics himself.

140 MARCUS] *Q1;* ROM[ANS] *Capell;* ALL *Cam*   141 SD] *this edn; To Attendants / Capell*   143
adjudged] *Q3, F (*adiudgd*);* adiudge *Q1*   144.1] *this edn; Exeunt Attendants / Cam*   144.2] *this
edn; All disappear from above / Ravenscroft; Lucius, and the rest, come down; with them, young Lucius
/ Capell*   145 ALL ROMANS] *Ravenscroft (*OMNES*);* ROM. *Capell; Q1 continues to* MARCUS   hail]
Q1; haile *to Q2–3, F*

LUCIUS

Thanks, gentle Romans. May I govern so
To heal Rome's harms and wipe away her woe.
But, gentle people, give me aim awhile,
For nature puts me to a heavy task.
Stand all aloof, but, uncle, draw you near   150
To shed obsequious tears upon this trunk.
[*Kisses Titus.*]
O, take this warm kiss on thy pale cold lips,
These sorrowful drops upon thy bloodstained face,
The last true duties of thy noble son.

MARCUS   [*Kisses Titus.*]

Tear for tear and loving kiss for kiss,   155
Thy brother Marcus tenders on thy lips.
O, were the sum of these that I should pay
Countless and infinite, yet would I pay them.

LUCIUS   [*to his son*]

Come hither, boy, come, come and learn of us
To melt in showers. Thy grandsire loved thee well: 160
Many a time he danced thee on his knee,
Sung thee asleep, his loving breast thy pillow;
Many a story hath he told to thee,
And bid thee bear his pretty tales in mind
And talk of them when he was dead and gone.   165

MARCUS

How many thousand times hath these poor lips,
When they were living, warmed themselves on
    thine!

148 **give me aim** stand by and observe
my efforts; metaphor from archery,
where the person who 'gave aim'
stood near the target and reported the
results of the shots
151 **obsequious** pertaining to obsequies,
funeral rites
156 **tenders** offers, as discharging a fin-
ancial obligation (hence the line of
imagery in 157–8), but *OED*, *v.*[2] 1,
'to be affected with pity', may be
subliminally present in the tone

150] *Q1; Capell adds SD: Kneels over Titus' body*   152 SD] *Johnson*   153 bloodstained] *F3* (blood-
stain'd*); blood slaine *Q1–2; bloud-slaine Q3, F*   155 SD] *Bevington; Kneeling by him / Capell*   159
SD] *Collier MS subst.*   162 Sung] *Q2; Song Q1*   163 story] *Q1; matter Q2–3, F*   164–8] *Q1;*
Meete and agreeing with thine infancie, / In that respect then, like a louing child. *(comma in Q3,*
F) / Shed yet some small drops from thy tender spring, / Because kind nature doth require it
so, / Friends should associate friends in griefe and woe *Q2–3, F*

O now, sweet boy, give them their latest kiss:
Bid him farewell, commit him to the grave;
Do them that kindness and take leave of them.   170
BOY   [*Kisses Titus.*]
O grandsire, grandsire, e'en with all my heart
Would I were dead, so you did live again.
O Lord, I cannot speak to him for weeping,
My tears will choke me if I ope my mouth.

[*Enter* AARON *under guard.*]

A ROMAN
You sad Andronici, have done with woes,   175
Give sentence on this execrable wretch
That hath been breeder of these dire events.
LUCIUS
Set him breast-deep in earth and famish him;
There let him stand and rave and cry for food.
If anyone relieves or pities him,   180
For the offence he dies. This is our doom;
Some stay to see him fastened in the earth.
AARON
Ah, why should wrath be mute and fury dumb?
I am no baby, I, that with base prayers
I should repent the evils I have done.   185
Ten thousand worse than ever yet I did
Would I perform if I might have my will.
If one good deed in all my life I did

---

170 **them ... them** referring back to the
     lips; F unnecessarily emended to 'him
     ... him' for consistency with the pre-
     vious line
171 BOY Picking up from this final kiss,
     the BBC production gave special
     emphasis to the Boy: its closing shot
     was 'YOUNG LUCIUS stares into

space' (BBC, 88).
172 **so** if only
175 A ROMAN This could be Emillius (as
     it is in Ravenscroft), but if the cast
     is large enough there is a case for
     having Roman Lord, Emillius and
     this Roman as three different mani-
     festations of the 'common voice'.

170 them ... them] *Q1;* him ... him *F*   171 BOY] *F; Puer Q1*   SD] *Bevington (after 172)*   174.1]
this edn; Enter Romans with Aaron / Rowe; Re-enter Attendants with Aaron / Dyce   175 A ROMAN]
Q1 (ROMANE); ROMANS F; EMIL. Ravenscroft; AEMIL. (Dyce)   183 Ah] *Q1; O F*

I do repent it from my very soul.

LUCIUS

    Some loving friends convey the emperor hence,   190
    And give him burial in his fathers' grave;
    My father and Lavinia shall forthwith
    Be closed in our household's monument;
    As for that ravenous tiger, Tamora,
    No funeral rite, nor man in mourning weed,   195
    No mournful bell shall ring her burial,
    But throw her forth to beasts and birds to prey:
    Her life was beastly and devoid of pity,
    And being dead, let birds on her take pity.

Exeunt [with the bodies].

Finis the Tragedy of Titus Andronicus.

191 **fathers'** no apostrophe in Qq,F. Could be singular (the father who died immediately before the action begins), but given the emphasis in 1.1 on the family vault and the fore-fathers, plural is better – though the distinction is not audible.

194 **ravenous** rapacious, but perhaps also hungry, ironic in view of what she's just eaten and the fact that she is about to be eaten

197 **throw ... prey** the fate of executed felons in Elizabethan England. *prey*: prey on – F's emendation to 'birds of prey' is unnecessary.

191 fathers'] *Cam (anon.);* fathers *Qq, F;* father's *Rowe* 194 ravenous] *Q1;* hainous *Q2–3, F* 195 rite] *Q1 (*right*)* mourning] *Q1;* mournefull *Q3, F* weed] *Q1;* weeds *Q2–3, F* 197 to prey] *Q1;* of prey *F* 198 beastly] *Q1;* Beast-like *F* 199] *Q1;* And being so, shall haue like want of pitty. / See iustice done on *Aron* that damn'd Moore, / By *(*From *F)* whom our heauie haps had their beginning: / Then *(*Than *Q2)* afterwards to order well the state, / That like euents may nere it ruinate. *Q2–3, F* 199.1 *with the bodies] Bevington subst.*

APPENDIX
PATTERNS AND
PRECEDENTS[1]

1 **The principal pattern**: the rape of Philomel, from Ovid, *Metamorphoses*, book six, translated by Arthur Golding (1567), lines 652–747, 804–53

[King Tereus marries Progne, but burns with desire for her sister Philomela]

> Assoone as *Tereus* and the Maide togither were a boord,
> And that their ship from land with Ores was haled on the foord,[2]
> The fielde is ours he cride aloude, I have the thing I sought
> And up he skipt, so barbrous and so beastly was his thought,
> That scarce even there he could forbeare his pleasure to have wrought.
> His eye went never off of hir: as when the scarefull Erne[3]
> With hooked talants trussing up a Hare among the Ferne,
> Hath laid hir in his nest, from whence the prisoner can not scape:
> The ravening fowle with greedie eyes upon his pray doth gape.   660
> Now was their journey come to ende: now were they gone a land
> In *Thracia*, when that *Tereus* tooke the Ladie by the hand,
> And led hir to a pelting[4] graunge that peakishly[5] did stand
> In woods forgrowen. There waxing pale and trembling sore for feare,
> And dreading all things, and with teares demaunding sadly where
> Hir sister was, he shet hir up: and therewithall bewraide[6]
> His wicked lust, and so by force bicause she was a Maide

---

1 Texts follow edns cited in list of abbreviations. Obsolete words in Golding are glossed at the foot of the page.
2 sea
3 eagle
4 paltry
5 ?remotely (only occurrence in *OED*)
6 revealed

And all alone he vanquisht hir. It booted nought at all
That she on sister, or on Sire, or on the Gods did call.
She quaketh like the wounded Lambe which from the Wolves
    hore[1] teeth   670
New shaken, thinkes hir selfe not safe: or as the Dove that seeth
Hir fethers with hir owne bloud staynde, who shuddring still
    doth feare
The greedie Hauke that did hir late with griping talants teare.
    Anon when that this mazednesse was somewhat overpast,
    She rent hir haire, and beate hir brest, and up to heavenward
        cast
Hir hands in mourningwise, and said: O cankerd Carle, O fell
And cruell Tyrant, neyther could the godly teares that fell
A downe my fathers cheekes when he did give thee charge of
    mee,
Ne of my sister that regarde that ought to be in thee,
Nor yet my chaast virginitie, nor conscience of the lawe   680
Of wedlocke, from this villanie thy barbrous heart withdraw?
Beholde thou hast confounded all. My sister thorough mee
Is made a Cucqueane:[2] and thy selfe through this offence of thee
Art made a husband to us both, and unto me a foe,
A just deserved punishment for lewdly doing so.
But to thintent O perjurde wretch no mischiefe may remaine
Unwrought by thee, why doest thou from murdring me refraine?
Would God thou had it done before this wicked rape. From
    hence
Then should my soule most blessedly have gone without offence.
But if the Gods doe see this deede, and if the Gods I say   690
Be ought, and in this wicked worlde beare any kinde of sway,
And if with me all other things decay not, sure the day
Will come that for this wickednesse full dearly thou shalt pay.
Yea I my selfe rejecting shame thy doings will bewray.
And if I may have power to come abrode, them blase I will
In open face of all the world: or if thou keepe me still
As prisoner in these woods, my voyce the verie woods shall fill,
And make the stones to understand. Let Heaven to this give
    eare
And all the Gods and powers therein if any God be there.
    The cruell tyrant being chaaft,[3] and also put in feare   700
    With these and other such hir wordes both causes so him
        stung,
    That drawing out his naked sworde that at his girdle hung,

1 greyish white
2 female cuckold
3 angered

He tooke hir rudely by the haire, and wrung hir hands behind
    hir,
Compelling hir to holde them there while he himselfe did binde
    hir.
When *Philomela* sawe the sworde she hoapt she should have
    dide,
And for the same hir naked throte she gladly did provide.
But as she yirnde and called ay upon hir fathers name,
And strived to have spoken still, the cruell tyrant came,
And with a paire of pinsons[1] fast did catch hir by the tung,
And with his sword did cut it off. The stumpe whereon it hung   710
Did patter still. The tip fell downe, and quivering on the ground
As though that it had murmured it made a certaine sound,
And as an Adders tayle cut off doth skip a while: even so
The tip of *Philomelaas* tongue did wriggle to and fro,
And nearer to hir mistresseward in dying still did go.
And after this most cruell act, for certaine men report
That he (I scarcely dare beleve) did oftentimes resort
To maymed *Philomela* and abusde hir at his will.
Yet after all this wickednesse he keeping countnance still,
Durst unto *Progne* home repaire. And she immediatly   720
Demaunded where hir sister was. He sighing feynedly
Did tell hir falsly she was dead: and with his suttle teares
He maketh all his tale to seeme of credit in hir eares.
Hir garments glittring all with golde she from hir shoulders
    teares
And puts on blacke, and setteth up an emptie Herce, and keepes
A solemne obite[2] for hir soule, and piteously she weepes
And waileth for hir sisters fate who was not in such wise
As that was, for to be bewailde. The Sunne had in the Skies
Past through the twelve celestiall signes, and finisht full a yeare.
But what should *Philomela* doe? She watched was so neare   730
That start she could not for hir life, the walles of that same
    graunge
Were made so high of maine[3] hard stone, that out she could not
    raunge.
Againe hir tunglesse mouth did want the utterance of the fact.
Great is the wit of pensivenesse, and when the head is ract
With hard misfortune, sharpe forecast of practise entereth in.
A warpe of white upon a frame of *Thracia* she did pin,
And weaved purple letters in betweene it, which bewraide
The wicked deede of *Tereus*. And having done, she praide

1   pincers
2   commemoration service
3   solid

A certaine woman by hir signes to beare them to hir mistresse.
She bare them and delivered them not knowing nerethelesse   740
What was in them. The Tyrants wife unfolded all the clout,[1]
And of hir wretched fortune red the processe whole throughout.
She held hir peace (a wondrous thing it is she should so doe)
But sorrow tide hir tongue, and wordes agreeable unto
Hir great displeasure were not at commaundment at that stound,[2]
And weepe she could not. Ryght and wrong she reckeneth to
    confound,
And on revengement of the deede hir heart doth wholy ground.

[Progne is driven to fury when her son Itys reminds her of her husband]

                                    No more delay there was.
She dragged *Itys* after hir as when it happes in *Inde*
A Tyger gets a little Calfe that suckes upon a Hynde,
And drags him through the shadie woods. And when that they
    had found
A place within the house far off and far above the ground,
Then *Progne* strake him with a sword now plainly seeing
    whother[3]
He should, and holding up his handes, and crying mother,
    mother,   810
And flying to hir necke: even where the brest and side doe
    bounde,
And never turnde away hir face. Inough had bene that wound
Alone to bring him to his ende. The tother sister slit
His throte. And while some life and soule was in his members
    yit,
In gobbits they them rent: whereof were some in Pipkins[4] boyld,
And other some on hissing spits against the fire were broyld:
And with the gellied bloud of him was all the chamber foyld.[5]
    To this same banket[6] *Progne* bade hir husband, knowing
        nought,
    Nor nought mistrusting of the harme and lewdnesse she had
        wrought.
And feyning a solemnitie according to the guise   820
Of *Athens*, at the which there might be none in any wise
Besides hir husband and hir selfe, she banisht from the same

1   shred of cloth
2   time, moment
3   whither (i.e. Itys sees what's going to happen to him)
4   pots
5   fouled (or printer's error for 'soiled')
6   banquet

Hir householde folke and sojourners, and such as guestwise
came.
King *Tereus* sitting in the throne of his forefathers, fed
And swallowed downe the selfe same flesh that of his bowels
bred.
And he (so blinded was his heart) fetch *Itys* hither, sed.
No lenger hir most cruell joy dissemble could the Queene,
But of hir murther coveting the messenger to beene,
She said: the thing thou askest for, thou hast within. About
He looked round, and asked where? To put him out of dout,   830
As he was yet demaunding where, and calling for him: out
Lept *Pholomele* with scattred haire aflaight[1] like one that fled
Had from some fray where slaughter was, and threw the bloudy
head
Of *Itys* in his fathers face. And never more was shee
Desirous to have had hir speache, that able she might be
Hir inward joy with worthie wordes to witnesse franke and free.
The tyrant with a hideous noyse away the table shoves,
And reeres the fiends from Hell. One while with yauning mouth
he proves[2]
To perbrake[3] up his meate againe, and cast his bowels out.
Another while with wringing handes he weeping goes about.   840
And of his sonne he termes himselfe the wretched grave. Anon
With naked sword and furious heart he followeth fierce upon
Pandions daughters. He that had bin present would have deemde
Their bodies to have hovered up with fethers. As they seemde,
So hovered they with wings in deede. Of whome the one away
To woodward flies, the other still about the house doth stay.
And of their murther from their brestes not yet the token goth,
For even still yet are stainde with bloud the fethers of them
both.
And he through sorrow and desire of vengeance waxing wight,[4]
Became a Bird upon whose top a tuft of feathers light   850
In likenesse of a Helmets crest doth trimly stand upright.
In stead of his long sword, his bill shootes out a passing space:
A Lapwing named is this Bird, all armed seemes his face.

1   flying
2   tries
3   vomit
4   swift

2   **The second pattern**: the rape of Lucrece, known to Shakespeare from Livy's *History of Rome* and Ovid's *Fasti*, here summarized in the Argument of his poem on the subject (1594)

Lucius Tarquinius (for his excessive pride surnamed Superbus), after he had caused his own father-in-law Servius Tullius to be cruelly murdered, and contrary to the Roman laws and customs, not requiring or staying for the people's suffrages, had possessed himself of the kingdom, went, accompanied with his sons and other noblemen of Rome, to besiege Ardea; during which siege, the principal men of the army meeting one evening at the tent of Sextus Tarquinius, the King's son, in their discourses after supper every one commended the virtues of his own wife; among whom Collatinus extolled the incomparable chastity of his wife Lucretia. In that pleasant humour they all posted to Rome, and intending by their secret and sudden arrival to make trial of that which every one had before avouched, only Collatinus finds his wife (though it were late in the night) spinning amongst her maids; the other ladies were all found dancing and revelling, or in several disports; whereupon the noblemen yielded Collatinus the victory, and his wife the fame. At that time Sextus Tarquinius being inflamed with Lucrece' beauty, yet smothering his passions for the present, departed with the rest back to the camp; from whence he shortly after privily withdrew himself, and was (according to his estate) royally entertained and lodged by Lucrece at Collatium. The same night he treacherously stealeth into her chamber, violently ravished her, and early in the morning speedeth away. Lucrece, in this lamentable plight, hastily dispatcheth messengers, one to Rome for her father, another to the camp for Collatine. They came, the one accompanied with [Lucius] Junius Brutus, the other with Publius Valerius; and finding Lucrece attired in mourning habit, demanded the cause of her sorrow. She, first taking an oath of them for her revenge, revealed the actor, and whole manner of his dealing, and withal suddenly stabbed herself. Which done, with one consent they all vowed to root out the whole hated family of the Tarquins; and bearing the dead body to Rome, Brutus acquainted the people with the doer and manner of the vile deed; with a bitter invective against the tyranny of the King, wherewith the people were so moved, that with one consent and a general acclamation the Tarquins were all exiled, and the state government changed from kings to consuls.

3 Some dramatic precedents

(a) Hieronimo's recognition speech (Kyd, *The Spanish Tragedy*, 2.5.4–23)

> Who calls Hieronimo? Speak, here I am.
> I did not slumber, therefore 'twas no dream,
> No, no, it was some woman cried for help,
> And here within this garden did she cry,
> And in this garden must I rescue her:
> But stay, what murd'rous spectacle is this?
> A man hang'd up and all the murderers gone,   10
> And in my bower, to lay the guilt on me:
> This place was made for pleasure not for death.
> > *He cuts him down.*
> Those garments that he wears I oft have seen –
> Alas, it is Horatio my sweet son!
> O no, but he that whilom was my son.
> O was it thou that call'dst me from my bed?
> O speak, if any spark of life remain:
> I am thy father. Who hath slain my son?
> What savage monster, not of human kind,
> Hath here been glutted with thy harmless blood,   20
> And left thy bloody corpse dishonour'd here,
> For me amidst this dark and deathful shades
> To drown thee with an ocean of my tears?

(b) Hieronimo's rhetoric of passion (Kyd, *The Spanish Tragedy*, 3.7.1–18)

> Where shall I run to breathe abroad my woes,
> My woes, whose weight hath wearied the earth?
> Or mine exclaims, that have surcharg'd the air
> With ceaseless plaints for my deceased son?
> The blust'ring winds, conspiring with my words,
> At my lament have mov'd the leaveless trees,
> Disrob'd the meadows of their flower'd green,
> Made mountains marsh with spring-tides of my tears,
> And broken through the brazen gates of hell.
> Yet still tormented is my tortur'd soul   10
> With broken sighs and restless passions,
> That winged mount, and, hovering in the air,
> Beat at the windows of the brightest heavens,
> Soliciting for justice and revenge:
> But they are plac'd in those empyreal heights
> Where, countermur'd with walls of diamond,
> I find the place impregnable, and they
> Resist my woes, and give my words no way.

(c) Hieronimo's quest for justice (Kyd, *The Spanish Tragedy*, 3.13.95–123)

See, see, O see thy shame, Hieronimo,
See here a loving father to his son!
Behold the sorrows and the sad laments
That he delivereth for his son's decease!
If love's effects so strives in lesser things,
If love enforce such moods in meaner wits,   100
If love express such power in poor estates:
Hieronimo, whenas a raging sea,
Toss'd with the wind and tide, o'erturneth then
The upper billows, course of waves to keep,
Whilst lesser waters labour in the deep:
Then sham'st thou not, Hieronimo, to neglect
The sweet revenge of thy Horatio?
Though on this earth justice will not be found,
I'll down to hell, and in this passion
Knock at the dismal gates of Pluto's court,   110
Getting by force, as once Alcides did,
A troop of Furies and tormenting hags
To torture Don Lorenzo and the rest.
Yet lest the triple-headed porter should
Deny my passage to the slimy strond,
The Thracian poet thou shalt counterfeit:
Come on, old father, be my Orpheus,
And if thou canst no notes upon the harp,
Then sound the burden of thy sore heart's grief,
Till we do gain that Proserpine may grant   120
Revenge on them that murdered my son:
Then will I rent and tear them thus and thus,
Shivering their limbs in pieces with my teeth.

Tear the papers.

(d) The art of villainy (Marlowe, *The Jew of Malta*, 2.3.176–214)

BARABAS
As for myself, I walk abroad a-nights,
And kill sick people groaning under walls;
Sometimes I go about and poison wells;
And now and then, to cherish Christian thieves,
I am content to lose some of my crowns,   180
That I may, walking in my gallery,
See 'em go pinion'd along by my door.
Being young, I studied physic, and began
To practise first upon the Italian;

286

There I enrich'd the priests with burials,
And always kept the sexton's arms in ure
With digging graves and ringing dead men's knells.
And after that, was I an engineer,
And in the wars 'twixt France and Germany,
Under pretence of helping Charles the Fifth,   190
Slew friend and enemy with my stratagems.
Then after that was I an usurer,
And with extorting, cozening, forfeiting,
And tricks belonging unto brokery,
I fill'd the gaols with bankrouts in a year,
And with young orphans planted hospitals,
And every moon made some or other mad,
And now and then one hang himself for grief,
Pinning upon his breast a long great scroll
How I with interest tormented him.   200
But mark how I am blest for plaguing them:
I have as much coin as will buy the town.
But tell me now, how hast thou spent thy time?

ITHAMORE

Faith, master,
In setting Christian villages on fire,
Chaining of eunuchs, binding galley-slaves.
One time I was an hostler in an inn,
And in the night time secretly would I steal
To travellers' chambers, and there cut their throats;
Once at Jerusalem, where the pilgrims kneel'd,   210
I strewed powder on the marble stones,
And therewithal their knees would rankle so
That I have laugh'd a-good to see the cripples
Go limping home to Christendom on stilts.

(e) The chopping of hands (*The First part of the Tragicall raigne of Selimus, sometime Emperour of the Turkes*, publ. 1594)[1]

ACOMAT

Nay let him die that liveth at his ease,
Death would a wretched caitive greatly please.

AGA

And thinkst thou then to scape unpu[n]ished,
No *Acomat*, though both mine eyes be gone,
Yet are my hands left on to murther thee.

1   Sigs F3ʳ–F4ʳ; line numbers from Malone Society Reprint.

ACOMAT

T'was wel remembred: *Regan* cut them off.   1430

> *They cut of his hands and give them Acomat.*

Now in that sort go tell thy Emperour
That if himselfe had but bene in thy place,
I would have us'd him crueller then thee:
Here take thy hands: I know thou lov'st them wel.

> *Opens his bosome, and puts them in.*

Which hand is this? right? or left? canst thou tell?

AGA

I know not which it is, but tis my hand.
But oh thou supreme architect of all,
First mover of those tenfold christall orbes,   1440
Where all those moving, and unmoving eyes
Behold thy goodnesse everlastingly:
See, unto thee I lift these bloudie armes,
For hands I have not for to lift to thee,
And in thy justice dart thy smouldring flame
Upon the head of cursed *Acomat*.
Oh cruell heavens and injurious fates,
Even the last refuge of a wretched man,
Is tooke from me: for how can *Aga* weepe?
Or ruine a brinish shew'r of pearled teares?   1450
Wanting the watry cesternes of his eyes?
Come lead me backe againe to *Bajazet*,
The wofullest, and sadd'st Embassadour
That ever was dispatch'd to any King....

> *Exeunt All.*

Enter Bajazet, Mustaffa, Cali, Hali, and Aga led by a souldier: who k[n]eeling
before Bajazet, and holding his legs shall say:

AGA

Is this the bodie of my soveraigne?
Are these the sacred pillars that support
The image of true magnanimitie?
Ah *Bajazet*, thy sonne false *Acomat*
Is full resolved to take thy life from thee:
Tis true, tis true, witnesse these handlesse armes,
Witnesse these emptie lodges of mine eyes,
Witnesse the gods that from the highest heaven
Beheld the tyrant with remorcelesse heart,
Puld out mine eyes, and cut off my weake hands.   1480
Witnesse that sun whose golden coloured beames
Your eyes do see, but mine can nere behold:
Witnesse the earth that sucked up my blood,

Streaming in rivers from my tronked armes.
Witnesse the present that he sends to thee,
Open my bosome, there you shall it see.
    Mustaffa opens his bosome and takes out his hands.
Those are the hands, which *Aga* once did use,
To tosse the speare, and in a warlike gyre   1490
To hurtle my sharpe sword about my head,
Those sends he to the wofull Emperour,
With purpose so [to] cut thy hands from thee.
Why is my soveraigne silent all this while?

BAJAZET

Ah *Aga*, *Bajazet* faine would speak to thee,
But sodaine sorrow eateth up my words.
Bajazet Aga, faine would weepe for thee,
But cruell sorrow drieth up my teares.
Bajazet Aga, faine would die for thee,
But griefe hath weakned my poore aged hands.   1500
How can he speak, whose tongue sorrow hath tide?
How can he mourne, that cannot shead a teare?
How shall he live, that full of miserie
Calleth for death, which will not let him die?

ABBREVIATIONS AND REFERENCES

In all references, place of publication is London unless otherwise stated.

ABBREVIATIONS

Typographic conventions used in text

[ ]   an editorial addition
{ }   a quarto passage which should perhaps be cut

Change of typeface indicates a Folio addition

Abbreviations used in notes

ed., eds	editor, editors
om.	omitted
Qq, F	the early printed texts: Q1, Q2, Q3 and F (see list of edns below)
SD	stage direction
SP	speech prefix
subst.	substantively
t.n.	the textual notes at the foot of each page
this edn	a reading adopted for the first time in this edition

* Precedes commentary notes involving substantive readings altered from the early edition on which this edition is based.
( ) surrounding a Q or F reading in t.n. indicates original spelling; surrounding an editor's or scholar's name indicates conjectural reading not actually included in an edited text.

Shakespeare's works

AC	*Antony and Cleopatra*
AW	*All's Well That Ends Well*
AYL	*As You Like It*

CE	*The Comedy of Errors*
Cor	*Coriolanus*
Cym	*Cymbeline*
Ham	*Hamlet*
1H4	*King Henry IV Part 1*
2H4	*King Henry IV Part 2*
H5	*King Henry V*
1H6	*King Henry VI Part 1*
2H6	*King Henry VI Part 2*
3H6	*King Henry VI Part 3*
H8	*King Henry VIII*
JC	*Julius Caesar*
KJ	*King John*
KL	*King Lear*
LC	*A Lover's Complaint*
LLL	*Love's Labour's Lost*
Luc	*The Rape of Lucrece*
MA	*Much Ado About Nothing*
Mac	*Macbeth*
MM	*Measure for Measure*
MND	*A Midsummer Night's Dream*
MV	*The Merchant of Venice*
MW	*The Merry Wives of Windsor*
Oth	*Othello*
Per	*Pericles*
PP	*The Passionate Pilgrim*
PT	*The Phoenix and the Turtle*
R2	*King Richard II*
R3	*King Richard III*
RJ	*Romeo and Juliet*
Son	*Sonnets*
TC	*Troilus and Cressida*
Tem	*The Tempest*
TGV	*The Two Gentlemen of Verona*
Tim	*Timon of Athens*
Tit	*Titus Andronicus*
TN	*Twelfth Night*
TNK	*The Two Noble Kinsmen*
TS	*The Taming of the Shrew*
VA	*Venus and Adonis*
WT	*The Winter's Tale*

Line references for other Shakespearean works are to Riv (to which *The Harvard Concordance to Shakespeare* is keyed), but quotations are sometimes emended.

Modern productions cited

BBC	BBC television, directed by Jane Howell, 1985
Brook	Shakespeare Memorial Theatre, Stratford-upon-Avon, Stoll Theatre, London, and European tour, directed by Peter Brook, 1955–7
Cambridge	Arts Theatre Trust, Cambridge, directed by Stephen Siddall, 1991
Santa Cruz	Shakespeare Santa Cruz, California, directed by Mark Rucker, 1988
Warner	Royal Shakespeare Company, Swan Theatre, Stratford-upon-Avon, The Pit, London, and European tour, directed by Deborah Warner, 1987–8

REFERENCES

Editions of Shakespeare collated

Adams	J. Q. Adams, *Shakespeare's Titus Andronicus: The First Quarto 1594*, facsimile with introduction (New York, 1936)
Allen & Muir	*Shakespeare's Plays in Quarto*, facsimiles, ed. Michael J. B. Allen and Kenneth Muir (Berkeley and Los Angeles, 1981)
Ard[1]	*Titus Andronicus*, ed. H. B. Baildon, The Arden Shakespeare (1912)
Ard[2]	*Titus Andronicus*, ed. J. C. Maxwell, The Arden Shakespeare (1953, 3rd edn 1961)
Bantam	*Three Classical Tragedies*, ed. David Bevington, The Bantam Shakespeare (New York, 1988)
BBC	*Titus Andronicus*, The BBC TV Shakespeare, text from Peter Alexander's 1951 *Complete Works*, with editorial matter and marginal commentary concerning 1985 television production (1986)
Bevington	*Complete Works*, ed. David Bevington (Glenview, Illinois, 1980)
Cam	*Works*, ed. W. G. Clark and W. A. Wright, 9 vols (Cambridge, 1863–6); text repr. in 1 vol. as 'Globe' edn (1864)
Cam[1]	*Titus Andronicus*, ed. John Dover Wilson, The New Shakespeare (Cambridge, 1948)
Capell	*Comedies, Histories, and Tragedies*, ed. Edward Capell, 10 vols (1767–8)
Collier	*Works*, ed. John Payne Collier, 8 vols (1842–4)
Craig	*Complete Works*, ed. W. J. Craig (Oxford, 1892)

Delius	*Werke*, ed. Nicolaus Delius, 3rd edn, 7 vols (Elberfeld, 1872)
Dyce	*Works*, ed. Alexander Dyce, 6 vols (1857)
Dyce[2]	*Works*, ed. Alexander Dyce, 9 vols (1864–7)
F	*Comedies, Histories, and Tragedies*, First Folio (1623)
F2	*Comedies, Histories, and Tragedies*, Second Folio (1632)
F3	*Comedies, Histories, and Tragedies*, Third Folio (1663)
F4	*Comedies, Histories, and Tragedies*, Fourth Folio (1685)
G1620	*Eine sehr klägliche Tragaedia von Tito Andronico und der hoffertigen Kaiserin, darinnen denckwürdige actiones zubefinden*, in *Englische Comedien und Tragedien* (1620); parallel German/English text in Albert Cohn, *Shakespeare in Germany in the Sixteenth and Seventeenth Centuries* (1865); quotations from English trans. in Ernest Brennecke, *Shakespeare in Germany 1590–1700 with Translations of Five Early Plays* (Chicago, 1964)
Hanmer	*Works*, ed. Thomas Hanmer, 6 vols (Oxford, 1743–4)
Hudson	*Works*, ed. H. N. Hudson, 11 vols (Boston, 1851–6)
Johnson	*Plays*, ed. Samuel Johnson, 8 vols (1765)
Keightley	*Plays*, ed. Thomas Keightley, 6 vols (1864)
Kittredge	*Complete Works*, ed. G. L. Kittredge (Boston, 1936)
Malone	*Plays and Poems*, ed. Edmond Malone, 10 vols (1790)
Oxf	*Complete Works*, gen. eds Stanley Wells and Gary Taylor (Oxford, 1986, Compact Edition 1988)
Oxf[1]	*Titus Andronicus*, ed. Eugene M. Waith, The Oxford Shakespeare (Oxford, 1984)
Pelican	*Complete Works*, The Pelican Text Revised, gen. ed. Alfred Harbage (1969)
Pope	*Works*, ed. Alexander Pope, 6 vols (1723–5)
Q1	*The Most Lamentable Romaine Tragedie of Titus Andronicus* (1594)
Q2	*The Most Lamentable Romaine Tragedie of Titus Andronicus* (1600)
Q3	*The Most Lamentable Tragedie of Titus Andronicus* (1611)
Ravenscroft	*Titus Andronicus, or The Rape of Lavinia. Acted at the Theatre Royall, A Tragedy. Alter'd from Mr Shakespears Works*, by Mr Edw. Ravenscroft (1687)
Red Letter	*Titus Andronicus*, ed. E. K. Chambers, The Red Letter Edition (1907)
Riv	*The Riverside Shakespeare*, textual ed. G. B. Evans (Boston, 1974)
Rowe	*Works*, ed. Nicholas Rowe, 6 vols (1709)
Rowe[2]	*Works*, ed. Nicholas Rowe, 2nd edn, 6 vols (1709)
Rowe[3]	*Works*, ed. Nicholas Rowe, 3rd edn, 8 vols (1714)

References

Serpieri	*Tito Andronico*, ed. and trans. Alessandro Serpieri (Milan, 1989). My trans. in quotation.
Signet	*Titus Andronicus*, ed. Sylvan Barnet, The Signet Classic Shakespeare (New York, 1963)
Steevens	*Plays*, ed. Samuel Johnson and George Steevens, 10 vols (1773)
Stoll	*Titus Andronicus*, ed. E. E. Stoll, The Tudor Shakespeare (New York, 1913)
Temple	*Titus Andronicus*, ed. M. R. Ridley, New Temple Shakespeare (1934)
Theobald	*Works*, ed. Lewis Theobald, 7 vols (1733)
Warburton	*Works*, ed. William Warburton, 8 vols (1747)
Yale	*Titus Andronicus*, ed. A. M. Witherspoon, The Yale Shakespeare (New Haven, 1926)

Other works

Abbott	E. A. Abbott, *A Shakespearian Grammar*, new edn (1872)
Aen.	Virgil, *Aeneid*, trans. Thomas Phaer, quoted from edn of 1584, rev. Thomas Twyne, ed. Steven Lally (New York, 1987)
Bacon	Francis Bacon, *The Essays*, ed. John Pitcher (Harmondsworth, 1985)
Baker	Howard Baker, *Induction to Tragedy* (Baton Rouge, 1939)
Barton	Anne Barton, 'Parks and Ardens', *Proceedings of the British Academy*, 80 (1991 Lectures), 49–71
Baskervill	C. R. Baskervill, 'A prompt copy of *A Looking Glass for London and England*', *Modern Philology*, 30 (1932–3), 29–51
Bate, 'Adaptation'	Jonathan Bate and Sonia Massai, 'Adaptation as edition' in *Margins of the Text*, ed. David Greetham (Ann Arbor, forthcoming)
Bate, *Ovid*	Jonathan Bate, *Shakespeare and Ovid* (Oxford, 1993)
Bennett	Paul E. Bennett, 'An Apparent Allusion to *Titus Andronicus*', *N&Q*, 200 (1955), 422–4, and 'The Word "Goths" in *A Knack to Know a Knave*', *N&Q*, 200 (1955), 462–3
Bernard	Samuel Bernard, *Andronicus Comnenus*, introduction by John L. Klause, Renaissance Latin Drama in England, 1st series, 6 (Hildesheim, 1986)
Billington	Michael Billington, 'Horror and Humanity', *The Guardian*, 14 May 1987, 24, repr. in Williamson
Bolton, 'Notes'	Joseph S. G. Bolton, 'Two notes on *Titus Andronicus*', *Modern Language Notes*, 45 (1930), 140–1
Bolton, 'Text'	Joseph S. G. Bolton, 'The Authentic Text of *Titus Andronicus*', *Publications of the Modern Language Association of America*, 44 (1929), 765–88

Bowers   Fredson Bowers, *Elizabethan Revenge Tragedy* (Princeton, 1940)

Braden   Gordon Braden, *Renaissance Tragedy and the Senecan Tradition* (New Haven, 1985)

Braekman   W. Braekman, 'The relationship of Shakespeare's *Titus Andronicus* to the German play of 1620 and to Jan Vos's *Aran en Titus*', *Studia Germanica Gandensia*, 9 (1967), 9–117 and 10 (1968), 9–65

Braunmuller   A. R. Braunmuller, 'Early Shakespearian Tragedy and its contemporary context: cause and emotion in *Titus Andronicus*, *Richard III*, and *The Rape of Lucrece*', in *Shakespearian Tragedy*, ed. David Palmer, Stratford-upon-Avon Studies 20 (1984), 97–128

Brooke   Nicholas Brooke, *Shakespeare's Early Tragedies* (1968)

Broude   Ronald Broude, 'Roman and Goth in *Titus Andronicus*', *SSt*, 6 (1970), 27–34

Brower   Reuben A. Brower, *Hero and Saint: Shakespeare and the Graeco-Roman Heroic Tradition* (Oxford, 1971)

Bullough   *Narrative and Dramatic Sources of Shakespeare*, ed. Geoffrey Bullough, 8 vols (1957–75)

Burnet   R. A. L. Burnet, 'Nashe and *Titus Andronicus*', *English Language Notes*, 18 (1980–1), 98–9.

Calvin   John Calvin, *Institutes of the Christian Religion* (1536), trans. Harro Höpfl, in *Luther and Calvin on Secular Authority*, Cambridge Texts in the History of Political Thought (Cambridge, 1991)

Cantrell &   Paul L. Cantrell and George Walton Williams, 'Roberts'
  Williams   compositors in *Titus Andronicus* Q2', *Studies in Bibliography*, 8 (1956), 27–38

Capell, *Notes* Edward Capell, *Notes and Variant Readings to Shakespeare*, 3 vols (1783)

Cartwright   Robert Cartwright, *New Readings in Shakespeare* (1866)

Cawdrey   Robert Cawdrey, *A Table Alphabetical, containing and teaching the true writing, and understanding of hard usual English words* (1604)

Cercignani   Fausto Cercignani, *Shakespeare's Works and Elizabethan Pronunciation* (Oxford, 1981)

Chambers   E. K. Chambers, *The Elizabethan Stage*, 4 vols (Oxford, 1923)

Collier MS   Manuscript emendations, probably by J. P. Collier, in his copy of F2, now in the Huntington Library

Cooper   Thomas Cooper, *Thesaurus Linguae Romanae et Britannicae … Accessit dictionarium historicum et poëticum propria vocabula* (1565)

David	Richard David, review of Peter Brook production, *ShS*, 10 (1957), 127
Dent	R. W. Dent, *Shakespeare's Proverbial Language: An Index* (Berkeley and Los Angeles, 1981)
Dessen	Alan C. Dessen, *Shakespeare in Performance: Titus Andronicus* (Manchester, 1989)
Dessen, Conventions	Alan C. Dessen, *Elizabethan Stage Conventions and Modern Interpreters* (Cambridge, 1984)
Eliot	T. S. Eliot, 'Seneca in Elizabethan translation', in his *Selected Essays 1917–1932* (1932), 65–105
Elyot	Sir Thomas Elyot, *The Book named The Governor* (1531; quoted from edn of 1580)
Fawcett	Mary Laughlin Fawcett, 'Arms/words/tears: language and the body in *Titus Andronicus*', *ELH*, 50 (1983), 261–77
Foakes	R. A. Foakes, *Illustrations of the English Stage 1580–1642* (1985)
Foxe	John Foxe, *Acts and Monuments* (1563)
George	David George, 'Shakespeare and Pembroke's men', *SQ*, 32 (1981), 305–23
Gossett	Suzanne Gossett, ' "Best men are molded out of faults": marrying the rapist in Jacobean drama', *English Literary Renaissance*, 14 (1984), 305–27
Greg	W. W. Greg, *The Shakespeare First Folio* (Oxford, 1955)
Guevara	*The Familiar Epistles of Sir Antonie of Guevara*, trans. Edward Hellowes (1584)
Haaker	Ann Haaker, ' "Non sine causa": the use of emblematic method and iconology in the thematic structure of *Titus Andronicus*', *Research Opportunities in Renaissance Drama*, 13–14 (1970–1), 143–68
Haggard	F. E. Haggard, 'The printing of Shakespeare's *Titus Andronicus*, 1594', unpubl. Ph.D. thesis, University of Kansas (1966)
Hallett	Charles A. and Elaine S. Hallett, *The Revenger's Madness* (Lincoln, Nebr., 1980)
Hattaway	Michael Hattaway, '*Titus Andronicus*: strange images of death', in his *Elizabethan Popular Theatre* (1982), 186–207
Henslowe	*Henslowe's Diary*, ed. R. A. Foakes and R. T. Rickert (Cambridge, 1961)
Herodian	*The History of Herodian, a Greeke Author, treating of the Romayne Emperors, after Marcus, translated oute of Greeke into Latin, by Angelus Politianus, and out of Latin into Englyshe, by Nicholas Smyth* (1550)
Heywood	Thomas Heywood, *The Golden Age or The Lives of Jupiter and Saturn, with the defining of the Heathen Gods* (1611)

Hinman
Charlton Hinman, *The Printing and Proof-Reading of the First Folio of Shakespeare*, 2 vols (Oxford, 1963)

Howard-Hill
Oxford Shakespeare Concordances: Titus Andronicus, ed. T. H. Howard-Hill (Oxford, 1972)

Hunter, 'Flatcaps'
G. K. Hunter, 'Flatcaps and bluecoats: visual signs on the Elizabethan stage', *Essays and Studies*, 33 (1980), 16–47

Hunter, 'Sources'
G. K. Hunter, 'The "Sources" of *Titus Andronicus* – once again', *N&Q*, 228 (1983), 114–16

Hunter, 'Sources and Meanings'
G. K. Hunter, 'Sources and meanings in *Titus Andronicus*', in *The Mirror up to Shakespeare*, ed. J. C. Gray (Toronto, 1983), 171–88

Ironside
Shakespeare's Lost Play: Edmund Ironside, ed. Eric Sams (1985). The ascription to Shakespeare is extremely dubious.

Jackson, *Attribution*
MacDonald P. Jackson, *Studies in Attribution: Middleton and Shakespeare* (Salzburg, 1979)

Jackson, 'Play'
MacDonald P. Jackson, '*Titus Andronicus*: play, ballad, and prose history', *N&Q*, 234 (1989), 315–17

Jackson, *ShS*
MacDonald P. Jackson, review of Oxf[1] in 'The year's contributions to Shakespearian study', *ShS*, 38 (1985), 246–50

James
Heather James, 'Cultural disintegration in *Titus Andronicus*: mutilating Titus, Vergil and Rome', in *Violence in Drama*, *Themes in Drama*, 13 (1991), 123–40

M. James
Mervyn James, *Society, Politics and Culture: Studies in Early Modern England* (Cambridge, 1986)

Jed
Stephanie H. Jed, *Chaste Thinking: The Rape of Lucretia and the Birth of Humanism* (Bloomington and Indianapolis, 1989)

Jones
Emrys Jones, *The Origins of Shakespeare* (Oxford, 1977)

Jonson
Ben Jonson, ed. C. H. Herford, Percy and Evelyn Simpson, 11 vols (Oxford, 1925–52), spelling modernized in quotations

Kerrigan
Motives of Woe: Shakespeare and 'Female Complaint': A Critical Anthology, ed. John Kerrigan (Oxford, 1991)

King
T. J. King, *Casting Shakespeare's Plays* (Cambridge, 1992)

Kliger
Samuel Kliger, *The Goths in England* (Cambridge, Mass., 1952; repr. New York, 1972)

Knack
A Knack to Know a Knave (1594), Malone Society Reprint, prepared by G. R. Proudfoot (Oxford, 1964)

Lambarde
William Lambarde, *A Perambulation of Kent* (1570), quoted from 1826 repr. of 2nd edn (repr. Bath, 1970)

Levy
F. J. Levy, *Tudor Historical Thought* (San Marino, 1967)

Livy
The Roman History Written by T. Livius of Padua, trans. Philemon Holland (1600)

Lodge, *Wounds*   Thomas Lodge, *The Wounds of Civil War*, ed. Joseph W. Houppert (Lincoln, Nebr., 1969)

Lyly   *The Complete Works of John Lyly*, ed. R. W. Bond, 3 vols (Oxford, 1902), spelling modernized in quotation

McMillin   Scott McMillin, 'Sussex's men in 1594: the evidence of *Titus Andronicus* and *The Jew of Malta*', *Theatre Survey*, 32 (1991), 214–23

Marienstras   Richard Marienstras, 'The forest, hunting and sacrifice in *Titus Andronicus*', in his *New Perspectives on the Shakespearean World* (Cambridge, 1985), 40–7

Marlowe   Christopher Marlowe, *Complete Plays and Poems*, ed. E. D. Pendry and J. C. Maxwell (1976)

Marshall &   Herbert Marshall and Mildred Stock, *Ira Aldridge: The*
Stock   *Negro Tragedian* (1958)

Met.   Ovid, *Metamorphoses*, quoted from Arthur Golding's trans. (1567). Line references to Golding, except where Latin original is quoted.

Metz, 'Stage'   G. Harold Metz, 'Stage history of *Titus Andronicus*', *SQ*, 28 (1977), 154–69

Metz,   G. Harold Metz, 'Disputed Shakespearean texts and styl-
'Stylometric'   ometric analysis', *TEXT: Transactions of the Society for Textual Scholarship*, 2 (1985), 149–71

Metz,   G. Harold Metz, '*Titus Andronicus*: a watermark in the
'Watermark'   Longleat Manuscript', *SQ*, 36 (1985), 450–3

Mincoff,   Marco Mincoff, 'The source of *Titus Andronicus*', *N & Q*,
'Source'   216 (1971), 131–4

Mincoff, *Steps*   Marco Mincoff, *Shakespeare: The First Steps* (Sofia, 1976)

Miola   Robert S. Miola, *Shakespeare and Classical Tragedy: The Influence of Seneca* (Oxford, 1992)

N&Q   *Notes and Queries*

Nashe   *The Works of Thomas Nashe*, ed. R. B. McKerrow, 5 vols (1904–10, repr., corr. F. P. Wilson, Oxford, 1958)

Nørgaard   Holger Nørgaard, 'Never wrong but with just cause', *English Studies*, 45 (1964), 137–41

OED   *Oxford English Dictionary* (citations from 2nd edn; where there is ambiguity as to which entry is cited, reference is given in the forms used in the dictionary itself)

Onions   C. T. Onions, *A Shakespeare Glossary*, rev. Robert D. Eagleson (Oxford, 1986)

Orgel   Stephen Orgel, 'Making greatness familiar', *Genre*, 15 (1982), 41–8

Palmer   D. J. Palmer, 'The unspeakable in pursuit of the uneatable: language and action in *Titus Andronicus*', *Critical Quarterly*, 14 (1972), 320–39

Partridge   Eric Partridge, *Shakespeare's Bawdy* (1947, 3rd edn 1968)

References

Peacham	Henry Peacham, *The Complete Gentleman, The Truth of Our Times, and The Art of Living in London*, ed. Virgil B. Heltzel (Ithaca, 1962)
Peele	David H. Horne, *The Life and Minor Works of George Peele* (New Haven, 1952)
Philomela	*Philomela*, in *The Christmas Prince*, introduction by E. J. Richards, Renaissance Latin Drama in England, 1st series, 11 (Hildesheim, 1982)
Plutarch	*The Lives of the Noble Grecians and Romans, compared together by that grave learned Philosopher and Historiographer, Plutarch of Chaeronea: Translated out of Greek into French by James Amyot ... and out of French into English, by Thomas North* (1579)
Politi	Jina Politi, ' "The gibbet-maker" ', *N&Q*, 236 (1991), 54–5
Price	Hereward T. Price, 'The authorship of *Titus Andronicus*', *Journal of English and Germanic Philology*, 42 (1943), 55–81
Ritson	Joseph Ritson, *Remarks, Critical and Illustrative, on the Text and Notes of the Last Edition of Shakespeare* (1783)
Robertson	John M. Robertson, *Did Shakespeare Write 'Titus Andronicus'?* (1905)
Romantics	*The Romantics on Shakespeare*, ed. Jonathan Bate (1992)
K. Rowe	Katherine Rowe, 'Dismembering and forgetting in *Titus Andronicus*', *SQ*, Fall, 1994
Schmidt	Alexander Schmidt, *Shakespeare-Lexicon*, 2 vols, through pagination (Berlin, 1874)
Selimus	*The Tragical Reign of Selimus* (1594), Malone Society Reprint, prepared by W. Bang (1908)
Seneca	Seneca, *Tragedies I & II*, Loeb Classical Library (1917, repr. 1968)
Sharpe	Kevin Sharpe and Christopher Brooks, 'History, English law and the Renaissance', *Past and Present*, 72 (1976), 133–42; repr. in Sharpe, *Politics and Ideas in Early Stuart England* (1989), 174–81
Sheahan	J. J. Sheahan, '*Titus Andronicus*: Ira Aldridge', *N&Q*, 4th series, 10 (1872), 132–3
ShS	*Shakespeare Survey*
Sisson	C. J. Sisson, *New Readings in Shakespeare*, 2 vols (Cambridge, 1956)
Sp. Trag.	Thomas Kyd, *The Spanish Tragedy*, ed. Philip Edwards (1959)
Spencer	T. J. B. Spencer, 'Shakespeare and the Elizabethan Romans', *ShS*, 10 (1957), 27–38
SQ	*Shakespeare Quarterly*

References

SSt	*Shakespeare Studies*
State-Trials	*A Complete Collection of State-Trials and Proceedings upon Impeachments for High Treason, and other Crimes and Misdemeanours; from the Reign of King Henry the Fourth, to the end of the Reign of Queen Anne*, 4 vols (1719)
Thompson	Ann Thompson, 'Philomel in *Titus Andronicus* and *Cymbeline*', *ShS*, 31 (1978), 23–32
Tilley	M. P. Tilley, *A Dictionary of the Proverbs in England in the Sixteenth and Seventeenth Centuries* (Ann Arbor, 1950)
Tobin	J. J. M. Tobin, 'Nomenclature and the dating of *Titus Andronicus*', *N&Q*, 229 (1984), 186–7
Tricomi	Albert H. Tricomi, 'The aesthetics of mutilation in *Titus Andronicus*', *ShS*, 27 (1974), 11–19
TxC	Stanley Wells and Gary Taylor, *William Shakespeare: A Textual Companion* (Oxford, 1987)
Tynan	Kenneth Tynan, 'Chamber of Horrors', *The Observer*, 21 Aug. 1955, 11, repr. in Williamson
Ungerer	Gustav Ungerer, 'An unrecorded Elizabethan performance of *Titus Andronicus*', *ShS*, 14 (1961), 102–9
Vickers	Nancy J. Vickers, 'Diana described: scattered woman and scattered rhyme', *Critical Inquiry*, 8 (1981–2), 265–79, and ' "The blazon of sweet beauty's best": Shakespeare's *Lucrece*', in *Shakespeare and the Question of Theory*, ed. Patricia Parker and Geoffrey Hartman (New York, 1985), 95–115
Waith, 'Met.'	E. M. Waith, 'The metamorphosis of violence in *Titus Andronicus*', *ShS*, 10 (1957), 39–49
Walker	W. S. Walker, *A Critical Examination of the Text of Shakespeare*, ed. W. N. Lettsom, 3 vols (1860)
Waugh	Evelyn Waugh, 'Titus with a grain of salt', *The Spectator*, 2 Sept. 1955, 300–1, repr. in Williamson
Wells, *Re-Editing*	Stanley Wells, *Re-Editing Shakespeare for the Modern Reader* (Oxford, 1984)
Wells, *ShS*	Stanley Wells, review of Deborah Warner production, *ShS*, 41 (1989), 178–81
Willbern	David Willbern, 'Rape and revenge in *Titus Andronicus*', *English Literary Renaissance*, 8 (1978), 159–82
Williamson	*Shakespearean Criticism: Excerpts from the Criticism of William Shakespeare's Plays and Poetry*, vol. 17, ed. Sandra L. Williamson (Detroit, 1992), 437–507
Wilson, 'Stage'	J. Dover Wilson, '*Titus Andronicus* on the stage in 1595', *ShS*, 1 (1948), 17–22
Wirszubski	Chaim Wirszubski, *Libertas as a Political Idea at Rome during the Late Republic and Early Principate* (Cambridge, 1968)

References

Wright   George T. Wright, *Shakespeare's Metrical Art* (Berkeley and Los Angeles, 1988)

Spelling of quotations follows the editions cited (unless otherwise stated), except that u/v and i/j have been silently modernized.

INDEX

TO INTRODUCTION AND COMMENTARY